DESIGN HISTORY READER

AN EMERGING VISION FOR A NEW NARRATIVE

EDITED BY KRISTEN COOGAN

with contributions by Alexina Federhen, Amina Hachimura, Anna Doctor, Annabella Pugliese, Bella Bennett, Charles Li, Dar Saravia, Ellen Johnson, Flora Kerner, Grace Chong, Haya AlMajali, Julia Cheung, Kristina Shumilina, Leila Garner, Maidha Salman, Natalie Seitz, Niharika Yellamraju, Olujimi Taiwo, Rayne Schulman, Rhea Jauhar, Risa Yamazaki, Ruxian Wang, Shaimaa Sabbagh, Sheryl Peng, Sophie Zimbler, Tyler Best, Tzu-Hsuan Huang, Winnie Mei, Xiuqi Ran, Yue Luo

AN EM

VISION

GRAPI

DESIG

HISTO

Design History Reader

BOSTON UNIVERSITY
HISTORY OF GRAPHIC DESIGN

Edited by
KRISTEN COOGAN

AN EMERGING VISION FOR GRAPHIC DESIGN HISTORY

The social-cultural awakening of 2020 became a mandate for self-reflection. How can we — as people, as designers, as educators — contribute to change? How can we foster more enhanced cultures of empathy and inclusion?

The central focus of this book is to promote a pluralistic approach to teaching and narrating graphic design history. Until now, traditional historical models have been monolithic and chronological. Those models were not comprehensive and alienated lesser-known and minority discourses. Change was needed.

This book asks how we can foster more enhanced cultures of empathy and inclusion and presents a design history that actually reflects the diversity in the profession and in the classroom. Building on the work of Nikole Hannah-Jones's groundbreaking *The 1619 Project* and Paulo Freire's *Pedagogy of the Oppressed*, the book confronts the status quo of American school curricula and also envisions educational spaces where the conventional teacher-student dynamic transforms into fertile ground for diverse contributions. This research also grapples with the paradox that while historians intentionally craft historical discourse based on collective knowledge, it often remains bound to a singular perspective.

Those perspectives multiplied when Boston University History of Graphic Design students embraced a plural design history pedagogy. Students challenged the Western design history canon through written research that targets under-known designers and design movements who they believe deserve representation. Students embraced the collective venture of shared responsibility — bringing their own authentic experiences and lived histories into conversation.

Those responses comprise the *Design History Reader*. Chapters are organized thematically, defining a framework for design history beyond chronology. These ideas broadly encompass a range of stories representing dominant and minority cultures. The concepts that tie these stories together become a contemporary vision of graphic design history and offer a new way to study, interact with, and perceive that narrative.

The *Design History Reader* is a dynamic starting point, open to interpretation and interrogation. It's not anywhere near being fully representative, but instead, a living archive that will continue to expand as our collective research advances.

These teaching experiences reveal that a plural model encourages a sense of agency within students. It teaches students to have a broader view of what the canon even is or includes, empowering them to represent more widespread cultural truths that mirror their own lived experiences. Taken together, those interests and perspectives form the basis of an emerging vision of a contemporary graphic design history discourse.

CONTENTS

CONTENTS

VISUAL SOVEREIGNTY

DEMOCRACY ON DEMAND

CONTENTS

HERSTORY

The stories emerging from the feminist struggle are etched with defiance against the backdrop of the popular canon. By and through design, herstories are steadily gaining widespread attention. Both historical and contemporary female designers are experiencing an ascent that aims to appropriately and adequately position them in the narrative of design history in a way that, until recently, was lacking. This effort revolves around acknowledging contemporaries and, more crucially, excavating stories of designers previously consigned to anonymity.

The Rise and Fall of Post-War Japanese Feminist Art

Post-war Japan witnessed remarkable economic growth and sweeping cultural transformations, particularly in the arts. The emergence of female artists paralleled a growing, albeit subtle, feminist consciousness; however, women faced significant challenges in gaining recognition for their work both domestically and internationally.

While some artists, including Yoko Ono (FIGURE 1) and Yayoi Kusama (FIGURE 2), broke through to international superstardom, it was only because of their activity in the United States — their impact in Japan went relatively unnoticed. In 1993, everything changed. Japanese art historian Kaori Chino codified the feminist dialogue with her essay "Gender in Japanese Art." This groundbreaking work introduced feminist theory to the Japanese art scene, both repositioning and empowering the female artist within a patriarchal system. Despite Chino's celebrity, progress was fragile and something to be protected. Conservatives who felt threatened by the more powerful and independent women used the system against them. Bureaucrats implemented *The Basic Law for a Gender Equal Society*, significantly hindering the organization of feminist exhibitions. This essay asks: What is the future of Japanese Feminism? Will it experience a resurgence or is Japan destined to become an unwavering feminist void?

THE EMERGENCE OF FEMALE ARTISTS IN POST-WAR JAPAN

After World War II, "Japan was left with almost nothing, [yet] their economy recovered at an incredible speed. Known as the Japanese Economic Miracle, Japan experienced rapid and sustained economic growth from 1945 to 1991, the period between post World War II and the end of the Cold War" *(Berkeley, 2023)*. The art world realized a similarly miraculous journey, growing from a homegrown institution to an international influencer. "Most scholars identify World War II as the critical turning point for Japanese art. After the war, Japanese artists shifted their interest from surrealism and other modernist forms of imagery to experimental mediums that rejected traditional styles and paved the way for the emergence of contemporary art manifestations" *(Valdes, 2022)*.

Women desperately searched for a position in this exciting new landscape. Unsatisfied with conventional notions of femininity, private institutions for female higher education were founded, providing a fertile backdrop for female artists seeking advanced study. Joshi Eigaku Juku, Joshi Bijutsu Gakko, and Jiyu Gakuen (FIGURE 3) provided spaces for more and more female students to learn *(Yasuko, 2008)*.[1-3] These

---

1–3 These institutions are now known as Tsuda College, Joshibi University of Art and Design, and Liberty School, respectively.

institutions nurtured the female artist, helping them forge a feminist identity which signified the beginning of a flourishing movement (FIGURE 4).

Few artists realized Kusama's and Ono's acclaim. In fact, Kusama's and Ono's experiences put the disparity of the female experience into high relief as the community of female artists struggled for acceptance. To gain any recognition, women felt they had to relinquish their individuality to a mainstream style governed by the male gaze (FIGURE 5). Not only that, but that same male-gaze resisted feminist and gender related subjects in contemporary art (Yoshimoto, 2006). This discrepancy between international acclaim and domestic recognition reflected the complex dynamics of post-war Japanese society and the role of women within it (FIGURE 6).

THE INTRODUCTION OF FEMINIST THEORY IN JAPANESE ART

The journey towards feminist awareness in the Japanese art scene can be traced back to 1993 when art historian Kaochi Chino published her groundbreaking work, "Gender in Japanese Art." Although Chino used the term "feminism" (feminizumu) infrequently, her project was inherently feminist.[4] Her use of the term "gender" suggests a deliberate and critical engagement with feminist ideas. Chino maintained that academic scholarship cannot be neutral or impartial, and that each artist must acknowledge how their environment and context shapes their individual perspective. Chino asserted that if women networked and learned from each other, they would better understand their own and their peers' perspectives, and that awareness could advance their collective scholarship. This form of criticality was something lacking in Japanese art history for so long — most female artists failed to acknowledge how their own intrinsic biases manifested in their work. The work created by women, informed by their own female experience read as bias, and that bias inadvertently created obstacles for any women who wanted to publicly exhibit their work.

Chino's work explored the intersection of gender and art, shedding light on the historical and contemporary contributions of female artists in Japan. Chino's 1995 *Image and Gender* learning seminar educated women, scholars and curators on the subject of feminine artistic emancipation. Tokyo Metropolitan Museum of Photography's first ever gender-themed exhibition *Gender – Beyond Memory* curated by Michiko Kasahara galvanized a long list of like-minded, gender-based exhibitions (FIGURE 7). Conservative male art critics denounced the new discourse around feminism and gender, attacking these "imported" ideas they felt were irrelevant to Japan — and in doing so, highlighted the persistence of an unyielding feudal ideology within Japanese society, which stifled broader social progress.

THE DECLINE OF FEMINISM AFTER 2000

The fragility of the feminist consciousness was again hindered in 1999 with the new and non-legally binding *Basic Law for a Gender Equal Society*. While the law ostensibly promoted gender equality, it actually suppressed the female voice even more. Conservatives claimed that the *Basic Law* destroyed traditional Japanese

---

4 It is for this reason that in this essay, I will often translate Chino's use of the term "jenda" as "feminism" when it is clear from the context that what is meant is a challenge to the status quo of gender difference rather than a mere description of it (Kano, 2003).

gender roles and launched the *Gender Bashing Movement* to restore historic norms. Chizuru Ueno, a pioneering Japanese feminist, was forbidden to use the term "gender freedom," throughout her lectures on the subject of feminism. Adachi Mariko, who established Japan's first *Institute for Gender Studies*, announced that the institute was to drop the term "Gender" in favor of "Women's Education" or it would lose its budget *(Chelsea Szendi Schieder, 2019)*. When Chino died in 2001, women felt they had lost their most powerful advocate, and their grief, frustration and helplessness simmered. Opportunities to showcase feminist, gender-based art, or even female led exhibitions all but disappeared. Chino's death intensified scrutiny against any notion of female independence. The use of terms like "girlie" became more prevalent, perpetuating ingrained stereotypes about women. The domestic culture curbed progressive discussions on gender and proved too limiting for women to thrive. Female artists gave up on Japan, and established studio practices internationally.

THE FUTURE OF JAPANESE FEMINISM

Today, the feminist experience is no less turbulent. According to the 2018 Gender Gap Index compiled by the World Economic Forum, Japan ranks 110th among 149 countries in terms of gender equality *(Berkeley Economic Review, 2023)*. Moreover, Japan seems to be one of the few countries that has not been greatly affected by the "Me Too" movement.

Will Japan perpetually remain the world's feminist black hole?[5] In 2018, a group named Tomorrow Girls Troop, self-identifying as a "fourth wave feminist art group," emerged (FIGURE 8). Founded three years earlier by a Japanese woman from California, the organization quickly attracted attention and worldwide support. The members of Tomorrow Girls wear pink bunny hoods and operate anonymously on the Internet. Their work predominantly revolves around addressing social and feminist issues, including topics such as sexual harassment on campuses and the persistence of "comfort women."[6] They engage in advocacy through various mediums, including performance art, public projects such as picnics and lectures, and promotional posters. Chino envisioned an art world with more equilibrium: "Some day, gender awareness (jenda no shiso) will be shared by many people, and these 'gender debates' of late-twentieth-century Japan will be regarded as historical events from the distant past. That day may not be tomorrow, but it will come, some day" *(Kano, 2003)*. These young groups may just hold the key to that hope.

The history of post-war Japanese feminism in art is marked by a complex interplay of emerging female artists, the introduction of feminist theory, and the challenges posed by a conservative male gaze. While female artists did indeed rise to prominence, both at home and abroad, their struggle for recognition and their role in promoting feminist values in the art world were subject to numerous obstacles. The

---

5 This writer hopes not.

6 Comfort women were women and girls forced into sexual slavery by the Imperial Japanese Army in occupied countries and territories before and during World War II.

legacy of figures like Yoko Ono, Yayoi Kusama, and Kaochi Chino has left an indelible mark on the history of Japanese art, shedding light on the need for continued efforts to bridge the gender gap and promote diversity in the field. With the emergence of new feminist groups like Tomorrow Girls Troop, will the historical cycle of rise and fall continue to repeat itself? Or one day will we truly see feminism taking root and spreading its branches in Japan? Let's wait and see.

BIBLIOGRAPHY

1. "ATSUKO TANAKA." AWARE Women artists / Femmes artistes. Accessed October 11, 2023. https://awarewomenartists.com/en/artiste/atsuko-tanaka/.

2. Berkeley Economic Review. "The Japanese Economic Miracle." Berkeley Economic Review. Accessed November 10, 2023. https://econreview.berkeley.edu/the-japanese-economic-miracle/#:~:text=Though%20Japan%20was%20left%20with,end%20of%20the%20Cold%20War.

3. BRYAN-WILSON, JULIA. "Remembering Yoko Ono's Cut Piece." Oxford Art Journal 26, no. 1 (2003): 99–123. https://doi.org/10.1093/oxartj/26.1.99.

4. "Gallery Moryta." , April 22, 2023. https://g-morita.com/archives/artist/%E5%A4%A7%E9%BB%92%E6%84%9B%E5%AD%90.

5. HASEGAWA, YUKO, and Pamela Miki. "The Spell to Re-Integrate the Self: The Significance of the Work of Yayoi Kusama in the New Era." Afterall: A Journal of Art, Context and Enquiry, no. 13 (Spring 2006): 46–53. https://doi.org/10.1086/aft.13.20711605.

6. "Hideko Fukushima." Taka Ishii Gallery / . Accessed October 11, 2023. https://www.takaishiigallery.com/en/archives/24638/.

7. KAWAHASHI, NORIKO, AND MASAKO KUROKI. "Editors' Introduction: Feminism and Religion in Contemporary Japan." Japanese Journal of Religious Studies, 4, 30, no. 3 (2003): 207–16. https://doi.org/10.18874/jjrs.30.3-4.2003.207-216.

8. KANO, AYAKO. "Women? Japan? Art?: Chino Kaori and the Feminist Art History Debates" Review of Japanese Culture and Society, 15 (December 2003): 25-38. https://www.jstor.org/stable/42801158.

10. MIDORI YOSHIMOTO. "Women Artists in the Japanese Postwar Avant-Garde: Celebrating a Multiplicity." Woman's Art Journal, 27, no. 1 (Spring - Summer, 2006):26-32, https://www.jstor.org/stable/20358068.

9. SHIMADA YOSHIKO. "Shortlist | The Defiant Fringed Pink: Feminist Art in Japan", Wed, 21 Aug 2019. https://aaa.org.hk/en/like-a-fever/like-a-fever/shortlist-the-defiant-fringed-pink-feminist-art-in-japan.

11. SUGA, YASUKO. "Modernism, Nationalism and Gender: Crafting 'modern' Japonisme." Journal of Design History 21, no. 3 (Autumn 1, 2008): 259–75. https://doi.org/10.1093/jdh/epn026.

12. VALDÉS, CONSTANZA Ontiveros. "Japanese Post-War Avant-Garde." Art Collection. Accessed November 5, 2024. https://artcollection.io/blog/japanese-post-war-avant-garde#:~:text=Most%20scholars%20identify%20World%20War,emergence%20of%20contemporary%20art%20manifestations.

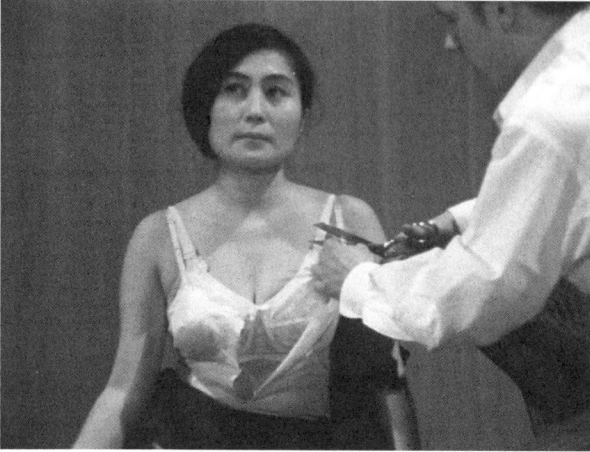

1.

3.

2.

FIGURES

1. Yoko Ono, *CUT PIECE*, Performed at Carnegie Recital Hall, New York, March 21, 1965. Credit: Andrew Westerman. Source: YouTube video screenshot, fair use for educational use.

2. Yayoi Kusama, *Store Window Installation for Louis Vuitton*, 2018. Credit: Yayoi Kusama.

3. Frank Lloyd Wright, *Jiyu Gakuen School*, Tokyo, Japan, 1921. Credit: Dr. Yasuko Suga.

4.

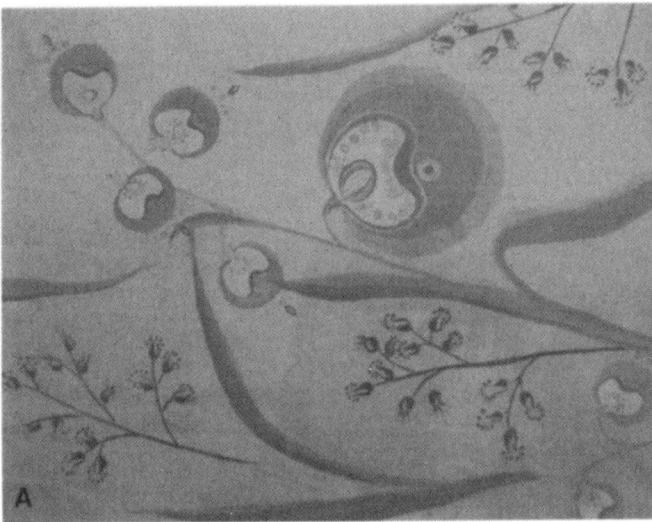

5.

4. Yoshikazu and Hani Motoko (founders), *Fujin no Tomo*, monthy women's magazine, Tokyo Japan, 1908. Credit: Jiyu Gakuen Library and Archives.

5. Imai Kazuko, Textile design. Credit: Jiyu Gakuen Library and Archives.

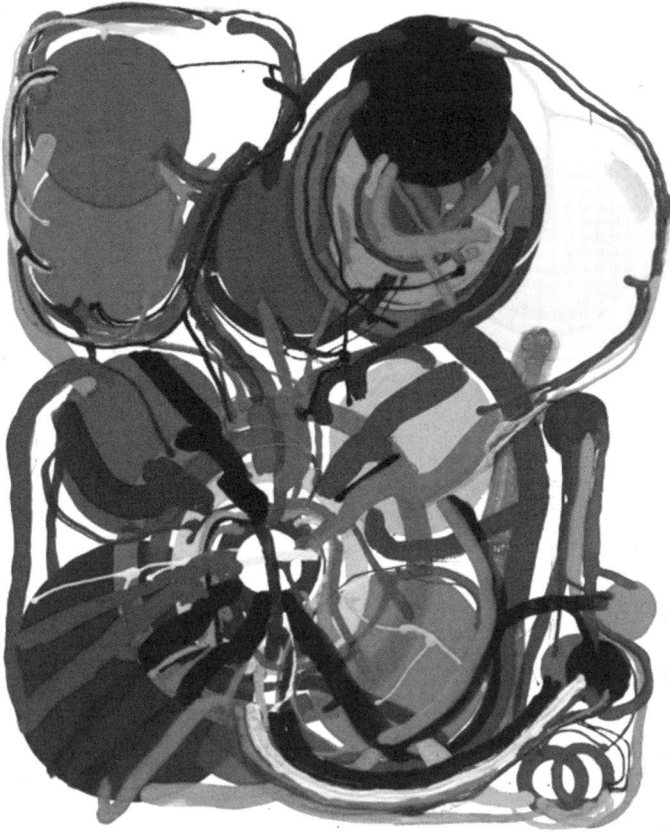

6.

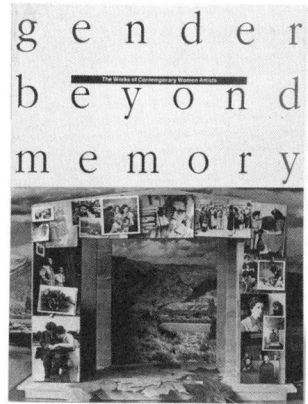

7.

6. Atsuko Tanaka, *Untitled*, 1976. Source: WikiArt, fair use for educational use.

7. Tokyo Metropolitan Museum of Photography, *Gender – Beyond Memory: The Works of Contemporary Women Artists*, 1997. Credit: Mari Mahr.

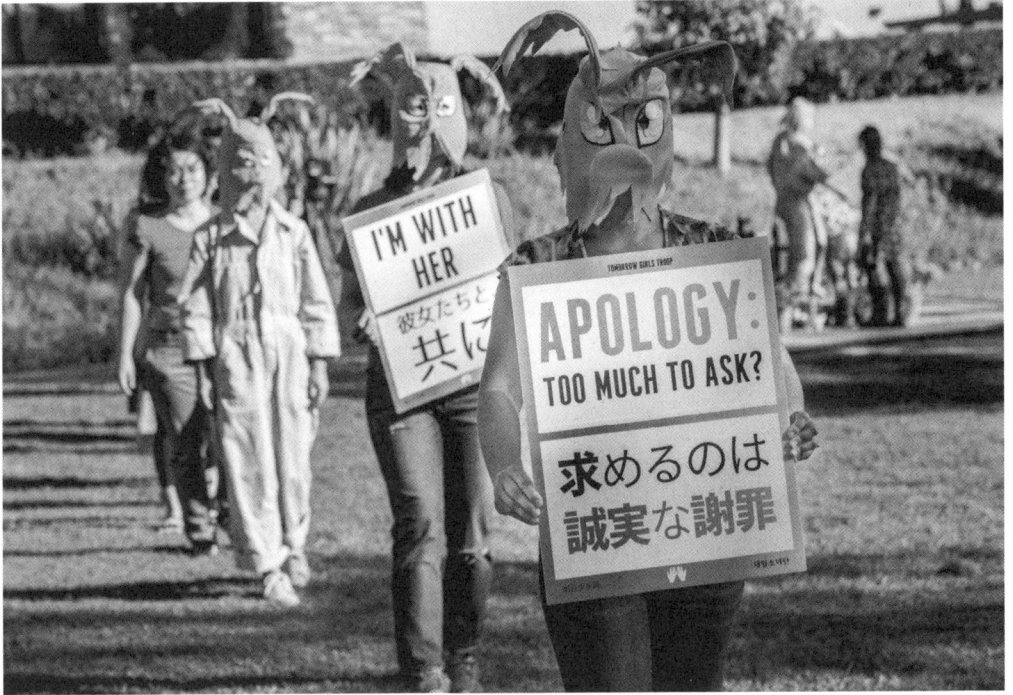

8.

8. Qianwen Jiang, *Tomorrow Girls Troop*, *Against Forgetting*, 2018. Credit: Tomorrow Girls Troop.

KRISTINA SHUMILINA

Women Designers in the Soviet Avant-Garde

Alexander Rodchenko, El Lissitzky, Vladimir Tatlin, and Alexander Vesnin have all become synonymous with the Soviet avant-garde. But where are the women? When women appear on history book pages, they are partners, daughters, wives, and lovers of the more familiar canonical men. This essay aims to showcase Soviet women as independent artists and designers who made equally compelling contributions to the Russian avant-garde as their male counterparts. The underknown stories of the female designers span handcraft, painting, graphic design, collage, publication design, textile design, costume design, stage design, and teaching. "They were gifted artists, well-trained, and articulate […] and their visual concepts were revolutionary for their day," noted Rebecca Cunningham in her article about theater designers (Cunningham, 1998).

Varvara Stepanova is one of the most underestimated Soviet designers from the revolutionary period. In one of Russia's most popular academic databases 'Cyber-Leninka', Stepanova is widely covered by only other female creatives. In her article, "The Life and Fate of the 'Amazon' of the Russian Avant-Garde," D. I. Akhmetova researches the early period of Stepanova's artwork, claiming Stepanova was "one of the most famous women of the Russian Avant-Garde […] one of the 'Amazons' of the Russian Avant-Garde, an artist, designer, and constructionist […] and an independent creative unit with an original vision of art" (Akhmetova, 2017). Akhmetova adds that: [Stepanova] "was an artist, designer, teacher, and also a wife of outstanding artist and photographer Alexander Rodchenko, which, probably, was the main and greatest mission in her life" (Akhmetova, 2017). Stepanova is usually remembered as Alexander Rodchenko's wife.

Varvara Stepanova was a prolific and versatile artist and designer. She and Lyubov Popova gained acclaim for their textile experiments. But Stepanova was also a painter, graphic designer, editorial designer, textile designer, and stage designer for Meyerhold's theater performances (FIGURES 1–8). Nonetheless, these accomplishments fail to compare to her status as the female force behind one of the most prominent Russian avant-gardists.

The Russian journal *LEF* (Left Front of the Arts) focused on the Soviet history, literature, journalism, and philosophy and is considered significant to the Soviet canon as a beacon of avant-garde innovation. As a student studying at a Russian University, I regularly discussed this journal and, in my own experience, recognized the disparity in how the journal's contributors were acknowledged. Vladimir Mayakovsky, Alexander Rodchenko, and other male writers and poets took center stage in our publication analysis. Yet, a deeper examination reveals the extraordinary work Varvara Stepanova and Lyubov Popova contributed throughout the *LEF* period. Within the journal, Rodchenko's name is almost always accompanied by Stepanova's and Popova's. Christina Kiaer notes: "As the celebratory *LEF* dedication makes vivid, Popova and Stepanova were central players in the Constructivist subset of the avant-garde" *(Kiaer, 2000)*.

Lyubov Popova's contribution to the Soviet avant-garde doesn't end with *LEF* (FIGURE 14). Popova was a stage designer, textile designer, painter, and poster and magazine designer *(Bowlt, 1976)* (FIGURES 15-20). Her contribution to textile design was immense (FIGURE 21). "Popova, above all, reached a new definition of movement perceived visually and did, indeed, extend 'art' into 'life'" *(Bowlt, 1976)*. Moreover, "with Popova's death in 1924 and Stepanova's transference of interest...the Constructivist experience in textiles was soon forgotten" *(Bowlt, 1976)*.

Popova is highlighted "above all" among those who created "an avant-garde of mode" and made lasting contributions to textile design *(Bowlt, 1976)*. Along with her work as a textile artist, she was a successful painter. In "What's in a Line? Gender and Modernit," Briony Fer examines the work of Lyubov Popova as a painter, examining how Popova expressed gender through abstraction. Popova was a member of the Textile Faculty at the VKhUTEMAS, Basic Course 1920–1924 *(Lodder, 2021)*. where she lectured in collaboration with Aleksandr Vesnin in such disciplines as "The Maximum Revelation of Color" and "Color Construction" *(Lodder, 2021)*. Her creative activities warrant more attention.

Gender equality, or lack thereof, did not register as a societal flaw in 1920s Russia. Stepanova and Popova worked and taught collaboratively with the more famous men. At VKhUTEMAS, they curated exhibitions together. In her review of the exhibition *Rodchenko & Popova: Defining Constructivism*, Patricia Railing writes: "If the '5 x 5 = 25' exhibition tells us anything, the message is that these five artists (three women, two men) shared common artistic convictions which they wanted to share with an art public" *(Railing, 2009)*. For Stepanova and Popova, the victory lay in the ability to engage in a creative career rather than the recognition that came with personal success. Yet, time distorts significance, and the history books tell only part of the story. Men led the charge; women were merely assistants or partners.

There are even more examples of women who failed to achieve adequate recognition for their contributions to the Soviet avant-garde. Alexandra Exter, who also designed for the theater, taught in VKhUTEMAS, "Color in Space," and was one of the Soviet avant-gardists who created an art studio school *(Lodder, 2021)* (FIGURES 22, 23). Nadezhda Udaltsova taught "Volume in Space" in VKhUTEMAS and "promoted her new approach to form and color in her teaching *(Lodder, 2021)*.

Ludmilla Maiakovskaia taught at VKhUTEMAS and introduced the spray paint and airbrush to create abstract elusive images in the Aerographics Department in the mid-1920s *(Lodder, 2021)*. While this essay aimed to spotlight the incredible achievements of women in the Soviet avant-garde, the hope is that it inspires even more interest. Recognizing these women takes a bit more persistence, patience, and curiosity, but the outcome is worth the investment.

BIBLIOGRAPHY

1. AKHMETOVA D. I. The life and fate of the 'Amazon' of the Russian Avant-Garde (V. F. Stepanova). In Russ. IN: Gasyrlaravazy — Eho vekov, 2017, no. 3/4, pp. 182-193. 12p.

2. BOWLT, JOHN E. 'From pictures to textile prints'. The Print Collector's Newsletter. Vol. 7, No. 1 (March-April 1976), pp. 16-20. 5p.

3. CUNNINGHAM, REBECCA. The Russian women artists/designers of the avant-garde. TD&T: Theatre Design & Technology; Spring98, Vol. 34 Issue 2, pp. 38-51. 14p.

4. FER, BRIONY. What's in a Line? Gender and Modernity. Oxford Art Journal. Vol. 13, No. 1 (1990), pp. 77-88. 12p.

5. GOUGH, MARIA. Faktura: The Making of the Russian Avant-Garde. REs: Anthropology and Aesthetics. No. 36, Factura (Autumn, 1999), pp. 32-59. 28p.

6. KIAER, CHRISTINA. The Russian Constructivist Flapper Dress. Critical Inquiry. Vol. 28, No. 1, Things (Autumn, 2001), pp. 185-243. 59p.

7. KIAER, CHRISTINA. The Short Life of the Equal Woman. Tate Etc.; Spring 2009, Issue 15, pp. 78-85. 8p.

8. LODDER, CHRISTINA. Avant-Garde as Method: Vkhutemas and the Pedagogy of Space 1920–1930. West 86th: A Journal of Decorative Arts, Design History & Material Culture; Spring/ Summer 2021, Vol. 28 Issue 1, pp. 163-165. 3p.

9. LODDER, CHRISTINA. Textiles for Revolutionary Russia: Training Textile Designers at the Moscow VKhUTEMAS. West 86th: A Journal of Decorative Arts, Design History & Material Culture; Fall-Winter2018, Vol. 25 Issue 2, pp. 139-159, 21p.

10. RAILING, PATRICIA. Rodchenko & Popova: Defining Constructivism. Structurist; 2009/2010, Issue 49/50, pp. 136-138. 3p.

1.

FIGURES

1. Lyubov Popova, *Spatial Force Construction*, 1920.
Credit: State Museum of Contemporary Art of
Thessaloniki. PD US/EU copyright expired.

2.

3.

4.

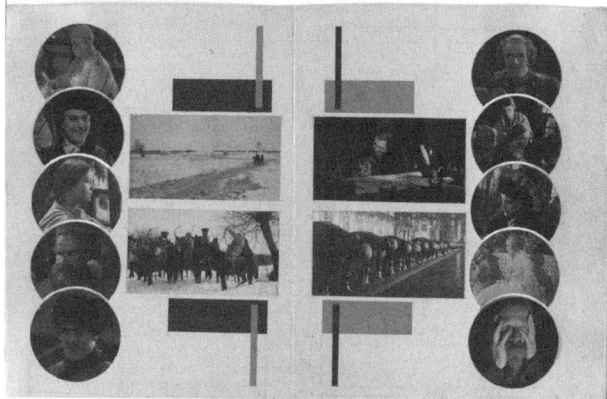

5.

6.

2. Varvara Stepanova, *Charlie Chaplin*, 1922. Credit:
Varvara Stepanova, UPRAVIS, 2024.

3. Varvara Stepanova, *SA. Sovremennaia Arkhitektura*,
no. 4, 1929. Credit: Varvara Stepanova, UPRAVIS, 2024.

4. Varvara Stepanova, *Gornye dorogi*, 1925. Credit:
Varvara Stepanova, UPRAVIS, 2024.

5. Varvara Stepanova, Maquette featuring the film
Kapitanskaya dochka in Sovetsky ekran, no. 32, 1928.
Credit: Varvara Stepanova, UPRAVIS, 2024.

6. Alexander Rodchenko, Lilya Brik wearing the headscarf
with pattern designed by Varvara Stepanova, 1924. Credit:
2024 Estate of Alexander Rodchenko.

7.   8.   9.   10.

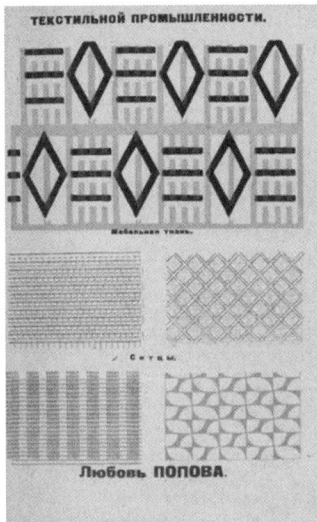  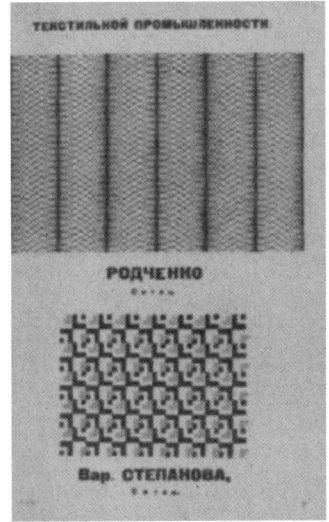

11.   12.   13.

7. Varvara Stepanova, Designs by Stepanova in *LEF Magazine of the Left Front of the Arts*, 1923. Credit: Varvara Stepanova, UPRAVIS, 2024.

8. Varvara Stepanova, *Students in Sports Clothing*, 1924. Credit: Varvara Stepanova, UPRAVIS, 2024.

9. Lyubov Popova, printed fabric sketches, 1924. Credit: *LEF: Magazine of the Left Front of the Arts*. No. 2 (6). PD US/EU copyright expired.

10. Alexander Rodchenko, Cover of *LEF: Magazine of the Left Front of the Arts*, No. 2 1924. Credit: Alexander Rodchenko UPRAVIS.

11. Lyubov Popova, Printed furniture fabric, 1924. Credit: *LEF: Magazine of the Left Front of the Arts*. No. 2 (6). PD US/EU copyright expired.

12. Varvara Stepanova, *Painted fabric designs*, 1924. Credit: Varvara Stepanova, UPRAVIS, 2024.

13. Alexander Rodchenko & Varvara Stepanova, *hintz design*, 1924. Credit: Alexander Rodchenko & Lyubov Popova, UPRAVIS, 2024.

14.

15.

16.

17.

18.

19.

14. Collage by Popova and Rodchenko, 1924. Credit: Alexander Rodchenko, Lyubov Popova, UPRAVIS, 2024.

15. Lyubov Popova, Stage design for *Earth in Turmoil*, Meyerhold Theater, Moscow, 1923. PD US/EU copyright expired.

16. Lyubov Popova, *The Tale of the Priest Balda* puppet show design, 1920. PD US/EU copyright expired.

17. Lyubov Popova, *The Magnanimous Cucklod* clothing sketch, 1921. PD US/EU copyright expired.

18. Lyubov Popova, Portrait of the Artist's Sister, 1909. PD US/EU copyright expired.

19. Lyubov Popova, Cubist landscape city, c. 1914. PD US/EU copyright expired.

20.

21.

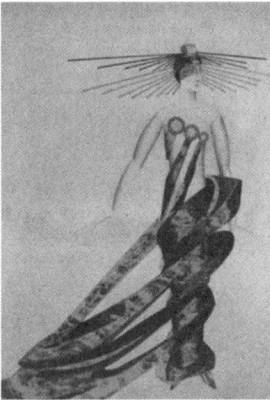

23.

22.

20. Lyubov Popova, *Questions of Stenography* magazine cover design, 1924. PD US/EU copyright expired.

21. Lyubov Popova, Textile design, c. 1924. PD US/EU copyright expired.

22. Alexander Exter, Moscow. Synthetic city, 1914. PD US/EU copyright expired.

23. Alexander Exter, *The Queen of The Martians* costume design for the movie Aelita, 1924. PD US/EU copyright expired.

rence for women who work with public visual and physical forms, March 20th at the

JULIA CHEUNG

Forging the Path for Radical and Feminist Design

Throughout history, female designers have often faced discrimination that restricted their artistic expression and professional growth. Despite these obstacles, many women have confronted inequity head-on, advocating for change through feminist activism. This activism has brought greater awareness to gender disparities within the design world, leading to increased recognition and celebration of women's contributions. Yet, historical narratives frequently overlook the pioneering feminists who laid the groundwork for equality in graphic design, failing to fully credit those who helped reshape the field.

As a progressive founder of women's feminist programs and talented designer, Sheila Levrant de Bretteville should be a monumental figure within design history (FIGURE 1). De Bretteville didn't just open up doors for feminist opportunities but established intensive and enriching educational methods that served as the emergence of postmodernism design.

Born in 1940 in Brooklyn, New York, De Bretteville's design experience began early in High School. Through the guidance of a graphic designer Leon Friend, De Bretteville was exposed to artistic education and history, which developed her interest in communitarian design. Soon after, De Bretteville attended Barnard College as an undergraduate, then gained her MFA at Yale University. Following De Bretteville's graduation in 1969, she was commissioned to rebrand the California Institute of the Arts (CalArts) visual identity. The principle around the re-branding embodied De Bretteville's philosophies drawn from her education at Yale University and the influences of her role model, Paulo Freire. Within this unique approach, De Bretteville applied the principle of positionality into these designs, referring to the shift in how social or political positions shape one's identity, which follows a more anthropological perspective. Instead of solely implementing ornamentation and technique, De Bretteville encouraged more context-based design, especially within her admissions poster (FIGURE 2). Through bold red typography, De Bretteville stated, "If the designer is to make a deliberate contribution to society, he must be able to integrate all he can learn about behavior and resources, ecology and human needs; taste and style just aren't enough" (Gourbe, 2020). This advertisement poster started one of the first discussions of how well-rounded or knowledgeable designers should be when exploring topics besides utilizing visual concepts.

This progressive method of design was carried into De Bretteville's pedagogy once she became a part of the faculty of CalArts as a graphic design professor. In the new curriculum De Bretteville developed, she took ideas from Freire's pedagogy and traditional Bauhaus teaching methods and followed a "horizontal exchange of information" *(Berenson, 2016)*. Along with visual skills, students needed to speculate and administer experiences into their work to gain conceptuality through their unique expression.

This pedagogy became even more prominent within De Bretteville's establishment of *The Women's Building* in 1973, a community center and school meant as a shared sanctuary for feminist culture (FIGURE 3). This organization focused on fighting oppression by empowering each female artist's exploration and strengthening their "performance and publication" *(Gourbe, 2020)*. The building hosted art galleries, providing studios and publishing contacts to stimulate artistic support, and arranged educational opportunities such as seminars, performances, and lectures. In an interview article, "Being Otherwise," by Silvia Sfligiotti, De Bretteville explains some of her assignment processes and successful student projects, which convey her program's impact.

De Bretteville noted her interest in using engagement within the design in response to an interview question about her pedagogy. Through the course "Private Conversations and Public Announcements," she experimented with this concept by pushing the students to visit a place that causes discomfort and creating a poster on how they could be more at ease *(Sfligiotti, 2016)*. De Bretteville explains her intentions, claiming that she was influenced by the disregard for women and their disrespectful treatment. As a result, some students "ended up having conversations with the men there about what would make a woman like her feel more comfortable" *(Knutson, 2023)*. Reflecting on her teaching style, De Bretteville states: "When I began to teach, I looked at all the assignments I was given and found them lacking in what I wanted to do" *(Sfligiotti, 2016)*. In another project, De Bretteville prompted students to choose a place they could develop through design. The students were more engaged, the assignment piqued their interest, and De Bretteville claimed, "I think that what catches your eye (your I) provides insight into yourself, and that's also very helpful to generating your work" *(Sfligiotti, 2016)*. Furthermore, this program also initiated Consciousness-Raising, which is a method that focuses a group of people on a cause or condition and has them acknowledge the vulnerabilities and social pressures faced by young women *(Berenson, 2016)*. Led by self-expression and individual experience, De Brettville had her students undergo unconventional educational methods, which allowed for the process of asking and answering questions.

Before the construction of these artistic platforms, women struggled to enable systems that opposed the obstacle of discrimination, but De Bretteville uplifted those designers to their highest potential. Despite these critical resources De Bretteville offered to these women, these contributions are hidden within design history, overlooking the praise she deserves. Therefore, artists should recognize these accomplishments more than they have been. However, De Bretteville's designs that impacted feminist activism also fall short of their deserved attention.

If De Brettville wasn't recognized for her pedagogy, she should at least be acknowledged for her *Women in Design: The Next Decade* poster (FIGURE 4) presented at the 2017 *Women's March on Washington* (FIGURE 5). This event, protesting the inauguration of Donald Trump, was one of the most historical moments of feminist resistance, gathering around 1,000,000 protesters (including myself). The "eyebolt" icon used within her poster was found throughout various items on protesters, becoming a symbol of revolt against Trump's misogynistic threats through its meaning, "strength without a fist" *(Ripost, 2017; Feminist Studio Workshop, 1973)* (FIGURE 6). The eyebolt icon, with hardware screw and female symbol, captures two ideas suggesting women are as strong as men. While De Bretteville's symbol wasn't made intentionally for this march — as it was presented at the *Women in Design Conference* poster in 1974 — it still left a compelling effect on viewers when it reappeared within one of the most worldwide organized feminist protests in existence, representing her work as an emblem of feminism. On De Bretteville's website, she describes how this poster was made, using a blueprint process which implied that their artistic visions could guide the future. Many other elements within the piece were influenced by personal connections to impactful imagery around [her], but emphasized that her "attraction to hardware led [her] to see the biological symbol of women in a simple eyebolt" *(De Bretteville, 1974)*.

De Bretteville's design work left a lasting effect — of at least 43 years — on those who witnessed it and proceeded to resurrect its symbolism. Nonetheless, when researching the iconic "eye bolt" symbol online, there is little to no documentation of its existence, despite the claims of its impact within the 2017 *Women's March*. It's absurd that the media has overlooked De Bretteville's artistic/activist contributions, especially since protesters purposely utilized her icon to symbolize their strength. The question arises: How can designers evolve without being able to identify essential periods of progress throughout history?

Feminist leaders have struggled against levels of persecution and hardship to gain the grounds of equality that we have today, but these leaps in progress won't necessarily sustain themselves. De Bretteville's efforts might have prompted equality, but we must remember these changes for them to remain intact. Some of the obstacles she experienced were high opposition towards integrating her program into Yale University (FIGURE 7) — as faculty resigned in conflict with her pedology — but De Bretteville emphasized in an interview in *Eye Magazine* that those moments didn't stump her mission, which was to evoke more purpose into the school's program *(Ellen Lupton, 1993)*. As female designers, we should use this perspective to guide our future — to persevere — and continue to educate others on these achievements to maintain our position of equal rights to others. Therefore, modern-day designers need to become the catalyst for feminist progression through historical awareness.

BIBLIOGRAPHY

1. ASTESANI, GIULIA. "Being Otherwise." Progetto Grafico. June 22, 2021. Accessed April 3, 2023. https://medium.com/progetto-grafico/being-otherwise-b9ccb-fca503a.

2. BERENSON, IZZY; HONETH, SARAH. "Clearing the Haze: Prologue to Postmodern Graphic Design Education through Sheila de Bretteville" The Gradient, 26, Apr, 2016. https://walkerart.org/magazine/clearing-the-haze-prologue-to-postmodern-graphic-design-education-through-sheila-de-bretteville-2.

3. DE BRETTEVILLE, SHEILA LEVRANT. "From Graphic Feminism and Feminist Design to Emancipation." Switch (On Paper). Accessed April 3, 2023. https://www.switchonpaper.com/en/society/feminism/sheila-de-bretteville-from-graphic-feminism-and-feminist-design-to-emancipation/.

4. DE BRETTEVILLE, SHEILA LEVRANT. Interviewed by Felix Burrichter. "Interview: Sheila Levrant de Bretteville on Graphic Design at Yale." Pin-Up Magazine, no. 8 (2009). Accessed April 26, 2023. https://archive.pinupmagazine.org/articles/interview-sheila-levrant-de-bretteville-graphic-designyale#20.

5. DE BRETTEVILLE, SHEILA LEVRANT. "SheilaStudio." SheilaStudio. 2023. https://sheilastudio.us/

6. KNUTSON, ERIN. "Interview: Graphic Designer, Artist, And Educator Sheila Levrant de Bretteville On Legacy." PIN—UP Magazine. https://archive.pinupmagazine.org/articles/interview-sheila-levrant-de-bretteville-graphic-designyale.

7. LUPTON, ELLEN. "Feature: Reputations: Sheila Levrant de Bretteville." Eye Magazine. Autumn, 1993. https://www.eyemagazine.com/feature/article/reputations-sheila-levrant-de-bretteville.

8. "Negotiating for Human Rights: The Inter-American Commission on Human Rights." Alexander Street. Accessed April 26, 2023. https://documents.alexanderstreet.com/d/1001001901.

9. "Riposte magazine meets graphic designer Sheila Levrant de Bretteville." It's Nice That. 23, November, 2017. https://www.itsnicethat.com/features/riposte-9-publication-231117

1.

If the designer is to make
a deliberate contribution to society,
he must be able to integrate
all he can learn about
behavior and resources,
ecology and human needs;

taste and style just aren't enough.

For information regarding admission,
graduate & undergraduate study, and financial aid
write:

School of Design

California Institute of the Arts
2404 West 7th Street
Los Angeles, California 90057

opening fall 1970

2.

3.

FIGURES

1. Activist Graphics from LACMA, *Sheila de Bretteville and the Woman's Building*, video, 2022. Source: YouTube screenshot, fair use for educational use.

2. Sheila Levrant de Bretteville, *Announcement poster for the CalArts School of Design*, 1970. Source: Are.na, fair use for educational use.

3. Maria Karras. Woman's Building opening at Grand View Street location, 1973. Credit: Maria Karras collection of Woman's Building papers and photographs. Getty Research Institute, Los Angeles (2018.M.16). © J. Paul Getty Trust.

4.

5.

6.

7.

4. *Women in Design: The Next Decade poster. Credit: Walker Art Museum.*

5. *Women's March, 2017. Credit: Shannon Stapleton / Reuters.*

6. Mikaela Krestesen, *Eyebolt necklace.* Credit: Mikaela Krestesen.

7. Sheila Levrant de Bretteville teaching at Yale University, 2021. Source: YouTube video screenshot, fair use for educational use.

HEROIC CRAFT

The examples in this chapter defy the pressures of capitalism. Here, craft captures the essence of local culture, focusing on creating handwork that asserts a folk or pre-colonial identity. This craft acts as a political force tied to a rich social heritage. Not only that, but the analog nature of craft sheds light on environmentally conscious design methods and materials, where concepts like slow industry prioritize quality and durability. Heroic craft serves as a reminder that design isn't solely about creating objects for consumption; it encompasses the politics of tradition, identity, and sustainability.

Peruvian Textiles: Weaving Patterns from History

Peru has the longest continuous tradition of textile production in the world, dating back over 12,000 years. The oldest documented textiles known are six fragments of woven fabric and twined cord found in Guerrero, Peru, which were carbon-dated to between 10100 and 9080 BCE.[1] Even though Peru was an important early innovator in textile production, their contribution to textile history must be addressed. An internet search for "history of the loom" and "history of weaving" found that almost all sites focused on Egypt, China, and the Middle East but did not mention Peru or South America.[2]

History of Weaving — Early Hand Weaving, written by Portland State University Associate Professor Emerita of History Karen Carr, did note that "people also invented weaving in the Americas, maybe around the same time as in Afro-Eurasia" but concludes that "they might have brought band-weaving with them from Asia, and then, as they settled down, they also invented wider looms and wider fabrics" *(Carr, 2017)*. Since the Andean textiles pre-date the Egyptian evidence by 5000 years and there is no evidence of a neolithic transoceanic trade between Egypt and the western coast of South America, Carr's suggestion is further documentation of how the contribution of Peruvian weavers is still overlooked. The significance of Peruvian textiles in the history of fabric production, the unequaled complexity and distinctive design of the fabrics, and their role in documenting thousands of years of Andean history demand recognition and deeper investigation in the narrative of design history.

Interest in Peruvian weaving languished until the early 20th century. Textiles from the Middle East and Asia had been coveted and traded from the 11th century when the Crusades opened up a cultural exchange with the East. On the other hand, South America was not on Europe's radar until 1492, when Columbus accidentally stumbled upon the continent and initiated the Spanish occupation. The high quality

---

1 Other ancient textile fragments have been found in Anatolia, Turkey, dated to 7000 BCE and Fayum, Egypt, dating to about 5000 BCE.

2 The sites included:
  a. "History of Weaving," Historyofclothing.com. 2021, www.historyofclothing. com/making-clothing/history-of-weaving/. No mention of Peru or South America.
  b. "History of the Loom: Know how your clothes are made." marylana.com. July 2020, https://marylana.com/blogs/news/ history-of-the-loom-know- how-your-clothes -are-made. This blog mentions a Mayan myth, but focuses only on Egypt when discussing the loom.
  c. "The History of Woven Textiles." June 15, 2017, www.tootal. nl/en/news/show/22/the-history-of- woventextiles. "The development of spinning and weaving began in ancient Egypt around 3400 before Christ (B.C.). The tool originally used for weaving was the loom." No mention of Peru or South America.

of Peruvian textiles was acknowledged in Europe in the 16th century but was decidedly secondary in importance to the Spaniards' single-minded quest for silver and gold. Several factors may have contributed to the lack of focus on Andean textiles over the last five centuries. Textiles are fragile and tend to disintegrate when exposed to the elements, so often, only fragmentary evidence survives at archaeological sites. The best-preserved textiles are found wrapped around mummified bodies in ancient cemeteries on coastal deserts or found on the frozen bodies of children sacrificed at the icy peaks of the Andes Mountains. The Peruvian government has passed laws preventing the desecration of ancient cemeteries to prevent looting, but this has also deterred scholarly investigations. The earliest scholarly articles on Andean textiles appear in the 1920s and 1930s, when interest may have been sparked by the photographs of Martin Chambi (1891–1973), a Peruvian photographer who documented the indigenous people of Cusco in the 1910s–1930s and took numerous images of native women wearing colorful garments with elaborately woven patterns (FIGURE 1). Writing for the *Penn Museum Journal* in 1920, Ethel Ellis Benners observed, "[c]onsidering the enormous wealth of decorative material to be found in prehistoric Peruvian art, it is strange more frequent use has not been made of this interesting and original type of design by the artist, designer and manufacturer" *(Benners, 1920)*. There have been several recent museum exhibits on Peruvian textiles. However, much more must be discovered and studied about Peruvian weavers and their textiles before they are fully integrated into mainstream design history.[3]

To better appreciate Andean textiles, it is necessary to understand the conditions under which they were created. An abundance of natural resources for fibers and dye contributed to the extraordinary development of textile production in Peru. The Andean people had access to three of the four major textile fibers: flax, cotton, and wool. Flax and other bast fibers were of low quality and were used for more practical purposes, such as rope, netting, and basketry. Despite the rugged Andean terrain, several cotton species could be cultivated in the coastal valleys. Cotton was available in white and several shades of brown. Wool was obtained from several members of the camelid family, including the alpaca, llama, and vicuna. Alpacas and llamas thrive in the high altitudes of the Andes, where the extreme temperatures cause them to grow extremely dense coats. The llama was domesticated as a pack animal for its wool by 1000 BCE. Camelid wool is graded based on its color, length, and softness. Wool from the vicuna is the highest grade, with one strand measuring about 12 microns; the finest cashmere measures 19 microns. The fibers are so delicate that they cannot be dyed with chemical dyes. Unlike their camelid cousins, the vicuna inhabits a limited geographic region in the Andes mountains, does not produce much wool, and can only be sheared every two years, making this fiber rare, expensive, and unique to this region.[4] Baby alpaca wool is next in quality, followed by adult alpaca fleece and llama wool, the coarsest camelid fiber. Traditional Peruvian textiles were dyed with natural substances to yield a bright variety of colors and hues (FIGURE

3 There were exhibitions of Andean textiles at the Museum of Fine Arts, Boston in 1994, the Metropolitan Museum of Art in 2004, and the Fashion and Textile Museum, London, in 2019. See Stone, Phipps, Ferguson, and Field Gray in the bibliography for catalogs or reviews of these shows.

2): blue corn for purple; Tara pods for blue; Yanali bark or Q'olle flowers for mustard yellow and orange; Ch'illca leaves for green; and Cochineal, a parasitic insect found on cacti, for red, pink, purple, and orange. Mineral salts were used to fix the colors, which have held up remarkably over the centuries. More research needs to be done on the properties of these dyes, as they might offer a color-fast natural substitute to chemical dyes. Few cultures inhabiting such a harsh environment have utilized their natural resources to this impressive degree. By ignoring the accomplishments of the Peruvian weavers, the design canon has missed an opportunity to highlight an inspiring example of creativity thriving in adversity.

Peruvian textiles utilized simple technology to create incredibly complex weaves and patterns. Peruvian weavers used three simple hand looms as early as the Neolithic period. The backstrap loom uses warp threads wrapped around two sticks or bars; one bar is secured by a rope to a tree or post, and the other is tied to the weaver, who supplies tension to the threads by leaning forward or backward (FIGURES 3-4). The four-peg loom has four posts set in the ground to support the two warp bars. Sometimes, two additional posts were added for a secondary warp to make more complicated tapestry weaves. The distance between the posts determined the width of the fabric. A vertical loom leans against a tree or building (FIGURE 6). It can have two warp bars or only a top bar with warp threads tied to rocks to maintain tension. With every loom, weavers would start at the bottom of the warp threads and work toward the top, so the length of the fabric was predetermined. Peruvians rarely cut their fabric; garments were created as one piece or constructed of several finished pieces sewn together. Working with simple looms, Peruvian weavers created fabrics of unparalleled complexity by using numerous heddles, supplemental warps, and discontinuous warps and wefts. They wove tapestries, brocades, damasks, double and triple cloth, stripes, and intricate patterns. Many of the fabrics they created cannot be duplicated on contemporary looms. Unconstrained by automated machines, Peruvian weavers could weave from any edge, start and stop patterns erratically, create idiosyncratic repeats, or put in diagonal or curved wefts. Benners observed:

> The Peruvian was unusually skilled in manipulating his simple hand loom where the weaver produces the design as the material grows [...] Some of the finest pieces contain nearly three hundred weft yarns to the inch and their cleverness in adapting the most intricate design and overcoming the technical difficulties of the loom is something that any other people have never accomplished—excepting perhaps the makers of the Coptic fabrics from Egypt (Benners, 1920).

In *To Weave for the Sun: Ancient Andean Textiles in the Museum of Fine Arts, Boston*, Rebecca Stone notes that "the creation of a typically complex Wari tap-

---

4 The vicuna has a limited range; it is indigenous to Peru, northern Chile, Bolivia, and parts of Argentina. A smaller population has been introduced to Ecuador. By the 1970s, the vicuna population had dropped to about 6,000 animals due to overhunting for its valuable wool. Since then, protective laws and controlled farming have increased the number of vicuna to around 125,000 animals.

estry tunic entails 6–9 miles of different colored thread interlocked as many as 1,500,500 separate times while being woven" (*Stone, 1994*). Surviving Andean textiles indicate that Peruvian weavers valued intricate patterns and intense color over labor efficiency. Their work represents some of the most elaborate woven work ever created, demonstrating a level of craft and artistry that has rarely been equaled. The difficulty of replicating Andean textiles may have contributed to their lack of interest during the 19th and early 20th centuries when mechanization and production were valued over hand craftsmanship.

The history of Peruvian textiles encompasses the cultural, economic, social, and political history of an extensive portion of a continent for twelve centuries. From 10000 to 3000 BCE, there is archaeological evidence of woven baskets made of plant fibers. From 3000 BCE to 1800 BCE, weavers on the north coast of Peru created non-loom and plain weave fabrics. By 1800 BCE, all the different weaving technologies were used, including double cloth, triple cloth, tapestry, embroidery, and discontinuous warp and weft. The centers of production had shifted to the Paracas and Nasca civilizations on the south coast and the Chavin culture in the central highlands. Surviving textiles from these cultures indicate that Andeans were already producing painted fabrics, intricate tapestries, and elaborate embroidery at a very early period (FIGURES 7-12). The Wari culture dominated the highland and coastal regions between 500–800 and was particularly adept at creating interlocked tapestries with highly abstracted figures and patterns (FIGURES 13-14). Their weaving was wonderful, often two hundred threads per inch. After 1000, several cultures flourished in the region for the next five centuries: Chimu on the north coast (FIGURES 15-16), Chancay (FIGURE 17) and Rimac (FIGURE 18) on the central coast, and Ica on the south coast (FIGURES 19-20). Some of these civilizations are only known by archaeological records, including textiles; the study of Peruvian textiles is critical to revealing the achievements of these cultures.

The Inca empire expanded across Peru after 1200, completely dominating the region by 1476; they absorbed all the weaving techniques used by the cultures they conquered. The Incas were the largest empire in pre-Columbian South America, and their economy was based on agriculture, metals, pottery, and textiles. In fact, they valued alpacas, vicunas, and fabrics made with their wool so highly that they were traded as currency throughout the empire. According to textile scholar Rutu Kanade, vicuna fabric was so valuable that only royal family members were allowed to wear it (*Kanade, 2020*). The most common Inca clothes were tunics with a tapestry border for men and one-piece garments gathered at the waist with woven belts for women; both genders wore mantles or shawls, often woven with motifs in many small squares or with a distinctive llama figure (FIGURE 21).

In 1531, Spanish explorer Francisco Pizzaro landed with a large force on the coast of Peru. He entered the primary Incan city of Cajamarca in 1532 and executed the Incan ruler Atahualpa in 1533. The Spanish ruled Peru until 1824, dramatically altering the political, economic, and social culture of the Indigenous people:

As the Spanish imposed their law and culture on the indigenous people of Peru, and the Incan empire was crushed, so was traditional textile production, as the Spanish did not want competition for
their artisans in Europe. A new system was created to produce Eu-
ropean-style cloth, introducing new materials from sheep, silk, and
metallic threads (Aracari, n.d.).

They introduced the treadle loom, allowing native weavers to produce fabric
rolls according to European preferences. Textiles produced for Spanish markets or
the Catholic Church included European figures, biblical scenes, inscriptions, and new
forms, such as seat covers, bedspreads, and rugs (FIGURES 22, 23). This pattern of
cultural obliteration was repeated in North America and Africa following European
colonization in an attempt to impose "civilized" standards on local populations who
were considered to be more "primitive." However, the traditional methods did not
die out completely, and local weavers continued to make warp-patterned textiles on
hand looms for their use. Ironically, the intricate textiles produced with the simple
Peruvian technology could be much more complex than the fabrics created with the
European looms.

The traditional language of the Andean people, Quechua, is an oral language;
lacking a written language, Peruvian weavers used symbols and patterns in their
textiles to communicate information and ideas, record historical events, and identify
individuals or communities. Individual motifs, called pallay, could be used throughout the Andes region, be specific to a particular community, or be unique to an individual weaver. Many patterns represent plants, animals, or items important to their
everyday life: corn, potato flowers, marine life, birds, llamas, and farming tools. Lakes,
waves, and mountain trails record the terrain of their homeland. Others have important symbolic associations. The condor, puma, and sun were Incan gods, while hearts
and hummingbirds represented love. Animals often represented qualities the wearer
possessed or wanted to achieve, such as sharp vision, ferocity, fertility, or strength.
Color, juxtaposition to other motifs, and placement on the textile added additional
meaning. Much of what we know about the Andean cultures comes from the woven
meanings in their textiles.

Fabric played an important role in Andean culture beyond its functional role
of providing clothing and warmth. The Incas regulated fabric production, establish-
ing regional textile centers throughout the empire. Weaving was not gender specific;
women and girls, men and boys participated in fabric production, passing on techniques and patterns from one generation to the next. Textiles were an indication of
social status and wealth. Only a select few were allowed to make or own the finest
vicuna wool cloth. The importance of textiles continued after death. The dead were
wrapped in hundreds of yards of fabric and buried with extra clothes; small versions
of clothing were made specifically to be buried with the deceased. Nasher Museum
curator Julia McHugh explains the central role of fabrics in Peruvian life:

> Textiles were powerful agents in the world of the living and the dead for numerous cultures across the region. In life, they conveyed political, social, and occupational status through their material, color, and motifs. In death, they served as wrapping for sacred mummy bundles and costumes for the afterlife (McHugh, 2000).

Textiles dominated Andean daily life to a degree rarely seen in any other culture; they are a portal to a vanished world.

Since the rediscovery of Peruvian textiles in the early 20th century, there have been periods of influence, appropriation, and revival. Bauhaus textile artists Anni Albers and Margarete Willers developed an interest in so-called "primitive art" and were inspired by Andean fabrics, particularly the brilliant colors and abstract patterns of the Wari weavers (FIGURES 24, 25). American fiber artists spurred a second wave of interest in Indigenous and Native Americans during the 1950s and 1960s. Andean weaving has been a rich design source for fashion; John Galliano's collection for Christian Dior in 2005 featured Peruvian textiles, and mid-range fashion house Escvdo offers their version of an Andean tunic. Contemporary Peruvian fashion designers Meche Correa, Chiara Macchiavello, and Mozhdeh Matin often feature modern interpretations of historic textile patterns (FIGURE 27). A more systematic effort to preserve traditional Peruvian weaving and dyeing techniques was established in 1996 by creating the Centro de Textiles Tradicionales del Cusco (CTTC). A partnership of ten weaving communities, the organization maintains weaving centers, promotes textile tourism, and mentors young weavers. But while these centers demonstrate hand weaving and natural dyeing, they cater to the tourist industry, creating tablecloths, table runners, placemats, belts, and bags with simplified versions of traditional designs (FIGURE 26). Some contemporary weavers continue the ancient tradition of creating motifs of significance to their daily lives, like the woman living in a landlocked village who weaves patterns of boats inspired by her son's toy. However, the fabrics are often striped, without the creative artistry of historic textiles. It is heartening that a 12,000-year tradition of textile production is continuing, but textile tourism may, in fact, undermine the integrity of the traditions it is trying to revive.

The history of Andean textiles is extremely complex and yet to be wholly documented or understood. Although textiles from this region are referred to as "Peruvian," the Andes region of South America includes portions of northern Chile, western Ecuador, Bolivia, and modern-day Peru. In addition, the area did not have a unified culture until the Inca created their empire in the 15th century. Over 12,000 years, dozens of autonomous civilizations emerged, flourished, and died out. While the textiles of these cultures are often studied as a group, their creators may not have had any connection with other societies in the region. For example, the Paracas civilization in southern Peru from 800–100 BCE, the Wari culture on the central highlands from 500–1000 CE, and the Chancay on the central coast from 1000–1470 CE would have had no contact with each other. While they appear to have shared an oral language and similar technology, each culture developed distinctive weaving innovations, styles, pallay, and patterns. It is important to understand and respect each civilization as a unique culture and not impose an artificial homogeneity. Unfortunately, cultural conflation seems to be a side effect of textile tourism. Some contemporary textiles combine pallay from different cultures and time periods; others misinterpret the meaning of ancient patterns. For example, the contemporary Umasbamba community of weavers near Cusco misinterprets the ancient cuttlefish motif. It claims unique ownership of the diamond pattern, which appears in almost every Andean culture across thousands of years. *(Ramos, 2019)* The canon of Western design must recognize the significant contributions of Andean textiles to design history — their artistry, diversity, technological skill, symbolic meaning, and social context — before 12,000 years of extraordinary creativity and talent are diluted beyond recognition.

BIBLIOGRAPHY

1. "Ancient Andean Textiles at the Yale University Art Gallery." HALI. 27 June 2016. https://hali. com/news/ancient-andean-textiles-at-yale-university-art-gallery/.

2. AUTHOR, ELISSA. "Andean Weaving and the Appropriation of the Ancient Past in Modern Fiber Art." Bauhaus Imaginista Journal. Edition 2: Learning From. www.bauhaus-imaginista. org/articles/824/andean-weaving-and-the-appropriation-of-the-ancient-past-in-modern-fib er-art.

3. "Backstrap Weaving in Peru." Threads of Peru, https://threadsofperu.com/pages/backstrap weaving-in-peru.

4. BANKHEAD, NATALIE. "Learning to Read Peruvian Textiles." Cusco Eats, 22 October 2016, http://cuzcoeats.com/learning-read-peruvian-textiles/.

5. BENNERS, ETHEL Ellis. "Ancient Peruvian Textiles." Penn Museum: The Museum Journal, vol. XI, no. 3, 1920, www.penn.museum/sites/journal/843/.

6. BRUMFIEL, ELIZABETH. "Cloth, Gender, Continuity, and Change: Fabricating Unity in Anthropology." American Anthropologist. Vol 108, no. 4, December 2006, pp. 862-877.

7. BUSKIRK, VAN AND ELIZABETH CONRAD. "Preserving Andean Weaving: The Center for Traditional Textiles of Cusco." Cultural Survival Quarterly Magazine, March 1999, www.culturalsurvival.org/publications/cultural-survival-quarterly/preserving-andean weaving-center-traditional-textiles.

8. C., W. A. "Peruvian Textiles." Bulletin of the Detroit Institute of the Arts of the City of Detroit. Vol 8, no 6, March 1927, pp. 67-72.

9. CARR, KAREN E. "History of weaving – Early hand weaving." Quatr.us Study Guides, June 8, 2017. https://quatr.us/clothing/history-weaving-early-hand-weaving.htm.

10. COHEN-APONTE, ANANDA. "Paracas Textiles: An Introduction." Smarthistory, October 16, 2020, https://smarthistory.org/paracas-textiles-introduction/.

11. "Colors of the Andes: Dyeing Wool the Peruvian Way." Adventures Within Reach Travel Blog. 7 January 2019. https://adventureswithinreach. com/travel/2019/02/07/dyeing-wool the-peruvian-way/.

12. CONFER, SARAH. "Andean textiles tell stories...literally." Threads of Peru Blog, 25 November 2014, https://threadsofperu.com/blogs/blog/88849670-andean-textiles-tell stories-literally.

13. CONKLIN, WILLIAM J. "Structure as Meaning in Andean Textiles." Chungara: Revista de Antropología Chilena, vol. 29, no. 1, January-June 1997, pp. 109-131.

14. "The Earliest Americans - Chavin." Nephicode.com. 7 March 2015. http://nephicode. blogspot. com/2015/03/the-earliest-americans-chavin.html.

15. FEMENÍAS, BLENDA, "Structure, Design, and Gender in Inka Textiles" PreColumbian Textile Conference VII / Jornadas de Textiles PreColombinos VII. 13 November 2017, pp. 341-348. http://digitalcommons.unl.edu/pct7/17.

16. FERGUSON, DIENEKE. "Weavers of the Clouds: Textile Arts of Peru." Hidden Art, 2019, https://hiddenart.co.uk/2019/08/02/weavers-of-the-clouds-textile-arts-of-peru/. Accessed 26 September 2021.

17. FERRARA, FLORA. "Peruvian Weaving: 4 Traditional Looms from Peruvian Textile Heritage." Huay Wasi. 22 January 2021. https://www.huaywasi.com/blogs/news/peruvian-weaving.

18. Field Grey. "Weavers of the Clouds: Textile Arts of Peru." Field Notes blog. 7 September 2019, http://field-grey.com/blog/weavers-of-the-clouds-textile-arts-of-peru/.

19. GOULDER, PAUL. "History of Peru Series – Part 8: Ancient Textiles." Andean Air Mail & Peruvian Times, 31 March 2011, www.peruvian-times.com/31/history-of-peru-series-part-8- ancient-textiles/11565/.

20. "History of Peruvian Textiles." Threads of Peru blog, 2021, https:// threadsofperu.com/pages/ peruvian-textiles-history.

21. KANADE, RUTU. "Textiles of Peru." Textile Value Chain blog, 8 August 2020, https://textilevaluechain. in/in-depth-analysis/articles/textile-articles/global-textiles of-peru/.

22. LIPKIN, ZWIA. "Peruvian Textiles and Tourism." Any Texture. 19 January 2018. www.anytexture. com/2018/01/peruvian-textiles-and-tourism/.

23. MCHUGH, JULIA. "Andean Textiles." Heilbrunn Timeline of Art History. New York: The Metropolitan Museum of Art, June 2000, https:// www.metmuseum.org/toah/hd/ adtx/hd_adtx.htm.

24. MEANS, PHILIP Ainsworth. A Study of Peruvian Textiles. Boston: Museum of Fine Arts, 1932.

25. MEISCH, LYNN A. "Messages From the Past: An Unbroken Inca Weaving Tradition in Northern

27. MURRA, JOHN V. "Cloth and Its Function in the Inca State." American Anthropologist. Vol. 64, no. 4, August 1962, pp. 710-728.

28. "Peru's Rich History of Textile Design." Indigenous blog, 2021, https://indigenous.com/blogs/we-are-knit-together/perus-rich-history-of-textile-design.

29. "Peruvian Textiles — Then and Now." Aracari Travel blog. 11 May 2016. www.aracari.com/blog/ luxury-travel-peru/peruvian-textiles-then-and-now/.

30. PHIPPS, ELENA. The Colonial Andes: Tapestries and Silverwork, 1530-1830. Metropolitan Museum of Art Publications, 2004.

31. "Quechua Symbols & Patterns." Threads of Peru blog. 2021, https:// threadsofperu.com/ pages/quechua-symbols-patterns.

32. RAMOS, JESUS. "Umasbamba Weaving Patterns." Kuoda blog, 15 March 2019, www.kuodatravel.com/ what-do-the-different-symbols-in-peruvian-textiles-mean/.

33. REETZ, SARAH. "Paracas and Other Andean Textiles at the Metropolitan Museum of Art." Bard Graduate Center. 26 September 2017. www.bgc.bard.edu/research-forum/ articles/354/paracas-and-other-andean-textiles.

34. REHL, JANE W. Weaving Metaphors, Weaving Cosmos: Structure, Creativity, and Meaning in Discontinuous Warp and Weft Textiles of Ancient Peru, 300 B.C.E.—1540 C.E. 2003. Emory University, PhD dissertation.

35. SCHER, SARAH. "All-T'oqapu Tunic." Smarthistory: A Center for Public Art History. 9 August 2015. https://smarthistory.org/all-toqa-pu-tunic/.

36. SCHROEDER, NAN EMMA. The Weaving of Original Textiles Influenced by Pre-Columbian Peruvian Weaving. 1976. Iowa State University, Master's Thesis.

37. SILVERMAN, HELAINE. "Touring Ancient Times: The Present and Presented Past in Contemporary Peru." American Anthropologist. Vol 104, no. 3, September 2002, pp. 881-902.

38. STONE, REBECCA, Anne Paul, Susan A. Niles, and Margaret Young-Sanchez. To weave for the sun: ancient Andean textiles in the Museum of Fine Arts, Boston. Thames and Hudson, 1994. "Textile Symbols." Mosqoy, nd. https://www.mosqoy. org/textile-symbols.

39. "The Colorful Fabrics and Textiles of Peru." LimaEasy. 20 April 2021. www.limaeasy.com/ peru-guide/history-of-peru/peruvian-archaeology/the-colorful-fabrics -and-textiles-of-peru.

40. "The Elsberg Collection of Peruvian Textiles." Bulletin of the Detroit Institute of the Arts of the City of Detroit. Vol. 19, no. 4, January 1940, pp. 34-42. http://www. dalnet.lib.mi.us/ dia/collections/ diaBulletins/19-4.pdf.

41. TROY, VIRGINIA GARDNER. "Anni Albers and Ancient Andean Textiles." Bauhaus Imaginista Journal. Edition 2: Learning From. http://www.bauhaus-imaginista. org/articles/771/anni-albers and-ancient-american-textiles.

42. "Wari Culture." Textiles in Context. 3 January 2019. https:// textilesincontext.net/tag/ wari-culture/.

43. "Weaving and Embroidery in Peru: Inspiring the Longevity of Tradition." Inkaterra. 9 July 2018, https://www.inkaterra.com/blog/ weaving-in-peru/.

44. WEIBEL, ADELE COULIN. "Peruvian Textiles." Bulletin of the Detroit Institute of the Arts of the City of Detroit. Vol. 8, no 6, March 1927, pp. 67-72.

PERUVIAN TEXTILES: WEAVING PATTERNS FROM HISTORY

1.

2.

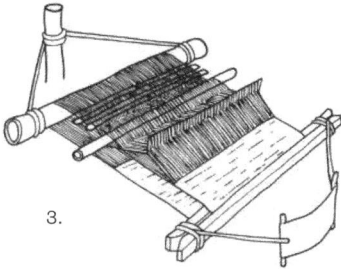

3.

4.

5.

6.

FIGURES

1. Martín Chambi, *Reina del mercado de Cuzco*, 1930. Source: Internet Archive, fair use for educational use.

2. Zwia Lipkin, *Peruvian dyed wool and the source of color*, 2018. Credit: Zwia Lipkin, ANY Texture Textile Art.

3. Backstrap Loom. Source: Researchgate.net, Creative Commons Attribution-NoDerivatives 4.0 International.

4. *Moche*, Vase, detail of woman using backstrap loom. 200-600 CE. Credit: British Museum.

5. Peter van der Sluijs, *Weaving Girls in Peru*, 2012. GNU Free Documentation License.

6. Felipe Huamán Poma de Ayala, *Frior Martín de Murúa mistreating a woman*, ca. 1600. Source: Wikimedia, PD US/EU copyright expired.

7.

8.

9.

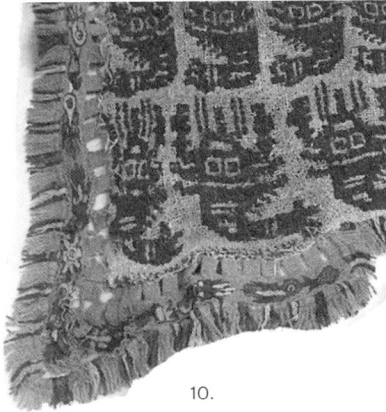

10.

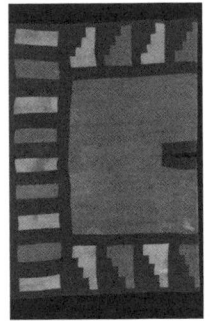

11.

12.

13.

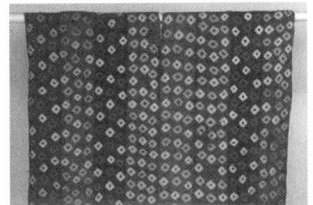

14.

7. Paracas, *Mantle fragment*, 5th-3rd century BCE. Credit: The Metropolitan Museum of Art.

8. Paracas, *Mantle*, 100 BCE - 200 CE. Credit: The Los Angeles County Museum of Art.

9. Paracas, *Embroidered mantle fragment*, 3rd-2nd century BCE. Credit: The Metropolitan Museum of Art.

10. Nasca, *Double-weave textile*, 1st-2nd century CE. Credit: The Metropolitan Museum of Art.

11. Nasca-Huari style, *Unku with staggered and linear designs*, 500-700. Credit: Lima Art Museum.

12. Chavin, *Painted textile fragment*, 4th-3rd century BCE. Credit: The Metropolitan Museum of Art.

13. Wari, *Tunic with discontinuous warps and wefts*, 750-950. Credit: The Textile Museum, Washington, D.C.

14. Wari, *Broad-striped Tunic*, 7th - 9th Century. Credit: The Metropolitan Museum of Art.

15.

16.

17.

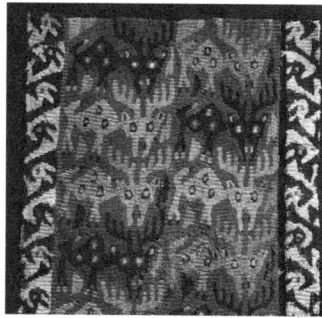

18.

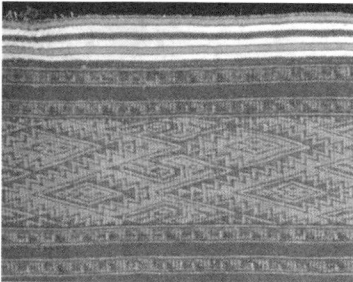

19.

20.

21.

15. Chimú, *Mantle with Pelicans and Tuna*, 1000-1476. Source: Wikipedia, PD US/EU copyright expired.

16. Chimú style, *Ceremonial textile*, 1350-1450. Credit: Lima Art Museum.

17. Chancay, *Sleeved Tunic with Flying Condors*, 1200-1400. PD US/EU copyright expired.

18. Chancay, *Tapestry with deer*, 1000-1450. Credit: Lombards Museum.

19. Ica, *Fragment of Tunic Band*, 1000-1532. Credit: Art Institute of Chicago.

20. Ica, *Miniature dress, featherwork*, 12th - 13th century. Credit: The Metropolitan Museum of Art.

22.

23.

24.

25.

26.

27.

21. Inca, *All-T'oqapu royal tunic*, 1450–1540. Credit: Dumbarton Oaks.

22. Peru, *Tapestry with figurative scenes*, 17th century. Credit: The Metropolitan Museum of Art.

23. Peru, *Woman's Mantle (lliclla)*, 17th-8th century. Credit: The Metropolitan Museum of Art.

24. Margarette Willers, *Slit Tapestry*, 1922. Credit: Bauhaus Imaginista.

25. Margarette Willers, *Textile designs*, 1920s. Credit: Bauhaus Archive, The Metropolitan Museum of Art.

26. Guy Marineau, *John Galliano for Christian Dior*, 2005. Credit: Guy Marineau.

27. Kate Riley, *Contemporary peruvian textiles*, 2019. Credit: Kate Riley, Centsational Style.

Tatreez:
The Art of Resistance Through Craft

Clothing is a profound expression of identity, and for Palestinians, it is a primary means of conveying national, cultural, and social heritage. Tatreez, the traditional Palestinian embroidery technique, is distinguished by its vibrant colors and intricate patterns. Beyond its visual beauty, Tatreez has been woven into the fabric of daily life for Palestinian women, marking marital status, economic standing, and regional origins.

Historically, Palestinian women honed the Tatreez craft. They commenced training as early as six years of age and passed down the skill through generations (Jeni, 2002). It offered a way for women to connect with their ancestors, fostering a robust and collective Palestinian identity. Despite its rich history and influence however, Tatreez has been largely excluded from the Western design history canon due to political and cultural factors that have obscured its visual and conceptual origins and its contemporary impact and legacy. This research delves into the historical roots, evolution, and symbolic significance of Tatreez as a representation of the Palestinian resistance, aiming to underscore the craft's pivotal role in nurturing a collective national identity and preserving a nation's cultural heritage.

The evolution of Tatreez is intricately linked to the shifting political landscape of Palestine. As the lives of Palestinians changed, so did the art form. A thobe, the traditional Palestinian costume, communicated an individual's status, age, and region of origin through unique motifs, patterns, and colors. Before the events of 1948, those elements differed heavily based on region. Palestine was made up of many small villages, which were all very independent of each other economically and socially. Each village developed a unique culture, with different dialects, foods, and stylistically diverse clothing. Initially, the traditional patterns used in Tatreez featured geometric shapes and elements inspired by a rural woman's daily life, including food, animals, politics, and nature (Saca, 2007). The motifs served as a visual cue to the embroiderer's village of origin. For example, the zigzag pattern in FIGURE 12, prevalent in Bedouin embroidery, represents the pattern goats make when urinating. Another motif named "Pasha's tent," and is a reference to the Ottoman occupation commonly featured in the garments produced in the village of Beit Dajan. In FIGURE 1, the pattern of two birds facing away from each other represents the relationship between a woman and her mother-in-law. Based on deeply-rooted religious beliefs, FIGURE 2 displays the custom of stitching an intentional "mark of imperfection" into the thobe to emphasize human imperfections, as only God was attributed with perfection.

Color also played a pivotal role in denoting regional and social identity. Different villages and regions within Palestine are associated with varying colors of fabric. For instance, while Ramallah favored a purer, brighter shade of red, Khalil employed a more brownish hue (*Saca, 2007*). The natural dyes to create these colors were produced from local plants and insects. Yellow was made from saffron flowers, purple from crushed murex shells (FIGURE 3), red from mixing pomegranate skins with other plants and insects (FIGURE 5), and so on. The selection of material and color used to create garments also conveyed one's social standing. Darker hues on clothing suggested wealthier backgrounds, as attaining those deep colors was costly as it required multiple dye baths. To quote Silvia Ulloa, "embroidery functioned as a 'social dictionary' in Palestinian society, serving as a potent symbol of cultural identity and a means of social distinction" (*Ulloa, 2020*).

Despite the differences in patterns, the embroidery process and overall structure of the dress remained the same. The thobes lacked any form-fitting design and were constructed from different parts attached using various stitching methods. At the heart of the thobe lies the Chest Panel (FIGURE 4), or qabbah. It is considered the key element distinguishing one village from another and indicates the wearer's social status. The dress's origin and regional affiliation are also reflected in its two distinct sleeve types. The first type, Irdan, features long, pointed triangular sleeves that are typically left unembroidered so that women can easily tie them behind their backs while working in the fields or around the house (FIGURE 6). The second type, Kum, features narrow sleeves that vary in length and include embroidery on the outer parts, arranged in vertical bands of varying thickness (FIGURES 7, 8). The decorative shoulder pieces (radah) serve various purposes and differ in size according to regional styles. They enhance the dress's aesthetic appeal, protect women from hair dyes such as henna, and increase the garment's durability. The skirt's side panels, or banayeq, consist of embroidered triangular fabric pieces to expand the dress's base and allow easy movement. The front portion of the dress, referred to as hijer, showcases regional distinctions. The dress components are united using two primary stitching techniques: manajel and sanabel stitches (*Saca, 2007*).

The catastrophic events of the Nakba, the 1948 mass displacement of Palestinians from their homeland, precipitated sweeping political, social, and economic changes in Palestinian society. Villages were destroyed or occupied, and many were forced to flee to the West Bank and Gaza, seeking refuge in neighboring countries (*Washington, 2020*). This upheaval profoundly impacted many aspects of everyday Palestinian life, including traditional dress and the art of Tatreez. For many women, the loss of their homes and livelihoods meant they could no longer afford the time or resources to embroider complex garments. Despite the political and economic difficulties, women in refugee camps across Jordan and Lebanon continued to practice the art of embroidery in the style of their original villages to preserve their displaced identity. By continuing this tradition and donning traditional dresses, these women were able to maintain a strong connection to their heritage and people. At this point, learning the art of embroidery and passing it on to younger generations became a way to preserve the collective Palestinian identity.

One main difference in the making of the garments is the motifs that were embroidered onto them. Special motifs were given names and held meanings. After the events of 1948, motifs developed into a way for women to express their hopes and struggles and also as a way to revive and maintain cultural heritage despite the Palestinian separation and mass displacement. New colors, designs, and motifs were introduced during this time. In the late 1980s, Palestinian women began to embroider symbols of their national identity onto their garments (*Allenby, 2002*). During the First Intifada Rebellion in 1987, Israeli soldiers confiscated the flags of Palestinian women protesting in the streets. In response, the women would repeatedly embroider the Palestinian flag onto their thobes' chests, sleeves, and back hems (FIGURE 9). They would also embroider depictions of the *Dome of the Rock in Jerusalem* (FIGURE 10), and the word "Palestine" itself.

In conclusion, the art of Tatreez has been an enduring and dynamic element of Palestinian culture. Beyond its aesthetic beauty, Tatreez has served as a powerful representation of national, cultural, and social identity, adapting to the shifting political landscape of Palestine. To quote scholar Jeni Allenby, Tatreez was the symbol of the "evolving Palestinian identity," as it "historically record[ed] individual interpretations of the political and cultural events that touched the lives of Palestinian village women" (*Allenby, 2002*). As Tatreez continues to evolve, future studies could explore how it is practiced and sustained in social media and contemporary contexts. In doing so, researchers can continue to shed light on this vital art form's historical and modern significance, ensuring its legacy is acknowledged and celebrated within the broader global design history.

BIBLIOGRAPHY

1. ALLENBY, JENI. "Re-inventing Cultural Heritage: Palestinian Traditional Costume and Embroidery since 1948." In Silk Roads, Other Roads: Proceedings of the Eighth Biennial Symposium of the Textile Society of America, September 26–28, 2002, Northampton, Massachusetts.

2. ARAFAT, BEISSAN and APEAGYEI, PHOEBE. Palestinian Cultural Heritage, Symbolic Costumes and Textile Designs. In: The 91st Textile Institute World Conference, 23 July 2018 - 26 July 2018, University of Leeds, UK.

3. "Diaspora and Tatreez: Reflections in Stitch." History of Design and Curatorial Studies. Accessed May 22, 2021. https://adht.parsons.edu/historyofdesign/objectives/diaspora-and-tatreez/.

4. "Folk Glory: Palestine." Folk Glory. Accessed April 26, 2023. https://www.folkglory.com/palestine.

5. GHNAIM, WAFA, AND FERYAL ABBASI-GHNAIM. Tatreez & Tea: Embroidery and Storytelling in the Palestinian Diaspora. Brooklyn: Self-published by Wafa Ghnaim, 2018.

6. IPS WASHINGTON, et al. "Nakba 1948: Selections from the Journal of Palestine Studies." Institute for Palestine Studies, 15 May 2020, https://www.palestine-studies.org/en/node/1650086.

7. KAWAR, WIDAD KAMEL. Threads of Identity: Preserving Palestinian Costume and Heritage. Cyprus: Rimal Books, 2011.

8. SACA, IMAN. "Oriental Institute Museum Publications (OIMP)." OIMP 25. Embroidering Identities: A Century of Palestinian Clothing | The Oriental Institute of the University of Chicago.

9. SKINNER, M. Palestinian Embroidery Motifs: A Treasury of Stitches 1850-1950. Rimal Publications, 2007.

10. ULLOA, SILVIA. "September Version - Tatreez Online - Silvia Ulloa Thesis (1)." Accessed May 22, 2021. https://www.diva-portal.org/smash/get/diva2:1470614/FULLTEXT01.pdf.

11. VOGELSANG-EASTWOOD, GILLIAN. Dressed with Distinction: Garments from Ottoman Syria. Los Angeles: Fowler Museum at UCLA, 2019.

12. WEIR, S. Embroidery from Palestine. University of Washington Press, 2006

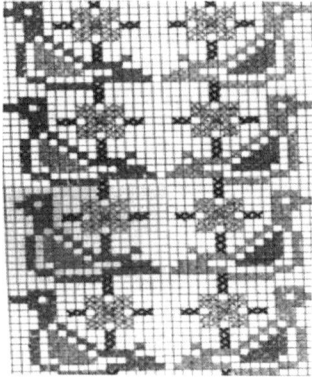

1.

2.

3.

4.

FIGURES

1. *"Birds Design" motif on a dress.* Credit: Wafa, G. & Abbasi-Ghnaim, F. Tatreez & Tea: Embroidery and Storytelling in the Palestinian Diaspora.

2. *Deliberate stitch imperfections on a thobe.* Credit: Weir, S., Embroidery from Palestine.

3. *Purple color made from crushed Murex shells.* Credit: Wafa, G. & Abbasi-Ghnaim, F. Tatreez & Tea: Embroidery and Storytelling in the Palestinian Diaspora.

4. *Detail of dress purchased in Ramallah,* 2000. Source: Wikimedia. Creative Commons Attribution-Share Alike 3.0 Unported.

5.

6.

7.

5. *Red color from mixing pomegranate skins, kermes, and insects.* Credit: Wafa, G. & Abbasi-Ghnaim, F. Tatreez & Tea: Embroidery and Storytelling in the Palestinian Diaspora.

6. *Ramallah dress*, 1880s. Credit: Folkglory, The Palestinian Thobe.

7. *Gaza area dress*, 1930s. Credit: Folkglory, The Palestinian Thobe.

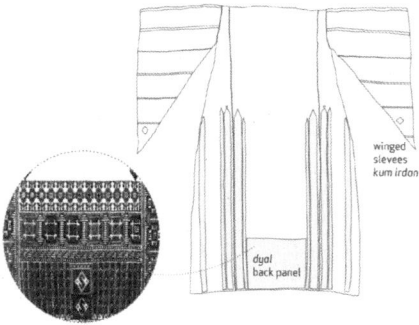

8.

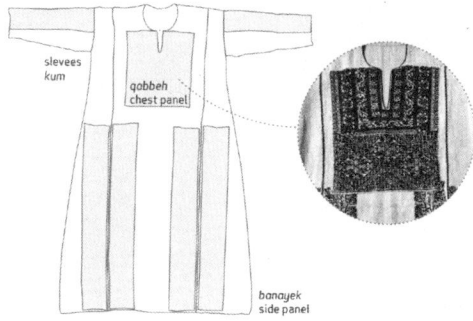

9.

10.

8. *The anatomy of a Palestinian dress*. Credit: Folkglory, The Palestinian Thobe.

9. *The anatomy of a Palestinian dress*. Credit: Folkglory, The Palestinian Thobe.

10. *Detail of Intifada dress showing Palestinian flag and map*, ca. 1989. Credit: DigitalCommons@University of Nebraska - Lincoln.

11.

12.

11. *Intifada dress with embroidered Dome of the Rock and flag.* Credit: Tiraz: Widad Kawar Home for Arab Dress.

12. *Zigzag motif on a Bedouin dress.* Credit: Ghnaim, Wafa, and Feryal Abbasi-Ghnaim. Tatreez & Tea: Embroidery and Storytelling in the Palestinian Diaspora. 2018.

Andean Textiles: Designing with the World in Mind

The archeological evidence of textiles from the Andes region stretches as far back as 800 BCE. Thousands of years later, from 500 BCE to 700 CE, the Paracas and Nasca cultures thrived in an arid desert region along the coast of Peru. These atmospheric conditions were ideal for the preservation of textiles. Instead of keeping a history record using written language, these societies used textiles and communicated through unique techniques, styles, and motifs.

Through a woven language, Paracas' and Nasca's design expresses their Indigenous cosmovision using the natural resources available. Andean textiles were symbolic, functional, and sustainable. In a world where sustainability needs to be a top priority, designers today should look to the past for design that has both a deeper meaning and a functional purpose.

Today's textile industry evolved from diverse hand-woven techniques from around the globe. Before the Industrial Revolution, textiles were made and sold locally on a very small scale. This method, known as a "cottage industry," did not scale with the needs of an increasing population. Based on one's perspective, the industrialization of textiles led to both the success and failure of the textile industry. As a brief review of modern history, industrialization began in England in the 1700s because of a rapidly increasing demand for textiles throughout England and in the colonies. Inventions such as the "spinning jenny," the water frame, the steam engine, and the cotton gin all improved the quality of thread and the overall textile production time. Cotton could be grown and harvested fifty times faster than before, allowing production on a much larger scale and at a lower price. Synthetic fibers were developed in the 1900s using chemicals that emit toxic waste and emissions. This new industrial method evolved into today's textile industry, which is responsible for 10 percent of global greenhouse gas emissions, 20 percent of global wastewater, 10 percent of microplastics, 92 million tons of waste each year, and $500 billion worth of material wasted annually. In addition to the environmental cost, an egregious human cost persists. Many workers in the textile industry, mostly women in less developed nations, are undervalued and mistreated; they face verbal and physical abuse, wage theft, lack of health protocols, and intense productivity expectations. This dismal environmental and human situation is due to financial greed, and large corporations need to maximize shareholder value through short-term profits and continual steep growth expectations. Effective marketing campaigns influence societies' perceived need to consume and keep up with current trends. Long overdue is a cultural shift: an effective initiative to change the public's priorities and reduce its desire for endless consumption of mass-produced disposable textiles. Andean weaving history may provide some insight into what a sustainable textile industry could look like.

Though I am focusing on textile weaving, their ideals about cloth can be transferred to any form of design. Every village was deeply reliant on the hand-crafted cloth. They even preserved woven textiles, baskets, and tools in the tombs of high-status individuals, "demonstrating that the act of textile production was just as sacred as the final product" *(McHugh, 2020)*. In "Cloth and Its Functions in the Inca State," John V. Murra states that there was a "much-quoted portrait of the never idle Andean peasant woman [who] took the spindle into her grave as a symbol of [her impact]." Weaving was a source of power for women; they were respected for their work.

In fact, the entire village took part in spinning and weaving, with older men and children making sacks and "rougher" items. An impressive amount of detail and effort went into creating these textiles, with thread spun finer than produced by most modern machines. Weaving was a valuable skill for every individual, and the practice itself symbolized many major ideals, such as the cyclical nature of life and death. Andeans recognized the work that went into creating their beautiful textiles, appreciating both the work and the worker. However, after Spanish colonizers arrived in the Andes, this highly specialized and time-consuming method of making textiles was replaced by faster-to-produce, less intricate designs. Ultimately, textile labor became associated with low social status *(Murra, 1962)*.

Andean families used woven cloth for ceremonial goods, ritualistic items, gifts for loved ones, and as a form of currency for trade and political purposes. Fiber never went to waste. Andean textiles' wide range of purposes displays their resourcefulness in using natural resources sparingly while acknowledging the inextricable tie between man and nature and the importance of respecting and preserving precious resources. Placing meaning beyond function on an object creates a deeper bond between the object and the owner (or consumer in today's terminology). Andean culture was rooted in their use of textiles; textiles were sacrificed for supernatural beings, which they believed controlled the natural world; they were used to display status through material, color, and motifs. Material such as cotton was used for lower-class citizens, while alpaca was reserved for citizens of higher status.

For example, only high-ranking men were allowed to wear four-cornered hats, such as the wool hat shown in FIGURE 1, and a checkerboard-patterned tunic which was often associated with the military (FIGURE 2). Natural dyes and pigments derived from plants and insects had their own meaning; red for conquest, green for rainforests, black for creation and death, yellow for maize or gold, and purple for Mama Oclla, the mythical founding mother of the Inca race *(Cartwright, 2023)*. Many of these colors can be seen in the geometric pattern in FIGURE 3.

Much of Andean textiles' beauty lies in their symbolism and hidden mythology. The nature of their designs also relied upon the tribal community, its geographical location, topography, natural resources, and spiritual contexts. As the Inca conquered different tribal communities, they absorbed the conquered peoples' spiritual beliefs into their own belief system resulting in techniques, patterns, and coloration being passed down for generations. Each small decision in the weaving process had significance, though it is difficult today to decode the meaning of many of the patterns. It's clear by their abstract depictions of felines, llamas, snakes, birds, sea creatures, and plants that they had a great appreciation for nature. Examples of this can be seen in FIGURES 4 and 5.

Not only did Andean textile designers have a great sense of balance between color and shape, but they also produced textiles that have meaning that is deeply rooted in Andean culture. This meaning began as a form of devotion to the supernatural beings that they honored. Still, meaning grew when community members found purpose by fabricating the textiles. Their communities allotted large amounts of their collective time to ensure their textiles were of the highest quality, from the spinning of the fibers to the natural dyeing process to the intricate weaving process. Today, we live in a world where mass production is the norm. Modern global citizens are often driven to acquire unnecessary material items that are not built to last or hold any inherent purpose or functionality. This mentality has led to our growing landfills, pollution of our remaining resources, and unsightly litter. The time has come for a process and design revolution that considers the future of our planet by looking to the past. Designing with multiple purposes in mind would be extremely beneficial for the world's long-term environmental and physiological health and population. To this end, we need a revival of slow-industry concepts: products and designs built to last and incorporate natural, sustainable materials while respecting the land and its cyclical nature. We need to think like the Andeans by cherishing the land and our local communities and finding meaningful purpose within our design practices.

BIBLIOGRAPHY

1. "Ancient Andean Textiles at Yale University Art Gallery." https://hali.com/news/ancient-andean-textiles-at-yale-university-art-gallery/.

2. "Andean Textiles." Centro De Textiles Tradicionales Del Cusco, https://www.textilescusco.org/andean-textiles.

3. CARTWRIGHT, MARK. "Inca Textiles." World History Encyclopedia, 2 Apr. 2023, https://www.worldhistory.org/article/791/inca-textiles/.

4. COHEN-APONTE, ANANDA. "Paracas Textiles: An Introduction." Smarthistory: The Center for Public Art History, https://smarthistory.org/paracas-textiles-introduction/.

5. DASS, RHONDA R. "The Spanish Unraveling of the Incan Empire: The Importance of Fibers and Textiles of the Past." Superior McNair Scholars Journal, Edited by William Morgan, vol. 2.

6. "Four-Cornered Hat." Museum of Fine Arts, Boston, https://collections.mfa.org/objects/36615/fourcornered-hat?ctx=d8de6dc3-5c64-4ae6-b45e-5b433e-6f5a88&idx=8.

7. IGINI, MARTINA. "10 Concerning Fast Fashion Waste Statistics." Earth.Org, 17 Feb. 2023, https://earth.org/statistics-about-fast-fashion-waste/.

8. "The Impact of Textile Production and Waste on the Environment." European Parliament, 26 Apr. 2022, https://www.europarl.europa.eu/news/en/headlines/society/20201208STO93327/the-impact-of-textile-production-and-waste-on-the-environment-infographic.

9. MCHUGH, JULIA. "Andean Textiles." In Heilbrunn Timeline of Art History. New York: The Metropolitan Museum of Art, 2000–. http://www.metmuseum.org/toah/hd/antx/hd_antx.htm (June 2020).

10. MURRA, JOHN V. "Cloth and Its Functions in the Inca State." American Anthropologist, vol. 64, no. 4, 1962, pp. 710–728., https://doi.org/10.1525/aa.1962.64.4.02a00020.

11. PROULX, DONALD A. The Nasca Culture: An Introduction. Edited by Judith Rickenbach, University of Massachusetts, https://people.umass.edu/proulx/online_pubs/Nasca_Overview_Zurich.pdf.

12. "Textile Fragment with Design of Stylized Birds and Humans." Google, https://artsandculture.google.com/asset/textile-fragment-with-design-of-stylized-birds-and-humans/2wHaQG-Ny9oLU4A.

13. "Votive Checkerboard Tunic: Inca." The Metropolitan Museum of Art, https://www.metmuseum.org/art/collection/search/751900.

14. "Wari Culture." Textiles in Context, https://textilesincontext.net/tag/wari-culture/.

1.

2.

3.

FIGURES

1. Tiwanaku or Wari, *Four-Cornered Hat*, 500—900 CE. Credit: The Metropolitan Museum of Art.

2. Inca, *Votive Checkerboard Tunic*, 1460 - 1626. Credit: The Metropolitan Museum of Art.

3. Wari, *Tunic*, 700-850. Credit: The Metropolitan Museum of Art.

4.

5.

4. Chancay, *Sleeved Tunic with Flying Condors*, 1200–1400. Source: Wikimedia, PD US/EU copyright expired.

5. Chancay, *Textile Fragment with Design of Stylized Birds and Humans*, 1000-1470. Credit: Los Angeles County Museum of Art.

THE DARK FANTASY

The Dark Fantasy weaves together the fantastical and the folkloric. Metaphors deliver a potent critique, where subversive ideas materialize as a coded language that challenges our perception of truth. While unsettling, these symbols aid us in understanding social politics. They shield the authentic, unfiltered voice, defiantly casting judgment toward a dominant colonial oppressor. Dark fantasies challenge preconceived notions of representation, blurring the boundary between truth and fiction, the fantastical and the critical.

ELLEN JOHNSON

Fairy Tales
as Souvenirs of
British Colonization

Fairy tales are as much children's stories as allegorical reflections of humanity. We imbue them with morals and symbolism. They shape not only the way we tell a story but what we consider to be a story. They are familiar and predictable; we search for patterns in our realities. Fairy tales are a way to simplify and categorize our worlds to be palatable and convenient. We can create and assign identity: hero and villain, beautiful and ugly, right and wrong, familiar and foreign. Yet, if we consider fairy tales a mirror of society, we must become aware of who's holding it.

Britain dominated the publishing of fairy stories and folklore at the same time that they were colonizing the East. The British fascination with Orientalism and an exotic "Other" that resulted from the expanding empire was reflected in their children's literature. These multicultural fairy tales reinforced the colonial fantasy of a dominant West. The end of the Victorian era saw an interest in collecting. Artifacts from far-off lands — made available through colonization and new trade — were seductive to the British public, as they were removed from their contexts and viewed from the "security" of London. In *Collecting the Empire: Andrew Lang's Fairy Books*, Sarah Hines writes, "Collection marks the space [...] where history is transformed into property" *(Hines, 2010)*. White Westerners were able to imbue these objects with their own stereotypes and meanings and create narratives that would not disrupt their narrow and comfortable worldviews. The objects became theirs, in a sense, as a continuation of colonization. The objects themselves became dominant.

Fairy tales were collected and transformed in the same way as any physical object. Fairy tale books were popular Christmas gifts for children, especially multicultural collections such as Andrew Lang's Fairy Book series, and fairy tales themselves became souvenirs of an Othered culture. When these tales were mediated through Western perspectives, they were viewed as singular representations of those Othered cultures. Lang's Fairy Books included tales from all over Europe, Africa, Asia, the Middle East, and even Indigenous American stories. "The originating culture of each story, as identified by Lang in the footnotes, is secondary to the new location of the story in an international collection of tales published in London" *(Hines, 2010)*. Westerners had complete control over how these cultures were translated and depicted. Sadhana Naithani, author and associate professor at Jawaharlal Nehru University in New Delhi, writes about "folklore collectors" who would extract the folktales from the areas being colonized to preserve the "savage" culture that the British would dominate. Folklore represents "the savage ideas out of which civilization has been evolved" *(Naithani,*

2001). Within this process, the colonizing folklore collector could weaponize the fairy tales against the culture from which they came. "These dualities too formed a harmonious whole: the folklore collector was greater than the folk and the folklore he studied" *(Naithani, 2001).* Colonizers had complete control. If there were mistranslations of these folktales, it only added to the depiction of the culture as mysterious, strange, and uncivilized rather than being a lack of intelligence on the part of the colonizer.

The development of three and four-color half-tone prints in the 1890s meant new levels of quality and accuracy when reproducing watercolor illustrations *(Shaw, 2019).* This shift paved the way for the luminary artists of the genre, like Edmund Dulac. Dulac worked in Britain and was known for his fantastical watercolors and linework. Illustrators like him helped popularize the "gift book," produced annually at Christmastime during the Edwardian period, and these decorative and expensive books furthered his success *(Lebedev, 2019).* Momentum was lost with the start of World War I in 1914 when resources became low, and the focus turned towards aiding the war efforts *(Shaw, 2019).* It was difficult to have a high-quality book printed at this time. The genre embraced the changing world, however, offering both a sense of nationalism and escapism with fairy tales. Thus came *The Allies' Fairy Book,* illustrated by Arthur Rackham and edited by Edmund Gosse, and *Fairy-book: Fairy Tales of the Allied Nations* by Dulac. Both books highlighted tales from the countries allied with Britain during the war. The contents page of both volumes indicates the nationality of each tale (FIGURES 1-2). These books became precious symbols: allies listed one by one, each represented with subsequent tales of heroism, victory, hope, and love. The introduction of *The Allies' Fairy Book,* written by Edmund Gosse, which is distinctly beautiful and poetic, defines a fairy as any "supernatural creature of the imagination" *(Rackham, 2019).*

Fairy- tales, therefore, must be understood as dealing with irresponsible beings and imaginary adventures which do not rest on any basis of experience or reason or physical possibility whatever [...] [T]he whole essence of a fairy-tale rests in its impossibility, in its dependence on a mysterious power above all mundane forces, which we call enchantment [...] One thing seems universally admitted, that these supernatural beings are gentle and pacific. "People of peace". [...] There is no record of the appearance of fairies upon a battlefield. It is when the hearts of country folk are hushed and silent that the mysterious voices of goblins are heard calling, at dewfall, from the terraces of the haunted hills (Rackham, 2019).

The introduction speaks of unity, peace, and belief — the belief that if so many nations have created their own versions of fairies and magic, how can it not be based in some reality? "There is an irrepressible tendency in mankind to believe that where there is smoke, there must be fire," Gosse points out *(Rackham, 2019).* These stories are the smoke. The sentiment that if there is enough belief, something must be true is one full of hope and thus perfect for its wartime audience. Both

Rackham's and Dulac's illustrations seem greatly influenced by the aesthetic of the cultures from which each story originates. While Rackham's hand is subtle here (FIGURES 3, 4), Dulac is much more obvious (FIGURES 5, 6). It is especially noticeable in Dulac's illustration for the Japanese tale *Urashima Taro* (FIGURE 7). While his other illustrations are visually dense, full of patterns and rich colors, the Japanese story is depicted with a completely different treatment of space. The figures are situated on a flat, atmospheric plane. The muted and misty color palette emphasizes the inky black details that bring the characters to the foreground. This illustration is easily recognizable as mimicking Japanese style and composition. The desire to understand Eastern aesthetics was something Dulac, and much of England, became enamored with. This obsession with Eastern illustration is specifically attributed to the British Museum's acquisition of Japanese paintings in the 1850s and is particularly easy to spot in Dulac's work (Lebedev, 2019). Dulac's illustrations for *Stories from the Arabian Nights*, versions of which were published between 1907 and 1914, are a clear example of the appropriation of Eastern art and Dulac's journey to Orientalism. Looking at this illustration (FIGURE 8) of a wave, for example, immediately brings to mind Hokusai's *The Great Wave Off Kanagawa* (FIGURE 9), which preceded it by approximately 45 years. Parallels can be seen in the hierarchical flat layers of the waves, the stylized white caps, and the limited development of a background. This depiction of nature as something more decorative than realistic defined Dulac's style; his figures take on an almost comic quality as the background fades away. His characters become typographic in their depiction of the scene. The paneled composition is another element adopted from Japan (FIGURE 10). Among the many fairy tales presented in *The Allies' Fairy Book*, perhaps one of the most fantastical is the notion of unity and collective history. How legitimate is it for the artists and editors in Edwardian England to claim their collection of works to be symbolic of peace and similarity when they have complete control over how these stories are portrayed?

During the same "golden age" of illustration, the Kobunsha publishing company in Japan was putting together a similar collection of fairy tales. Takejiro Hasegawa was at the helm, originally compiling the stories as a textbook for Japanese students learning English. The Japanese fairy tales were translated into English by Hasegawa's missionary friends and illustrated by Japanese woodblock artists. The collections became wildly popular internationally due to the growing trend of Orientalism spreading across Europe. The stories were new to the English audience and the illustrations were already similar in style to what was being mimicked by their own artists. Hasewaga took advantage of the Western craze over the publications and started marketing them as souvenirs rather than educational materials. He incorporated the use of more traditional materials with this strategy in mind, producing copies on Chirimen paper, similar to crepe paper. These textured versions of the volumes attracted an even wider audience.

The dangerous side effect of this enthusiasm for Eastern content is that collections such as Hasewaga's were absorbed and understood as authentic symbols of Japanese culture rather than as English translations of Japanese folktales (*Guth, 2008*). If one of the primary examples of a culture one consumes is a collection of fairy tales, how is that culture perceived? Fairy tales are traditionally considered children's media, with simple morals and imaginative imagery. The act of translation becomes part of the appropriation. It is not just the art that is being taken, but the morals, ideas, history, and voice. This is not to say that translation is inherently problematic; it is only necessary to recognize that translators are making choices that may or may not include the nuance of the original. Christine M. E. Guth argues, in "Hasegawa's Fairy Tales: Toying with Japan," that this simplification is part of the appeal for a Western audience. By infantilizing Japanese culture in this selective consumption of it, it further situates Western culture as superior and dominant. "In this developmental scheme, Western civilization is positioned at the top of an evolutionary ladder with other non-Western nations at various stages beneath it. Thus, Japan is considered the childhood of the West" *(Guth, 2008)*.

Fairy tales were one way in which colonizers could display and reinforce power dynamics and stereotypes. In narrating and illustrating a culture's folklore, the British decided how that culture would be perceived in the West. Translation and collection were weapons used to further the British empire, and these watered-down relics of the cultures they conquered were wrapped up and presented to children as proof of righteousness. What is missing from the Western canon of fairy tales? Can representation without an authentic voice be true representation? When we examine our canon, it is not only the question of whose stories we are hearing that must be addressed, but, as importantly, we must examine who is telling them.

BIBLIOGRAPHY

1 DECOU, CHRISTOPHER. "Woodblocks in Wonderland: The Japanese Fairy Tale Series." The Public Domain Review, 2 Sept. 2019, https://publicdomainreview.org/essay/woodblocks-in-wonderland-the-japanese-fairy-tale-seri es.

2. DULAC, EDMUND. Fairy Tales of the Allied Nations. Hodder & Stoughton, 1916.

3. GUTH, CHRISTINE M. E. "Hasegawa's Fairy Tales: Toying with Japan." RES: Anthropology and Aesthetics, no. 53/54, [President and Fellows of Harvard College, Peabody Museum of Archaeology and Ethnology], 2008, pp. 266–81, http://www.jstor.org/stable/25608821.

4. HINES, SARA. "Collecting the Empire: Andrew Lang's Fairy Books (1889-1910)." Marvels & Tales, vol. 24, no. 1, Wayne State University Press, 2010, pp. 39–56, http://www.jstor.org/stable/41389025.

5. LEBEDEV, DMITRY. "Edmund Dulac's Book Graphics and the Problem of Orientalism in British Illustration of Edwardian Era and the Second Decade of Xxth Century." Edmund Dulac's Book Graphics and the Problem of Orientalism in British Illustration of Edwardian Era and the Second Decade of XXth Century | Atlantis Press, Atlantis Press, 1 Nov. 2019, https://www.atlantis-press.com/proceedings/icassee-19/125923517.

6. NAITHANI, SADHANA. "Prefaced Space: Tales of the Colonial British Collectors of Indian Folklore." Imagined States, edited by Luisa Del Giudice and Gerald Porter, University Press of Colorado, 2001, pp. 64–79, https://doi.org/10.2307/j.ctt46nxsn.5.

7. RACKHAM, ARTHUR, AND EDMUND GOSSE. The Allies' Fairy Tale Book. J.B. Lippincott, 1916. Shaw, Lucy. "Wartime Fairy Tales • V&A Blog." V&A Blog, 18 Dec. 2019, https://www.vam.ac.uk/blog/museum-life/wartime-fairy. tales.

8. SHAW, LUCY. "Wartime Fairy Tales • V&A Blog." V&A Blog, 18 Dec. 2019, https://www.vam.ac.uk/blog/museum-life/wartime-fairy-tales.

1.

2.

3.

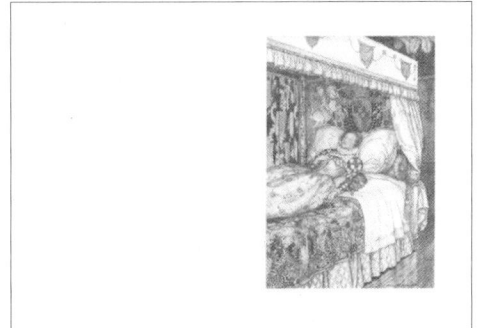

4.

FIGURES

1. Edmund Dulac, *Fairy Tales of the Allied Nations*, table of contents, 1916. PD US/EU copyright expired.

2. Edmund Dulac, *Fairy Tales of the Allied Nations*, 1916. PD US/EU copyright expired.

3. Edmund Dulac, *Fairy Tales of the Allied Nations*, 1916. PD US/EU copyright expired.

4. Edmund Dulac, *Fairy Tales of the Allied Nations*, 1916. PD US/EU copyright expired.

5.

6.

7.

5. Edmund Dulac, *Fairy Tales of the Allied Nations*, 1916.
PD US/EU copyright expired.

6. Arthur Rackham, The Allies Fairy Book, 1939. PD US/
EU copyright expired.

7. Arthur Rackham, The Allies Fairy Book, 1939. PD US/
EU copyright expired.

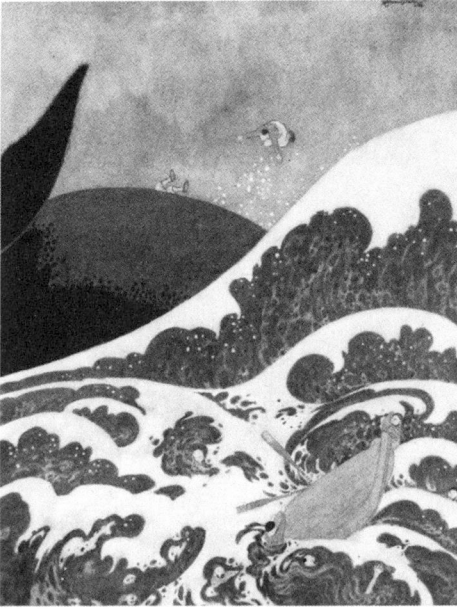

8.

9.

10.

8. Edmund Dulac, "The Episode of the Whale," 1914, from Sindbad the Sailor and Other Stories from the Arabian Nights, Credit: Bodleian Library Publishing, 2019.

9. Hokusai, *The Great Wave Off Kanagawa*, 1831. PD US/ EU copyright expired.

10. Edmund Dulac, Stories From the Arabian Nights, 1911. PD US/EU copyright expired.

China's
Modern Woodcut Movement

The Western historical canon situates Chinese visual culture in an Orientalist framework, undermining its rich and dynamic history. This perspective makes it hard to appreciate how China positioned its art as a weapon of communication and a tool of resistance for oppressed people. China's New Woodcut Movement of the late 1920s and 1930s represents an underknown chapter of Chinese art that broke out of the Orientalist cliches. Emerging out of the New Culture movement, the New Woodcut movement responded to China's complex social, political, and cultural landscape during its early modernization period.

The New Woodcut Movement played a critical role in the development of China's art and design history. It acted as the voice of resistance during a time of political upheaval, constructed a new visual language and identity of Chinese modernism, and challenged established artistic conventions of consumption and distribution.

BIRTH OF A MOVEMENT

In the early 20th century, the fall of the Qing dynasty and the rise of a new but volatile republic establishment produced a monumental paradigm shift in cultural, literary, and artistic realms, culminating in what is known as the New Culture Movement. Originally spearheaded by a circle of literary figures, scholars, and thinkers surrounding the *New Youth Magazine*, active between 1915 and 1926 (FIGURE 1), the movement's central philosophy sought to revitalize and liberate the Chinese spirit. They rejected Confucius values—values representative of thousands of years of unjust feudalist hierarchies— and instead rallied for liberalism, democracy, women's emancipation, modern science, and access to vernacular literature *(Xu, 2009)*.

Renowned writer Lu Xun (1881-1936) resides at the center of China's New Woodcut Movement. As a visual manifestation of Lu's intellectual and cultural ethos, the movement drew on the volatility of German expressionism and the grassroots efforts of Russian activists during the November Revolution (FIGURE 2). Having utilized woodcuts as a means of mass communication in slogans, banners, and posters, Lu hoped woodcuts would become the definitive art form of modern China. As he promoted the art form via exhibitions, workshops, and publications of foreign prints by artists such as Käthe Kollwitz and Frans Masereel, his influence drew in flocks of young students and artists toward Shanghai as the epicenter of revolutionary thoughts, literature, and art *(Sun, 1974)* (FIGURE 3).

ART OF RESISTANCE

In a brutal political climate with violent suppression from both domestic republican power and foreign imperialist forces, woodcuts became the dominant mode of artistic resistance, true to Lu's visions. The art of Chinese modern woodcut served the role of the people's resistance via the expression of emotion and the depiction of real-life experiences.

Modern Chinese woodcuts aimed to reflect the harsh realities of the masses, portraying themes including the hardship of those facing exploitation, poverty, and war. This content diverged from conventional Chinese art-making seen throughout history. The familiar artwork, considered art-for-art-sake by the youth population, catered to the privileged literati and aristocrats *(Yuan, 2020)*. However, we see the grim reality of laborers and workers in Chen Puzhi's *Rickshaw Puller* (FIGURE 4) and Jiang Feng's *Workers on the Wharf* (FIGURE 5). These woodcuts capture the excruciatingly overworked, exhausted, and sickly figures with unflinching and unflattering detail *(Tang, 2006)*.

The rawness of these depictions became a political message unto itself, fomenting resistance against the tragic social conditions faced by the working class. Hu Yichuan's *To The Front!* (FIGURE 6), created in response to the Japanese bombing of Shanghai and the invasion of Manchuria, communicates the need to stand up against Japanese imperial aggression. The image engages directly with the viewer with an unabashed depiction of the common working man with rolled-up sleeves *(Tang, 2006)*.

BEAUTY OF STRENGTH

Woodcuts first appeared in the early 700s as illustrations for Buddhist manuscripts, although they were overlooked in the late Qing Dynasty and early republic. Eventually, they were seen as effective forms of communication and miraculously revitalized. Distinct visual and stylistic languages — described as the "beauty of strength" — that combined international and traditional influences recast the historical form into a modern setting.

The New Woodcut Movement produced unforgiving messages that were widely consumed by Chinese audiences. Artists borrowed techniques and visual tropes from stone engravings (FIGURE 7), traditional New Year prints (FIGURE 8), book illustrations, and the West's manipulation of monochrome color palettes to create arresting imagery. Li Hua's *Road Worker at Rest* (FIGURE 9) reflects a striking resemblance to Soviet artist Vasily Kasian's *Workers in the West* (FIGURE 10). Yet, Li stylizes and simplifies compositional details to evoke a certain sense of blunt empowerment *(Tang, 2006)*.

Li coined the phrase "beauty of force" to describe the woodcuts, observing stark, linear contrasts of black and white palettes and vicious, slashing line works (Sun, 1974). The muscularity of the visual language actively rejected the conventional slender gracefulness seen in traditional Chinese art. The stylistic velocity distinguishes the woodcuts from any work that came before it and is visible in the work of a range of artists. Hu's devastating anti-war message, *A Scene in Zhabei* (FIGURE 11), depicts an urban landscape littered with fallen men *(Tang, 2007)*. Li Hua's *Roar, China* (FIGURE 12) is perhaps the most iconic image of the movement, visually and spiritually. A naked and contorted figure outlined in bold, twisting lines evokes a primal sense of despair and fury. The identity-less rendering — eyes covered, stark naked, with no identity markers — became a universal expression for the movement. The dagger at the composition's corner suggests hope at the end of the tunnel *(Tang, 2006)*.

ART OF THE PEOPLE

Part of the movement's success can be attributed to its use of simple imagery and universal messages that were accessible to broad audiences. By the end of the 1930s and following intense government persecution, the movement shifted from its center in Shanghai to southern China.

In southern China, efforts were made to make the woodcuts accessible to an expanded working class. Farming villages became the focus of the touring exhibits, often in People's Education Halls. Artists worked directly with local communities, showcasing narratives of empowerment and further instructed locals on the woodcut printing technique *(Sun, 1974)*. To this end, the New Woodcut Movement was true to its spirit as an art for the people and by the people.

The New Woodcut Movement of China was a key part of China's visual and design history, as it not only ushered in a new visual language but did so in a way that effectively connected audiences and artists. Whether or not the transition of the movement from a concentrated underground effort to a mainstream phenomenon was a net positive remains debatable. Following the fall of the old republic in 1949, woodcut culture permeated the public realm. In a starkly ironic twist, the People's Republic of China ultimately institutionalized the woodcut form by coopting the style in its official propaganda *(Ferrari, 2009)*.

BIBLIOGRAPHY

1. EMRICH, ELIZABETH. "Modernity Through Experimentation: Lu Xun and the Modern Chinese Woodcut Movement." Print, Profit, and Perception 28: 64–91, 2014.

2. FERRARI, R. (2009). Reviewed Work(s): Origins of the Chinese Avant-Garde: The Modern Woodcut Movement by Xiaobing Tang. China Review International, 16(2), 271–275. https:// doi.org/10.1353/cri.2009.0050.

3. TANG, X. (1992). Lu Xun's "Diary of a madman" and a Chinese modernism. PMLA/Publications of the Modern Language Association of America, 107(5), 1222–1234. https://doi.org/10.2307/462876.

4. TANG, XIAOBING. Origins of the Chinese Avant-Garde: The Modern Woodcut Movement. University of California Press, 2007.

5. SUN, SIRLEY HSIAO-LING. 1974. Lu Hsun And The Chinese Woodcut Movement: 1929-1936. Ph.D. diss., Stanford University, https://ezproxy.bu.edu/login?qurl=https%3A%2F%2Fwww.proquest.com%2Fdissertations-theses%2Flu-hsun-chinese-woodcut-movement-1929-1936.

6. XU, JILIN. "The May Fourth Spirit, Now and Then." China Heritage Quarterly, no. 17, Mar. 2009, http://www.chinaheritagequarterly.org/features.php?-searchterm=017_mayfourthspirit.inc&issue=017.

7. YUAN, FARREN. 2020. "Blades of Resistance: Early Twentieth-Century Woodcuts in Revolutionary China." Broad Street Humanities Review. https://broadstreethumanitiesreview.com/publicationsfarren/.

1.

2.

3.

FIGURES

1. *La Jeunesse, Vol. 2, no. 1*, 1916. PD US/EU copyright expired.

2. Woodcut, Cao Bai, *Portrait of Lu Xun*, 1935. Source: Internet Archive. Credit: Tang, X., Origins Of The Chinese Avant Garde The Modern Woodcut Movement.

3. Fei Sha, *Lu Xun meeting with young woodcut artists*, 1936. Credit: The Hong Kong University of Science and Technology Library.

4.

5.

4. Chen Puzhi (Langa, Lanchia), *Rickshaw Puller*, 1934.
Source: Internet Archive. Credit: Tang, X., Origins
Of The Chinese Avant Garde The Modern Woodcut
Movement.

5. Jiang Feng, *Workers on the Wharf*, 1932. Source:
Internet Archive. Credit: Tang, X., Origins Of The
Chinese Avant Garde The Modern Woodcut Movement.

6.

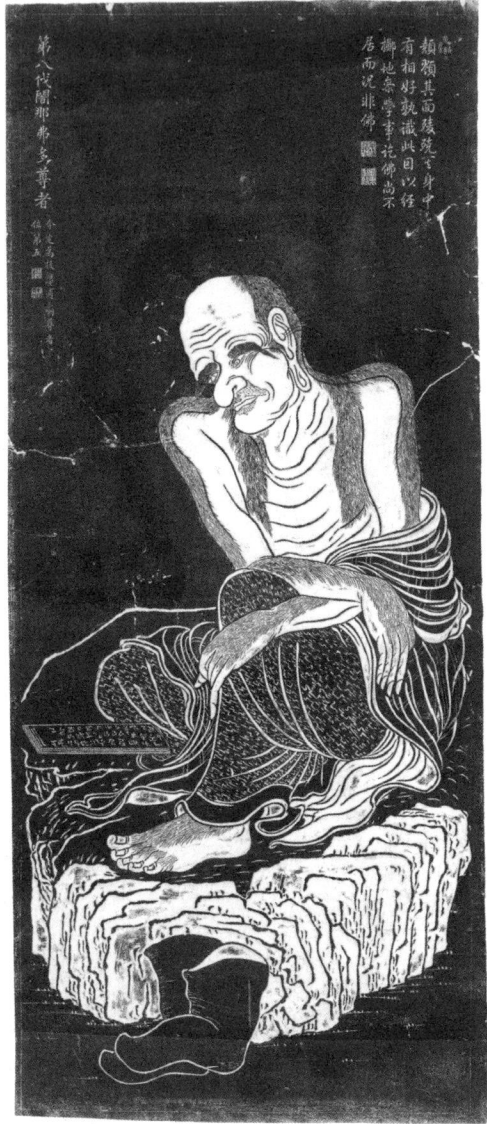

8.　　　　　　　　　　　　　　　7.

6. Hu Yichuan, *To the Front*, 1932. Source: Internet Archive. Credit: Tang, X., Origins Of The Chinese Avant Garde The Modern Woodcut Movement.

7. *Rubbing of Luohan*, attr. to Guanxiu, 1757. Credit: The Meotropolitan Museum of Art.

8. Unknown artist, *Nianhua: The Spirit of the Doors*, ca.1900. Source: Wikimedia. PD US/EU copyright expired.

9.

10.

11.

12.

9. Li Hua, *Road Worker at Rest,* 1934. Source: Internet Archive. Credit: Tang, X., *Origins Of The Chinese Avant Garde The Modern Woodcut Movement.*

10. Vasily Kasian, *Workers in the West (Breaktime),* 1926. Source: Internet Archive. Credit: Tang, X., *Origins Of The Chinese Avant Garde The Modern Woodcut Movement.*

11. Hu Yichuan, *A Scene in Zhabei,* 2932. Source: Internet Archive. Credit: Tang, X., *Origins Of The Chinese Avant Garde The Modern Woodcut Movement.*

12. Li Hua, *China Roar!,* 1938. Source: Internet Archive. Credit: Tang, X., *Origins Of The Chinese Avant Garde The Modern Woodcut Movement.*

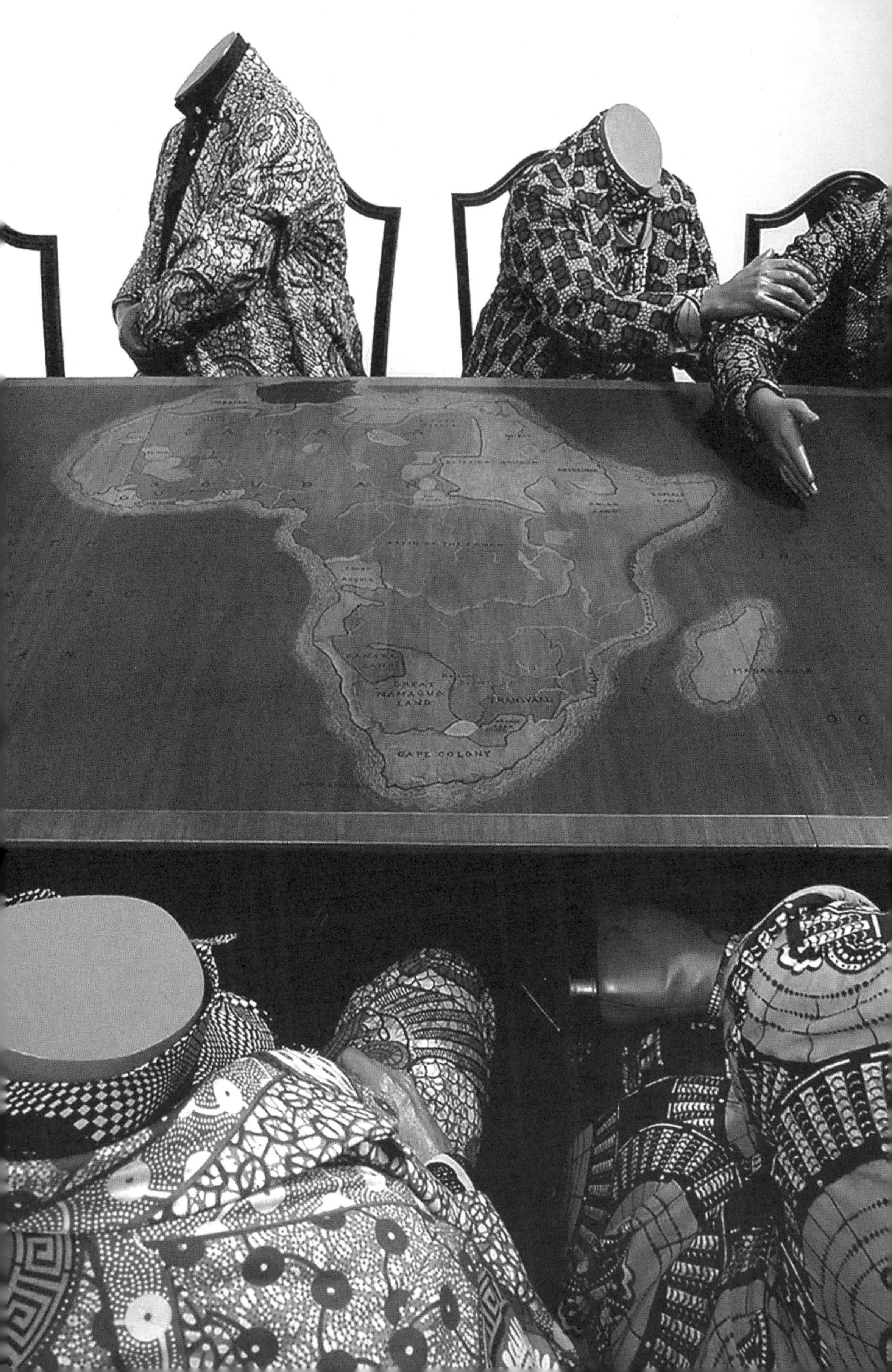
GREAT
NAMAQUA
LAND
TRANSVAAL
CAPE COLONY

Culture and Identity Through the Lens of Yinka Shonibare

What does it mean to be a global citizen? How does one integrate living in Britain and its brutal history of colonization of countless people and countries? Yinka Shonibare explores these questions and so much more through his work. He is a Nigerian-British multimedia artist born in London but raised in Nigeria during most of his formative years. The collision of Shonibare's Nigerian identity combined with that of its British colonial oppressor is a theme that guides Shonibare's creative oeuvre.

Shonibare works with various mediums, including painting, sculpture, photography, installation, film, and performance art. He explores the history of colonialism and how it influenced how we identify with race and class. He questions the idea of identity and the shared, messy history of things we see in our day-to-day lives that reveal how interconnected the world actually is.

Shonibare was born in London in 1962 and moved to Nigeria when he was three, where he lived until he was sixteen. His father was a wealthy lawyer, and his parents expected him to follow a similar career path. Fortunately, Shonibare discovered a passion for art as a young child and aspired to be an artist when he grew up. His parents' disappointment is a typical response from immigrant parents who have to wrestle with the disparity between their own social circumstances and that of their more privileged children. Despite this, Shonibare's family's wealth provided the much-needed financial freedom to explore a career path that was not solely focused on generating money, a privilege he now recognizes as totally unique. With his talents and passion for art, he was accepted into an art school in England. Just a few weeks after classes started, he developed transverse myelitis, a disorder that causes inflammation within the spine that left half of his body paralyzed. He was hospitalized for a year before returning to school (Kuiper, 2023).

Despite his paralysis, Shonibare's art improved. His teachers were instrumental and influential in the development of his artistic vision. When one teacher questioned why he took influence from Russian culture instead of making "African art," Shonibare questioned his influences as they related to his own cultural roots. He says, "People always want to categorize things. I'm much more interested in this idea of a hybrid" (Wofford, 2016). He later explores ideas relating to mixed cultures and identities within his work, especially between Europe and Africa.

Shonibare explores mixed cultures and identities most visibly when he uses Dutch wax print fabrics, which many assume originated in Africa due to their popularity in Central and West Africa (FIGURE 1). "The fabrics are not really authentically African the way people think," says Shonibare. "They prove to have a crossbred cultural background quite of their own. And it's the fallacy of that signification that I like. It's the way I view culture – it's an artificial construct." The wax prints were brought to Africa by the Dutch during their colonial reign (FIGURE 2). The Dutch admired the bright wax print fabrics seen throughout modern-day Indonesia and replicated the look. But, instead of intricate handwork favored by the Indonesians, the Dutch mechanized the batik production process with machinery. The Dutch then tried to sell these knockoffs back to Indonesia but failed in their markets (FIGURES 3, 4). The replica wax prints eventually took hold in West Africa, where they were very well received and became a cultural staple despite their origin elsewhere. Shonibare draws on the fabric's culturally intertwined history to comment on identity and the relationship between cultures. He states, "I'm very interested in the colonial relationships between Africa and Europe, and the fabrics have become a metaphor for that" (Caldwell, 2016). In addition to making political commentary, these fabrics add tons of color and vibrancy to his work making his pieces pop beautifully.

In *Scramble for Africa*, Shonibare visualizes the Berlin Conference where European imperialists met to agree on how to colonize Africa (FIGURE 5). Fourteen fiberglass mannequins are set up around a table manipulated to represent a debate, where each member is eager to claim a piece of the continent. Each figure is headless and wears a Dutch wax fabric that covers their bodies. Shonibare explains, "I wanted to represent these European leaders as mindless in their hunger for what the Belgian King Leopold II called a slice of this magnificent African cake" (Caldwell, 2016). Each mannequin's varying skin tones capture the idea that the domination of one culture over another is a timeless phenomenon.

Shonibare reimagined ideas of rationality and religion in iconic Western classical art in his solo exhibition at Stephen Friedman Gallery *and the wall that fell away*. He is an artist who takes inspiration from the zeitgeist. Shonibare reacted to heightened xenophobic attitudes across social and political spectrums — Trump wanted to build a wall dividing the United States and Mexico, and the Brexit vote passed — that stoked increasing acrimony, division, and discord (Peterson, 2017). The gallery experience opens with da Vinci's *Vitruvian Man* (FIGURE 6). The original *Vitruvian Man* is a white man representing a Renaissance belief in the perfection of the human body as a microcosm of the universe. Shonibare's *Vitruvian Man* depicts an androgynous figure that suggests ideals found in the original can and should be applied to every human being. Residing on the wall above is a mural painted directly on the wall. The circles represent universalism. Shonibare incorporates patterned textures of the Dutch wax fabric that carry the weight of its colonial provenance (Olowu, 2007). The piece was intended to be inclusive, inviting to the viewer, and challenging those who wish for division. He states, "Imagine the world's civilizations without the influence of other cultures. Imagine Britain without Rome. Imagine Rome without Greece...you do have to build from what you've learned from other people" (Olowu, 2007). Shonibare used this exhibit to show that breaking down walls provides the opportunity to learn and grow. He demonstrates how much humanity has to gain from being open-minded and accepting of other cultures.

Shonibare loves to work with complexities and multiple layers, which play with the viewer's preconceived notions and beliefs. When describing his work, he states, "It's important that there is this ambiguity, that it doesn't answer these questions, and that no definite statements are being made" *(Stilling, 2013)*. His experience living in different cultures allowed him to witness interconnectedness and exchange, a reality he celebrates and critiques. He argues that those who discriminate not only cause harm to others but also themselves. Avoiding other cultures deprives a person of the opportunity to learn different perspectives.

BIBLIOGRAPHY

1. CALDWELL, ELLEN C. "Yinka Shonibare: Postcolonial Film and Fabrication." Arts & Culture. May 11, 2016.

2. "Dutch Wax Prints: Aka African Wax Prints Think Africa." Think Africa, July 5, 2020. https://thinkafrica.net/dutch-wax-prints/.

3. KUIPER, K.. "Yinka Shonibare." Encyclopedia Britannica, February 10, 2015. https://www.britannica.com/biography/Yinka-Shonibare.

4. OLOWU, DURO. Yinka Shonibare MBE in Conversation with Duro Olowu. Stephen Friedman Gallery, 2007. https://www.stephenfriedman.com/video/17-yinka-shonibare-mbe-in-conversation-with-duroolowu/.

5. PETERSEN, ANNE RING. Migration into Art: Transcultural Identities and Art-Making in a Globalised World. Manchester University Press, 2017. http://www.jstor.org/stable/j.ctvnb7rb5.

6. SHONIBARE, Y. (2018). Biography. Retrieved from Yinka Shonibare MBE (RA) Becoming an Artist: Yinka Shonibare. YouTube. YouTube, 2020. https://www.youtube.com/watch?v=UamZkDsmcFk&ab_channel=TateKids.

7. STILLING, ROBERT. "An Image of Europe: Yinka Shonibare's Postcolonial Decadence." PMLA 128, no. 2 (March 2013): 299-321.

8. Tate. "Who Is Yinka Shonibare?" Tate Kids, July 20, 2020. https://www.tate.org.uk/kids/explore/who-is/who-yinka-shonibare.

9. WOFFORD, TOBIAS. "Whose Diaspora?" Art Journal 75, no. 1 (Spring 2016): 74-79.

10. "Yinka Shonibare in 'Transformation.'" Art21, October 21, 2009. https://art21.org/watch/art-in-the-twenty-first-century/s5/yinka-shonibare-cbe-in-transformation-segment/.

1.

FIGURES

1. Tom Jamieson, *Portrait of Yinka Shonibare*, 2021.
Credit: James Cohan.

2.

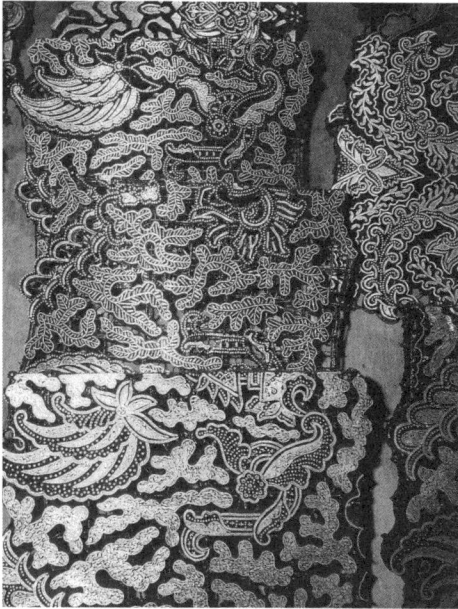

3.

4.

2. Alexander Sarlay, *African Wax Prints*, West Africa, 2009. Source: Wikimedia, Creative Commons Attribution-Share Alike 3.0 Unported.

3. Ian Alexander, *Tjap printing blocks with traditional Batik patterns*, 1996. Source: Wikimedia, Creative Commons Attribution-Share Alike 3.0 Unported.

4. Loek Tangel, *Vlisco Factory*, 2000. Credit: Rijksdienst voor het Cultureel Erfgoed. Source: Wikimedia, Creative Commons Attribution-Share Alike 3.0 Unported.

5.

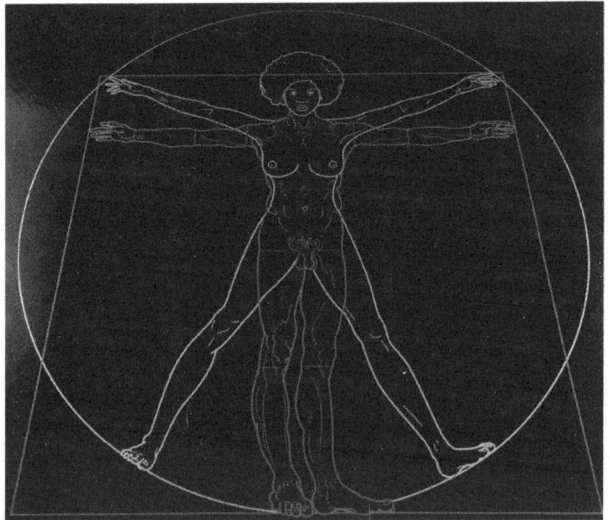

6.

5. Yinka Shonibare, *Scramble for Africa*, 2003. Credit: Yinka Shonibare CBE.

6. Yinka Shonibare, *...and the wall fell away*, 2018. Credit: Yinka Shonibare CBE.

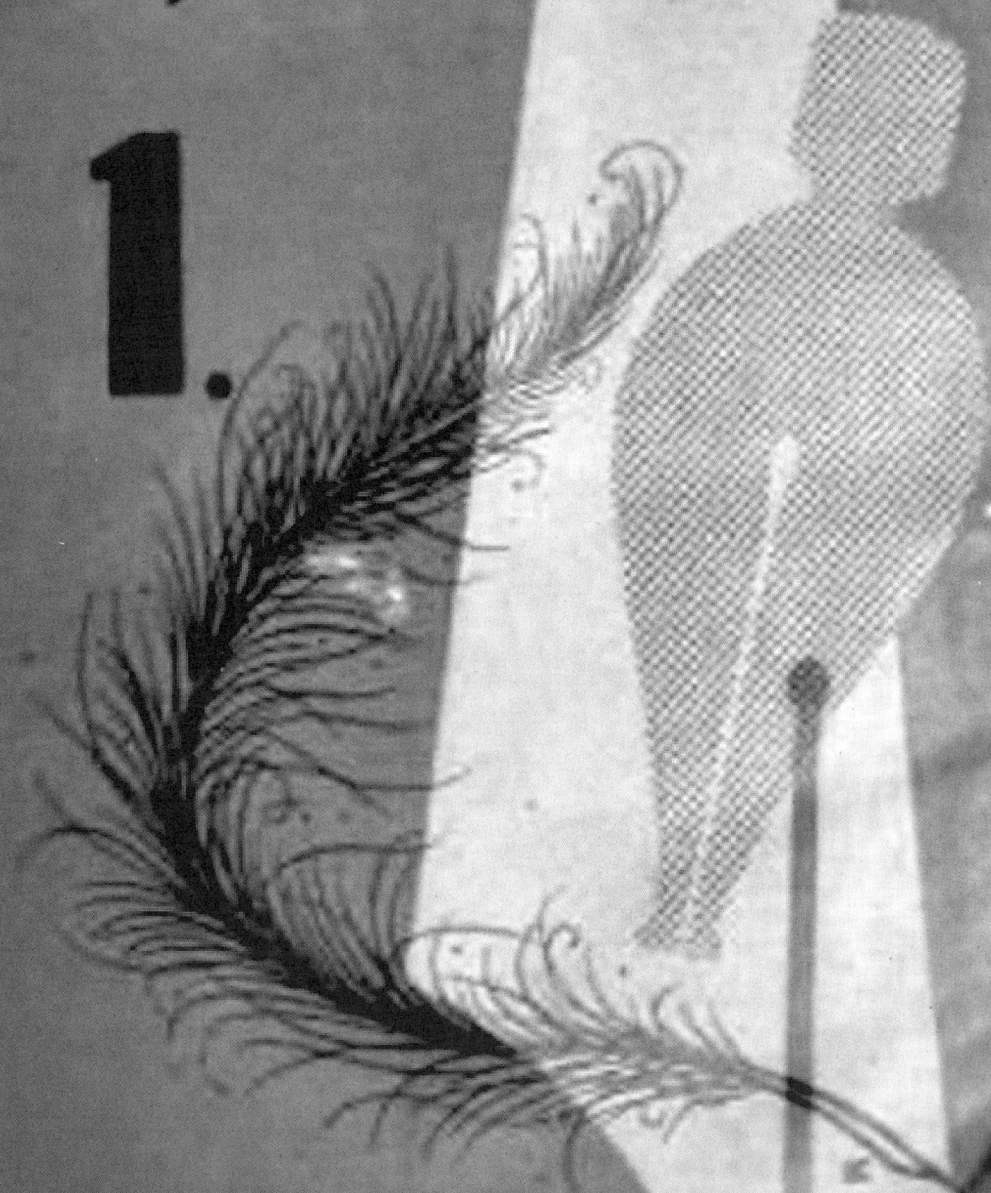

作家

1.

第一卷 · 第一期

一 · 中華民國二十五年五月十五日出版

RAYNE SCHULMAN

Taiwan:
A Hybridization of Style

Taiwan's design legacy derives from colonial occupation, industrial aspirations, and a desire to be more like the West. To fully appreciate Taiwan's unique design culture, it is critical to understand how these factors shaped its development and yielded a unique aesthetic landscape. "Race, colonialism, manufacturing and production practices, and the multi-layered political environment," along with the long period of Japanese occupation, all play into the visual language that has grown within the country (Chou, n.d.).

Researchers commonly divide the history of Taiwan into three distinctive periods: the Japanese occupation from 1895–1945, the era of Kuomingtang (KMT) authoritative government from 1949–1987, and the modern democratic period from the 1980s to the present day (*Yao, 2015*). However, it is essential to recognize that the roots of design in Taiwan predate all of these periods. The earliest foundations of design in Taiwan lie in the living conditions and utensils used by the aboriginal communities of the island (*Chou, n.d.*). Traditional Taiwanese aboriginal communities designed everyday objects, including intricately woven textile designs (FIGURE 1) and hand-carved wooden objects (FIGURE 2). Both of these examples feature elaborately ornamented details and exhibit the level of craftsmanship that Taiwanese design encompasses without the influence of foreign powers. Although these designs are not overtly referenced in most design works, recognizing the artistry of aboriginal design heritage allows for a more holistic understanding of Taiwan's diverse and evolving design history.

The period of colonial Japanese rule in Taiwan, which lasted fifty years, following the Sino-Japanese War, brought significant transformations in the social structure and catalyzed economic development (*Yao, 2015*). During this time, Japan was determined to catch up with Western imperial powers, and art, culture, and design played a substantial role in their reformation (*Yao, Sun, and Lin, 2013*). As a result, Western aesthetic principles and design conventions were adopted in Japanese society and trickled down to Taiwan. This cultural exchange put Taiwan in the unique position of being introduced to Western principles that had already been filtered through a Japanese lens, highlighting the interaction between colonial influences and how Taiwanese design was essentially a blend of Western and Eastern principles (*Yao, Sun, and Lin, 2013*).

One compelling influence on Taiwanese designs at the time was the Bauhaus movement and its construction of visual style. They distinctively found inspiration from Bauhaus artists who composed color in their works and utilized space (*Yao,*

Sun, and Lin, 2013). Designs coming out of Taiwan during this time show a "succinct modernist design style" *(Yao, Sun, and Lin, 2013)*. Book covers show an example of the modernist influence (FIGURE 3). The cover features a minimalist graphic approach to show pens and quills. It embraces clean lines and geometric shapes, keeping only the necessary ornamentation to communicate the figure as a pen. The way the text and figures interact also shows that the designers were mindful of a balance in the piece, a characteristic of the Bauhaus movement. Marketing for colonial government industries at the time also highlights the blend of influences in Taiwan (FIGURE 4). While it retains elements of Japanese styles — namely, the woodblock print techniques and muted colors — there are also compositional elements reminiscent of Art Deco posters. The arrangement of the ships running up the piece with the perpendicular horizon lines and the bold use of contrasting red and blue tones gives the design a grandiose and extravagant feeling — distinctly characterizes Art Deco design.

Along with Japan's modernization efforts came industrialization and the "pursuit of economic development," leading to the growth of commercial design *(Yao and Hsu, 2016)*. Western symbols and language were seen as modern and progressive, leading many Taiwanese companies to use English lettering in their trademark symbols *(Yao and Hsu, 2016)* (FIGURE 5). The Mitsubishi Corporation's *Kewpie Canned Pineapples* even used the kewpie doll figure in their advertising as it was a popular character in Western countries (FIGURE 6).

Following the Japanese occupation, Taiwan fell under almost four decades of the KMT's authoritative regime of martial law *(Fu and Zhao, 2021)*. he regime suppressed freedom of speech and strictly enforced censorship; anyone seen as a threat to the KMT was punished. In addition to internal suppression, Taiwan found itself at the center of political conflicts between China and the United States during the Cold War period, making it a politically tense time for the country. To gain insights into the design of this period, a focal point can be placed in the works of Huang Hua-Cheng. Huang Hua-Cheng has been credited as a figurehead in Taiwanese design, leading the country through its first design revolution. One of his most famous works is *Five Coins for Trudeau* (FIGURE 7). When Taiwan was invited to participate in the 1976 Montreal Olympics, the discourse over "Two Chinas" was heavily debated. Prime Minister Trudeau would not allow Taiwan to compete with the "Republic of China," it was speculated that it was due to a major economic deal between mainland China and the Canadian government *(Fu and Zhao, 2021)*. As a response, Huang designed the poster featuring five coins arranged in the Olympics logo formation on a dish shaped like a maple leaf to represent the "economic greed and games of international politics" *(Fu and Zhao, 2021)*.

During the 1970s and into the 1980s, Taiwan witnessed a rapid expansion of its economy, and publishing companies began to invest more in book cover designs. Here, Huang's influence as a graphic designer became truly noticeable *(Fu and Zhao, 2021)*. Many covers at the time focused more on illustrations, whereas Huang featured "high-contrast, close-up crop photographs" *(Fu and Zhao, 2021)* (FIGURE 8). These images were eye-catching and dramatic — far outside the Taiwanese public's norm. Over his career, Huang designed over three hundred book covers, with many referencing US pop artists and influenced by US culture (FIGURE 9).

Currently, the design culture in Taiwan is complicated. Graphic design is still seen as a medium for advertising, and "designers in Taiwan are mostly subordinate to design departments in manufacturing companies" as opposed to freelance designers and design studios in the West (Chou, n.d.). Designers in Taiwan have fewer opportunities to include their own perspectives in their designs and are "bound to the constraints of manufacturing production and profit" (Chou, n.d.). A studio defying this is Five Metal Shop, a small independent creative studio that brings a Taiwanese perspective to the forefront of their designs. One of their most popular projects is their annual tear-away calendar designs that bring a modern take on an everyday product. For years, design history in Asia, apart from Japan, has been seen as an imitation of Western culture, leading it to be largely disregarded in the Western design canon (Chou, 2006). However, for a marginalized area such as Taiwan, it is impossible to ignore the influences the colonial powers had on its development. Rather than viewing Taiwanese design as an imitation, the unique hybridization of Western and Eastern philosophies should be acknowledged. Recognizing Taiwanese design in the Western canon can foster a more inclusive and comprehensive understanding of global design history.

BIBLIOGRAPHY

1. CHOU, WEN HEUI. 2006. "Design History in Globalization and the Place of East Asian Design." Engineering and Product Design Education Conference, (September).https://readings.design/ PDF/design-history-in-globalization.pdf.

2. CHOU, WEN HUEI. Reorient1: Researching Taiwanese Design History in the Context of World Design History. Asia University, Taiwan. Accessed June 11, 2023.

3. FU, FLORENCE, AND ZHANG ZHAO. 2021. "The Life of Huang Hua Cheng, the Idiosyncratic Designer Who "Led Taiwan into the First Design Revolution."" AIGA Eye on Design. https://eyeondesign. aiga.org/the-life-of-huang-hua-cheng-the-idiosyncratic-designer-wholed-taiwan-into-the-first-design-revolution/

4. YAO, TSUN-HSIUNG. 2015. "Enlightenments and Development in Modern Taiwanese Visual Design from the Japanese Colonial Period to the Present (1895-2015)." Review of Arts and Humanities 4, no. 1 (June): 42-49. http://dx.doi. org/10.15640/rah.v4n1a6

5. YAO, TSUN-HSIUNG, CHU-YU SUN, AND PIN-CHANG LIN. 2013. "Modern Design in Taiwan: The Japanese Period, 1895-1945." Design Issues 29, no. 3: 38—51. http:// www.jstor.org/stable/24267088

6. YAO, TSUN HSIUNG, AND MEI YUN HSU. 2016. "Western Culture Influences on Taiwanese Trademark Design during Japanese Colonial Period." International Journal of Art and Art History 4, no. 2 (December): 63-77. https://doi. org/10.15640/ijaah.v4n2p5

1.

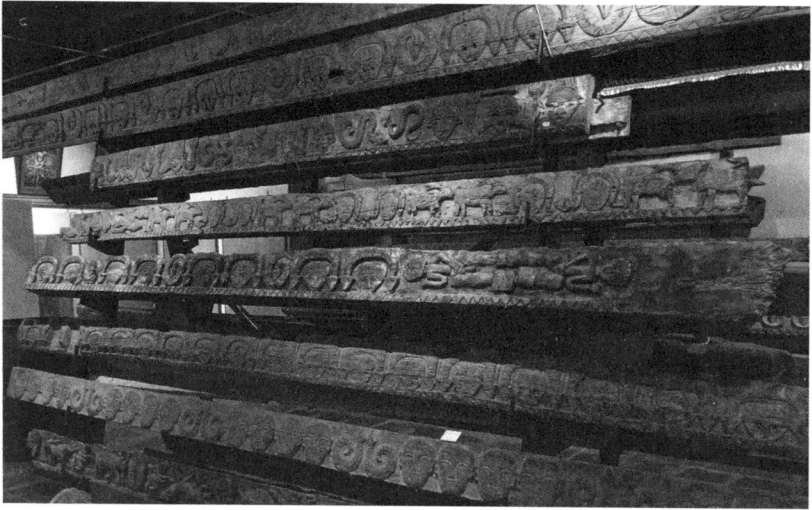

2.

FIGURES

1. Taiwan, *Paiwan people, Leg Wrappers*, 19th to early 20th century. Source: Wikimedia, Creative Commons CC0 1.0 Universal Public Domain Dedication.

2. Bernard Gagnon, *19th century Carved lintels in the Formosan Aboriginal Culture Village Museum*, 2011. Source: Wikimedia, Creative Commons Attribution-Share Alike 3.0 Unported, 2.5 Generic, 2.0 Generic and 1.0 Generic.

3.

4.

3. *Cover of Modern Style*, 1932. PD US/EU copyright expired. Yao, T.-H. Enlightenments and Development in *Modern Taiwanese Visual Design from the Japanese Colonial Period to the Present*.

4. Kaohsiung Museum of History, *Kaohsiung Port Exhibition*, poster, 1931. Credit: MIT Press *Design Issues*, Vol. 29, No. 3.

5.

6.

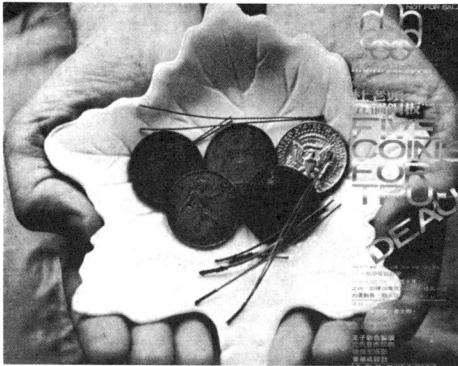

7.

5. Taiwan Daily News, *Advertisement with Western letters*, early 20th century. Source: Internet Archive. Credit: Yao, T. H. & Hsu, M. Y., *Western Culture Influences on Taiwanese Trademark Design during Japanese Colonial Period*.

6. *Pineapple Labels*, 1910s-1920s. Source: Internet Archive. Credit: Yao, T.-H. & Hsu, M. Y., *Western Culture Influences on Taiwanese Trademark Design during Japanese Colonial Period*.

7. Huang Hai-Cheng, *Five Coins For Trudeau*, 1976. Credit: Taipei Fine Arts Museum.

8.

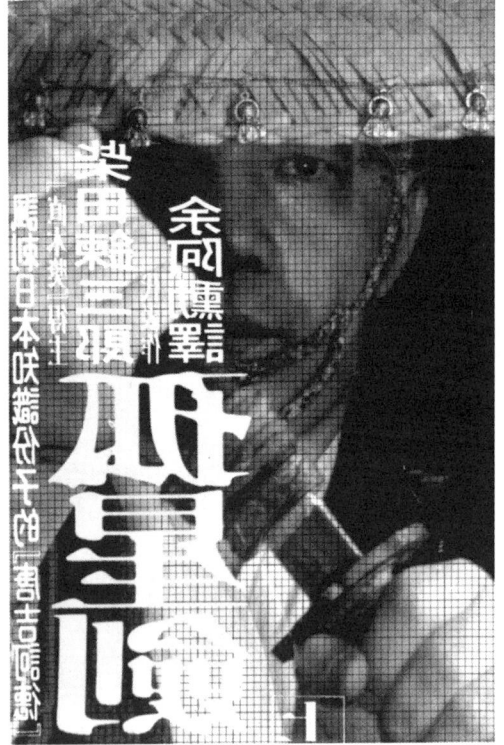

9.

8. Chuang Ling, *I Love Black Eyes* cover photograph, 1976. Credit: Taipei Fine Arts Museum.

9. Huang Hai-Cheng, *The Lone Star Swordsman* cover photograph, 1980. Credit: Taipei Fine Arts Museum.

Maula Jut:
Beyond the Film's Surface

Late 1970s. Punjab, Pakistan. Cinema is coming out of "A Decade of Endurance," resurrecting itself in Pakistan from the ashes of the subcontinent's partition (Naveed, 2019). The industry is booming, at the peak of "A Decade of Change," pouring out sentimental and romantic movies loved by the public (Naveed 2019). The decade is coming to an end, and more changes follow. General Zia-Ul-Haq comes into power, bringing about the "Decade of Decadence" (Naveed, 2019).

A newly introduced Code of Censorship stifles cultural innovation, and Pakistani cinema declines. Any and every subsequent idea for films, newspapers, and commercials is fueled by fear of surveillance. Anyone found going against "The Code" is severely penalized. Microphones are placed near the mouths of those flogged "to amplify their agonized screams for the edification of the huge crowd" *(Naveed, 2019)*. Cue the introduction of a new genre in cinema, seemingly inspired by combatting surveillance, a film so bloody and violent it puts the severity of the actions administered by those in power to shame: *Maula Jut*, 1979. This essay investigates the importance of *Maula Jut* as a film that reignited the rise of Pakistani cinematic culture and the accompanying poster that shaped the development of Pakistani graphic design.

Following its release, Maula Jut almost immediately gained phenomenal popularity in the nation. The news of a new film in the cinema that managed to pass "The Code" spread like wildfire. People flocked to the cinema to watch this new film, making it an overnight success. This also made the film a poster child for future films to succeed under the new rules *(Kapadia, 2015)*. The rising popularity of the film made Zia uneasy and threatened his dictatorship. Unsuccessful attempts were made to censor and eventually ban the film. "The Code" imposed censorship policies against displays of affection but not violence. Any attempt to restrict access to the film only piqued even greater public interest and enhanced *Maula Jut's* reputation as a cultural beacon. *Maula Jut* dominated cinema houses for an astounding 310 weeks and gained the title of "the undisputed glittering prize of Pakistani film" *(Rabe, 2019)*.

In terms of design, the film's poster (FIGURE 1) also became a subject of interest. Featuring the main protagonist and antagonist of the film, the poster itself speaks of the violence to be depicted in the film. Maula Jut, the protagonist, grips his Gandasa (weapon), dripping with the blood of his enemies, ready to strike down any threat that comes his way. The antagonist, Noori Natt, points a finger heavenwards in the background. In films from this era, the hero was shown to be an ordinary man dressed in clothing that matched what people wore normally. Usually, this was someone who challenged the administration, much like how people wanted to rebel against General

Zia's dictatorial rules. This made the film very relatable for the nation. As Mushtaq Gazdar notes: "In such a proletariat environment, a new hero was born who seemed attuned to their way of life. Sultan Rahi (Maula Jut) was the embodiment of all that the common man was waiting for" (*Naveed, 2019*). Such designs were popular back in the day as they accurately represented Pakistani folk art. The bright, vibrant colors and equally vibrant imagery are reminiscent of the Punjabi culture, which is known to be loud and vivid. According to Saima Zaidi, "Pakistani design cannot truly be confined to a few adjectives: each design carries its own influences and inspirations" (*Heller, 2011*).

Typefaces would be manipulated to reflect the genre of the film. For this specific example, the title is reshaped to look like dripping blood, hinting at the violence depicted in the film. This practice of manipulation often ended with experimental and unique results. These posters also featured Arabic calligraphy (FIGURE 2) as part of their set of typefaces. The importance of Arabic calligraphy in Pakistani culture stems from its importance to Muslims. The entirety of the Qur'an, the holy book of Islam, is written in Arabic and holds a sacred place in the hearts of Muslims in a religious context as well. Being that almost 97 percent of Pakistanis are Muslims, the significance of the text gains some perspective.

People were able to analyze the poster with ease, appreciating what they could see there. They eagerly watched the film and contributed to its huge success. The way the poster ties together many cultural aspects of Punjab, seemingly almost speaking the language of the region where it's from, was a large part of why the design worked so well. Similar design choices were implemented for films released inspired by *Maula Jut* (FIGURE 3).

The influence of the poster design bled into other mediums as well. Slowly, rickshaws with Sultan Rahi's (Maula Jut) portrait began to pop up (FIGURE 4), his face was painted onto walls as murals (FIGURE 5), and the backs of trucks were seen proudly boasting similar images (FIGURE 6). The entire country was extremely taken with *Maula Jut*. As observed by Iftikhar Dadi, cinema stars from Pakistan find themselves on calendars, posters, and postcards, in broadly circulated Pakistani magazines, as decor in people's homes, in *pān* (betel leaf) shops, on vehicles, and in restaurants (*Dadi, 2022*). The poster itself would be printed out and repeatedly plastered all over the walls. The uniqueness of this design made it into a form of street art and eventually an iconic part of Pakistani culture. This phenomenon also resulted in the rural and urban populations coming together and bridging the class divide through cinema.

Maula Jut's influence persists. A 2022 remake of the movie embodying the original formula of violence and gore proved to be a success. Although the film was well received, the promotional campaign was a shocking contrast to the original (FIGURE 7). Stripped of all its iconic elements, the poster designed for the remake showed an absurd amount of Western influence. The resemblance to posters designed for Marvel movies is visible (FIGURE 8). However, during the time between the release of the two films, Pakistani design culture became deeply homogenized, marking a stark shift in the poster for the original and much-anticipated remake. One of the most disheartening differences was the complete elimination of Arabic calligraphy from the poster —

even though Arabic text holds a sacred meaning to the people of Pakistan, eradicating the text conveys adversity to inclusion. One may argue that it was done to boost the film internationally, but that is easily achievable by using both Arabic and English texts, as the original piece did.

Deliberate steps taken to commercialize this release undermine a lot of what the original *Maula Jut* film stood for. As a form of political resistance, the 1979 version became iconic. The 2022 remake feels as if it was made without a clear purpose or intent beyond mere existence in mind, without any real significance, as a part of the hordes of mass-produced films. In contrast, the poster for the original film reflects the extensive thought and effort that went into making it culturally accurate. This carelessness may also result in stripping other mediums of their unique craftsmanship. As mentioned above, trucks, rickshaws, street art, and many other mediums saw the influence of the hype generated by the original poster. If the root of that influence is altered to this level, it may cause unprecedented changes throughout Pakistan's design world.

Moreover, the people whose livelihoods depend heavily on this craftsmanship would suffer. The ones who saw *Maula Jut* rise as a ray of hope in times of tyranny would experience a profound sense of loss and lack of belonging as what holds immense importance to their identity is being taken from them. Now that Pakistani craft is gaining attention on a global level, the implications associated with revising the iconic poster are vast. Every decision taken to portray Pakistani culture will ultimately change the way we are perceived in the world beyond just design. The fate of the contemporary revision of the *Maula Jut* poster harkens to how Lorraine Wild's "Great Wheel of Style" charts how an aesthetic gets commodified. Unfortunately, the revival stage did not garner much interest for the poster in question. Rather, it fumbled its iconic status and failed to recreate it.

Maula Jut was a film created as a form of political resistance. The accompanying visuals for the film therefore have a deeper significance as well. Each element making up those visuals has a meaning of its own. The poster for *Maula Jut* and the posters for films that followed it unapologetically celebrated the heroes of these films, but more than that, they celebrated the culture of Punjab. Why did the attitude towards that culture shift to a negative one? Why was it looked down upon and no longer celebrated? Why was it swept under the rug, covered up, and hidden from the world? Why was that individuality given up on?

Not only does this poster represent a certain era in Pakistani cinema, but it also represents the identity of Pakistan. Changing these elements to suit an audience belonging anywhere other than where the design originates is a deliberate loss of self. Visual languages can and will continue to evolve, but designers should be wary of maintaining multicultural visual expression when they do.

BIBLIOGRAPHY

1. ASGHAR, MUHAMMAD, AND MUHAMMAD A. REHMA-NI. "Macho Icons Going Places." https://pdfs.semanticscholar.org/59b3/9a6603126a045493b-cc9b7e357d185840ae.pdf May 22, 2019. https://doi.org/10.5614/j.vad.2019.11.1.1.

2. DADI, IFTIKHAR. "Introduc-tion: The Lahore Effect." In Lahore Cinema: Between Realism and Fable, 1—28. University of Washington Press, 2022. http://www.jstor.org/stable/j.ctv31nzk1s.6

3. DIBBERN, DOUG. "Revising the Canon: Outline for an Alternative History of the Cinema." In Cinema's Doppelgängers, 33—302. Punctum Books, 2021. http://www.jstor.org/stable/jj.2353883.4

4. ELIAS, JAMAL J. "On Wings of Diesel: Spiritual Space and Religious Imagination in Pakistani Truck Decoration." RES: Anthropology and Aesthetics, no. 43 (2003): 187—202. http://www.jstor.org/stable/20167598

5. HELLER, STEVEN. "Pakistan: An Emerging Design Nation." The Atlantic, May 26, 2011. https://www.theatlantic.com/entertainment/ar-chive/2011/05/pakistan-an-emerg-ing-design-nation/2 39505/

6. KAPADIA, MUHAMMAD A. "The Philosophy of Maula Jatt." Medium, May 18, 2015. https://medium.com/the-outtake/understanding-the-most-powerful-pakistani-fim-of-all-time-55c5c19d8a9d

7. NAVEED, FAHAD. "Exploring the History of Pakistani Cinema." Herald, June 28, 2019. https://herald.dawn.com/news/1398913/exploring-the-history-of-paki-stani-cinema

8. RABE, NATE. "The Philosophy of Maula Jatt." Scroll.in, Janu-ary 15, 2019. https://scroll.in/reel/909311/severed-limbs-and-rivers-of-blood-the-film-that-in-spired-fawad-khans-the-legend-of-maula-jatt

9. SCHIMMEL, ANNEMARIE, AND BARBAR RIVOLTA. "Islamic Calligraphy." The Metropoli-tan Museum of Art Bulletin 50, no. 1 (1992): 1—56. https://doi.org/10.2307/3263914

10. VISWANATH, GITA, AND SALMA MALIK. "Revisiting 1947 through Popular Cinema: A Comparative Study of India and Pakistan." Economic and Polit-ical Weekly 44, no. 36 (2009): 61—69. http://www.jstor.org/stable/25663519

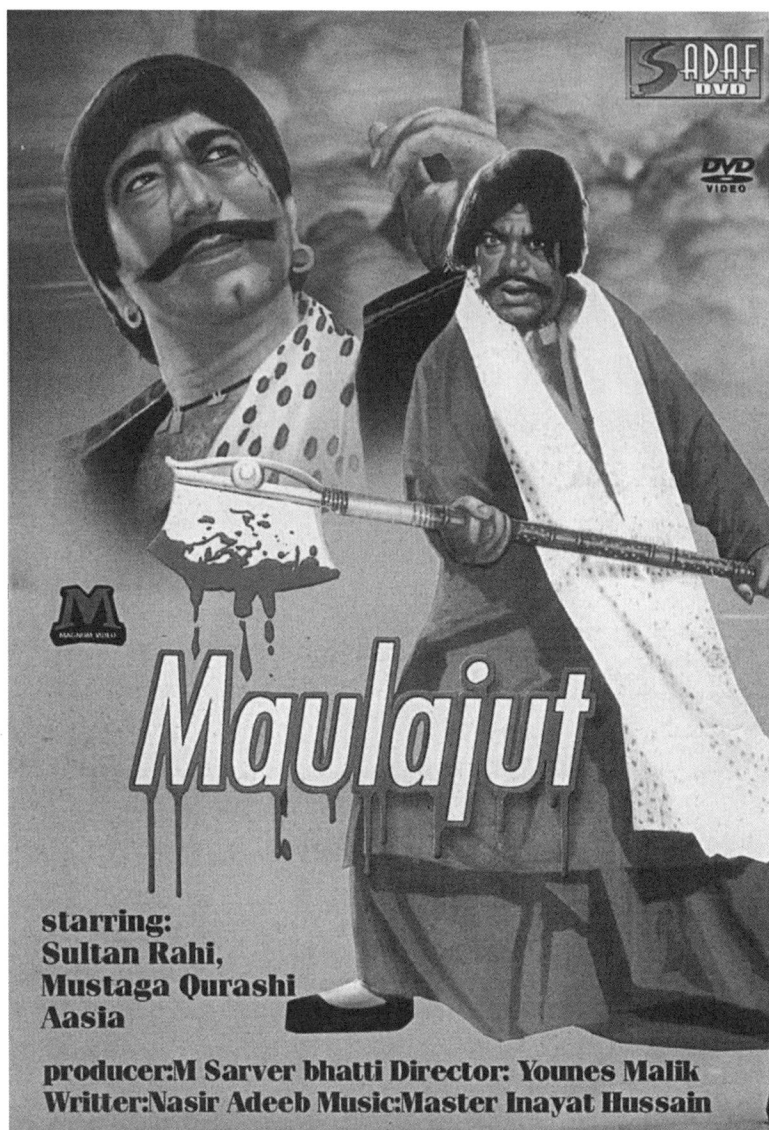

1.

FIGURES

1. Unknown Artist, *Maulajut* movie poster, 1979. Source:
IMDb, fair use for educational use.

2.

3.

2. Mir `Imad al-Hasani, *Folio with Verses in Nasta'liq Script*, 1608—9. Credit: The Metropolitan Museum of Art.

3. Unknown artists, *Maula Jatt*, 1979. Source: IMDb, fair use for educational use.

4.

---

4. *Sultan Rahi*, Lahore street mural, 2018. Credit:
Jacqueline Hadel, Tokidoki Nomad Blog.

5.

6.

5. Abdullah Haris Films, *The Legend of Maula Jatt* film promotional poster, 2022. Credit: Bilal Lashari.

6. Walt Disney Studios Motion Pictures, *Avengers: Endgame* theatrical release poster, 2019. Source: IMDb, fair use for educational use.

VISUAL SOVEREIGNTY

Design as a tool for visual sovereignty represents the voice of the unsung. These voices rise and challenge dominant frameworks that historically stifled diversity and "othered" marginalized communities. The examples in this chapter replace subtlety with strikingly literal, visceral messages that require no translation, no decoding. It's an unfiltered dialogue that commands attention through inventive new visual languages seen in posters, prints, books, and fashion. Visual sovereignty celebrates the power of design to transcend limitations, to amplify the marginalized, and to proclaim a reality marked by inclusivity and change.

The INDIANS' BOOK

AN OFFERING BY THE AMERICAN INDIANS OF
INDIAN LORE, MUSICAL AND NARRATIVE, TO
FORM A RECORD OF THE SONGS AND LEGENDS
OF THEIR RACE

RECORDED AND EDITED

BY

Natalie Curtis

ILLUSTRATIONS FROM PHOTOGRAPHS AND
FROM ORIGINAL DRAWINGS BY INDIANS

NEW YORK AND LONDON
HARPER AND BROTHERS PUBLISHERS
MCMVII

A. de L.

Design as a Tool
for Indigenous
Visual Sovereignty:
The Impact of Angel DeCora

History is a narrative shaped by the historian. Whether consciously or not, a historian's beliefs shape both what is included and omitted—reflecting biases rooted in identity, politics, social views, religion, and more. As the field of graphic design history began to take form, it was largely driven by a Eurocentric, patriarchal lens, often marginalizing contributions outside of this worldview. Consequently, designers who don't fit this narrative—such as Angel DeCora, a 20th-century Indigenous artist, designer, and educator—are frequently absent from academic curricula. This essay explores DeCora's story, highlighting her creative and educational impact on Native artists and designers, both historically and in contemporary contexts.

When describing her drive, DeCora says: "My people are a race of designers. I look for the day when the Indian shall make beautiful things for all the world" *(Curtis, 1920)*. More often than not, mainstream American culture and media relegate Indigenous people and cultures to the past and reduce them to stereotypes that fail to recognize the diversity in indigeneity. Academia does only slightly better with its more nuanced understanding of Indigenous topics but still comes up short as the classes stay stuck in the anthropology department or get labeled as "special topic" courses. To look at the design field specifically and to understand why Indigenous design resides on the periphery of higher education is to reckon with the notion that colonialism is the bedrock of the development of our country — and that colonialism shape-shifted the advancement of the United States' visual culture. As Chippewa designer Neebin Southall puts it, "[m]ost educators inherit this situation with absolutely no ill intent, but the truth is, the situation is historically rooted in some very ugly things: white suprematism, genocide, displacement, cultural suppression, and forced assimilation. It's important to acknowledge the truth" *(Andersen, 2017)*. Recognition is key, but the conversation does not end there.

   Although Indigenous voices belong in the Western design discourse, designers and historians must also acknowledge the shortcomings borne out of erasure and racial discrimination that continue to bias non-Native perspectives of this diverse racial group. As historian Devon A. Mihesuah notes, "no other ethnic group in the United States ha[s] endured greater and more varied distortions of its cultural identity than American Indians" *(Mihesuah, 1996)*. To avoid perpetuating misrepresentations and misinterpretations by non-Natives, Professor Christine Ballangree-Morris stresses the importance of understanding the phenomenon of multiplicity seen across Indigenous identities, understandings, and aesthetics in the article "Indigenous Aesthetics." While embarking on this brief exploration of the inimitable Angel DeCora and the impact she had, it is important to apply a "trans-Indigenous understanding," as noted by Ballangree-Morris. This means developing our understanding of Indigenous arts as they are situated in a space "informed by multiple, distinct systems of Indigenous aesthetics across tribal, national, geographic, and cultural borders" (Ballangree-Morris, 2008). In short, non-Natives should incorporate a nuanced understanding of indigeneity that parallels a nuanced understanding of their own racial and ethnic identity.

In her obituary, Angel DeCora was described as the first American Indian artist to openly embrace an Indigenous identity amid an oppressive reality shaped by the interests of white men (Curtis, 1920). DeCora, known as "Hinook-Mani' wi-Kilina'ka" in her mother tongue, was born in the latter half of the 19th century on the Winnebago reservation in Nebraska. DeCora's educational history spans geography and level of study, including the Hampton Institute in Virginia; Miss Burnham's Classical School for Girls in Massachusetts; Smith College; Drexel Institute; Cowles Art School in Boston, and the Boston Museum of Fine Arts. During that time, she was a student of various well-known artists of the period, such as landscape artist Dwight W. Tyron at Smith, illustrator Howard Pyle at Drexel, American impressionist Joseph De Camp at Cowles Art School, and American impressionists Frank Benson and Edmund Tarbell. Before directing her energy towards teaching young Native students, DeCora had a successful career working as an independent artist in New York and Boston, when few women were afforded the opportunity. Her résumé includes two paintings appearing in the 1910 Salon, the publication of two of her illustrated stories in *Harper's Monthly Magazine* 1899 issue, and illustration for several books. Her work generally had Native individuals as the subject matter, providing a platform to represent Native identity from a Native perspective that divorces from the primitivist stereotypes created by the white population and instead asserts the nuanced existence of the diverse cultural community. Although DeCora was exceptionally skilled and well-trained in early 20th-century American art techniques, she expressed disdain for drawing like a white man (Curtis, 1920).

In 1906, DeCora joined the faculty at the Carlisle Indian School in Pennsylvania. DeCora accepted the position on the condition that she "shall not be expected to teach in the white man's way, but shall be given complete liberty to develop the art of [her] own race and to apply this, as far as possible, to various forms of art industries and crafts" (Gere, 2004). To illuminate the rich cultural diversity of American Indian tribes and preserve the traditions associated with them, DeCora helped her students learn about one another's tribal design language in a space that was originally designed to force students to abandon their identity to adopt the "right," or white, way of being. In DeCora's art class, students studied the ornamentation of tribal groups such as the Sioux, the Arapahoe, the Winnebago, the Diné (Navajo), the Zuni, the Pueblo people, and the Hopi. In her role as an educator, DeCora determined that design was the most accessible and authentic form to teach her students. In her autobiography, she expressed that "although at times, I yearn to express myself in landscape art, I feel that designing is the best channel in which to convey the native qualities of the Indian's decorative talent" *(DeCora, 1911)*. Through copious amounts of research that came from reading papers, studying the object themselves, and visiting practitioners (who were mainly women) of various tribes to gain firsthand knowledge, DeCora pieced together a curriculum that empowered her students to embrace their unique identity while also building upon the inherent artistic talent she argued all Natives possessed. DeCora sought to show that Native art belonged in the American art canon as it was the truest version of American art due to where and from whom it originates.

During this time, DeCora took up a few design projects, some of her most revolutionary work appearing in ethnomusicologist Natalie Curtis' *The Indians' Book*. This publication compiled the songs, stories, and drawings of Indigenous communities nationwide, organized by tribe. Initially, DeCora was commissioned to create the title page for her tribe, the Winnebago people. When she presented her design, it became apparent to the publishing team that all the title pages needed this intentional and beautifully designed hand-lettering (FIGURES 1, 2). The in-house designer rejected the request to copy the style, advising them to work with the artist who created the page. When DeCora's identity was revealed, the designer was not surprised, admitting that "no white man could have done this" *(Curtis, 1920)*.

For each tribe showcased in the book, DeCora used a system of ornaments and symbolic imagery to hand-letter tribe-specific title pages that reflected the nuances of each group. DeCora's typography unified decorative elements with tribe-specific graphics and styles (FIGURE 3). DeCora often included brief explanations to identify the features in her lettering since the book's audience was most likely unfamiliar with the imagery (FIGURE 4). An example is her description of the lettering for the Kwakiutl people that accompanies the illustrations of Kwakiutl artist Kialish reads: "The letters are composed of motives peculiar to the Kwakiutl design: the tail and fin of the whale, the hawk, and the eye joint" *(Curtis, 1907)*. The inclusion of this simple and brief statement was a revolutionary act.

Her trans-Indigenous approach when designing the title pages for *The Indians' Book* embodies her approach as an educator. Rather than mimicking white European art, DeCora stressed literacy in one's own tribal design language within her curriculum. This supported the growth of individualized voices and preserved the diversity in cultural practices. DeCora's classroom was a space for "interchanging ideas" between students and teachers.

Around the time of DeCora's departure from Carlisle in 1915, the presidential administration became less accepting of this approach to teaching at residential schools, which stifled DeCora's work. In 1919, Angel died, and not long after, her connection to the countless successful Native artists and designers who were once her students vanished. A designer who took such a radical approach in their work is rarely uttered in the design history classroom.

However, it must be clarified that it is not as if once DeCora died, the flourishing of Native artists and designers ceased to exist. Native art soon began to receive attention from the white art world in the early 20th century. Throughout the century, artists like contemporary painter Jaune Quick-To-See-Smith have knocked down the barriers of the white male-dominated art world. Artists like Diné (Navajo) printmaker Melanie Yazzie continually challenge non-Natives' notion of what Native art should look like by using her own system of symbols to represent her tradition (FIGURE 5).

In the context of graphic design, Lakota graphic designer Sadie Red Wing seeks to increase Native representation in the design curriculum and to disseminate the notion of visual sovereignty within Native graphic design. Similar to DeCora's argument for students to learn and develop their understanding of their specific tribe's design elements, Red Wing underscores the importance of Native designers increasing the visual literacy of their tribal visual systems. This practice of resiliency combats the prevalence of pan-Indianism that has crept into Native designs to cater to a white audience. Red Wing's graduate thesis, *Learning the Traditional Lakota Visual Language Through Shape Play*, puts this notion into practice and is meant to serve as a reference for other Indigenous designers. As Red Wing puts it, "Native American students are colonized to think that they are artists and not designers. The way they practice is always 'craft.' I put my efforts into getting Native American students away from that thinking when it comes to designing artifacts" *(Andersen, 2017)*. In summation, it is past due for American design curricula to incorporate the work and stories of designers like Angel DeCora for the benefit of everyone.

BIBLIOGRAPHY

1. ANDERSEN, MARGARET. 2017. "Why Can't the U.S. Decolonize Its Design Education?" AIGA Eye on Design, January 2, 2017. https://eyeondesign.aiga.org/why-cant-the-u-s-decolonize-its-design-education/.

2. BARKATAKI, SUSSANA. 2008. "Om Tattoos & Cultural Appropriation (4 Min Read)." Om-Stars, 12 Oct. 2020, omstars.com/blog/yoga-philosophy-insight/om-tattoos-cultural-appropriation-4-min-read/.

3. CURTIS, NATALIE. 1907. The Indians' Book: An Offering by the American Indians of Indian Lore Music and Narrative, to Form a Record of the Sounds and Legends of Their Race. New York: Harper.

4. CURTIS, NATALIE. 1920. "The American Indian Artist." The Outlook, January 14, 1920. https://www.neebin.com/nativedesign/wp-content/uploads/2020/11/Angel_DeCora_The_Outlook_feature_obituary.pdf.
DeCora, Angel. 1911. "Angel DeCora—An Autobiography." The Red Man by Red Man (March): 279-285. https://carlisleindian.dickinson.edu/sites/all/files/docs-publications/RedMan_v03n07c.p df.

5. GERE, ANNE RUGGLES. 2004. "An Art of Survivance: Angel DeCora at Carlisle." American Indian Quarterly 28, no. 3/4 (Summer-Autumn): 649-684. https://www.jstor.org/stable/4138937.

6. MIHESUAH, DEVON A. 1996. American Indians: Stereotypes and realities. Atlanta: Clarity.

7. RED WING, SADIE. 2016. "Learning the Traditional Lakota Visual Language Through Shape Play." Graduate thesis, North Carolina State University. https://issuu.com/sadieredwing/docs/srw_thesis_2016.

8. YAZZIE, MELANIE. 2018. "Geographies of Memory Exhibition Video." The WheelWright Museum. YouTube video, 20:19. https://www.youtube.com/watch?v=Xwl44De-J0gU&t=28s.

1.

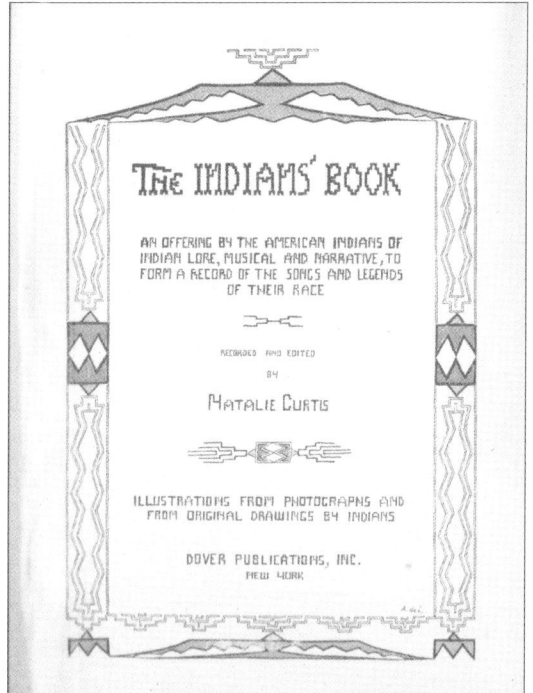

2.

FIGURES

1. Angel DeCora, *The Indians' Book*, 1907. PD US/EU copyright expired.

2. Angel DeCora, *The Indians' Book*, winnebago lettering, 1907. PD US/EU copyright expired.

3.

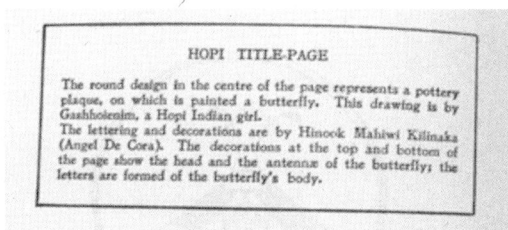

HOPI TITLE-PAGE

The round design in the centre of the page represents a pottery plaque, on which is painted a butterfly. This drawing is by Gashhokenim, a Hopi Indian girl.
The lettering and decorations are by Hinook Mahiwi Kilinaka (Angel De Cora). The decorations at the top and bottom of the page show the head and the antennæ of the butterfly; the letters are formed of the butterfly's body.

4.

3. Angel DeCora, *The Indians' Book*, kwakiutl lettering, 1907. PD US/EU copyright expired.

4. Angel DeCora, *The Indians' Book*, title and caption overlays, 1907. PD US/EU copyright expired.

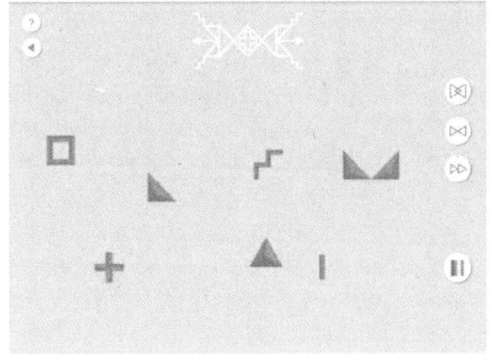

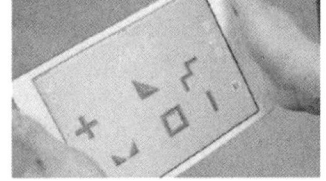

5.

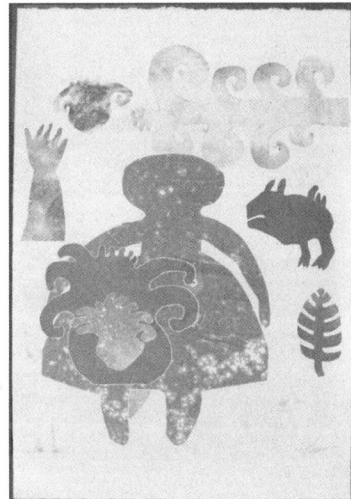

6.

5. Sadie Red Wing, *Oúnchage*. Credit: Sadie Red Wing.

6. Melanie A. Yazzie, *Blue Corn Girl*, 2011. Credit: Glenn Green Galleries.

NIHARIKA YELLAMRAJU

Unveiling the
Political Resonance
of Indian Modern Art

Political posters emerged as a powerful medium for expressing dissent, fostering nationalism, and mobilizing the masses against British imperialism in India. These posters served as a means of communication and played a crucial role in shaping the narrative of the Indian independence movement. The subsequent emergence of an Indian modern art style marked a quest for identity and independence, blending traditional symbolism with Western techniques. This essay outlines the key instances in and the pioneers of modern Indian art.

Indian modern art is a style that established India's voice across a political landscape that challenged its very identity in Western media. Often associated with the abundant wealth and crafts of the past, Western representation of Indian art tends to overshadow the hardships endured during colonization. By examining this largely overlooked art movement, we can establish a foundation for showcasing diverse perspectives on art and history, emphasizing the necessity of adopting a transcendent viewpoint when analyzing the dynamics of non-Western modernisms.

The inception of the Indian modern art style can be traced back to the late 19th and early 20th century, primarily through traditional paintings and craft. One of the notable pioneers to emerge during this period was the Bengal School of Art, founded by Abanindranath. The Bengal School aimed to revive traditional Indian art forms and techniques, emphasizing the utilization of indigenous materials, themes, and narratives in their artistic expressions, similar to the ideology of William Morris on craft (*Mitter, 2007*). This institution played a significant role in shaping the visual representation of political posters, as artists incorporated elements of Indian mythology, folklore, and historical narratives to evoke a sense of national pride and cultural identity. Notably, renowned artists of the early 20th century, such as Nandalal Bose and Jamini Roy (FIGURES 1, 3), showcased this innovative technique. They utilized their artworks to challenge colonial oppression and advocate for the cultural emancipation of India. Through their paintings, which depicted rural life, peasant struggles, and the resilience of the common people, they shed light on the socio-political disparities prevalent in colonial India. Consequently, their works invoked a collective consciousness and resistance against foreign domination.

These artists played significant roles in shaping the visual language of protest posters, with one notable example being the Ghadar movement. From 1903 to 1913, approximately ten thousand South Asian immigrants arrived in North America, predominantly from the rural areas of central Punjab (*Puri, 1980*). A considerable number of these Punjabis had previously served in the British military. In response to this influx, the Canadian government implemented a series of laws aimed at restricting the entry of South Asians into the country and limiting the political rights of those already residing there. To combat these discriminatory measures, the migrants formed Hindustani Associations, and intellectuals such as Har Dayal and Taraknath Das endeavored to mobilize students from the University of Berkeley, educating them in anarchist and nationalist ideologies (*Philatelic Incarnation, 2014*). Additionally, they established a weekly newspaper to incite rebellion and recruit courageous soldiers for the Indian independence struggle. During this period, the production of Indian alphabets on metal type was limited, resulting in the newspaper being primarily handwritten. In the words of the paper *Revolutionary Organization*, the term "Ghadar" itself signifies revolt or rebellion. The first issue of the publication announced a war against English rule and that the plan was an armed rebellion similar to the one waged by Indians in 1857. This edition of the newspaper conveyed the group's main message, "The time will soon come when rifles and blood will take the place of pens and ink" (*Singh, 2015*). To further emphasize this message, a later compilation of nationalist and socialist literature of the movement utilized illustrations, as seen in FIGURE 2, which exhibited elements of the Indian modern style of art. Through their experimentation with various techniques, such as the use of bold colors like saffron and blood red, strong lines, and symbolic imagery, they effectively conveyed a sense of urgency, solidarity, and national pride among the masses.

During the onset of WWII, the experimental and revolutionary spirit of the movement continued to thrive, as seen in the form of typographic posters used for spreading nationalist propaganda of Mahatma Gandhi. One example is FIGURE 4, a WWII propaganda leaflet issued in 1928 by Indian Independence League members Rash Bihari Bose and Jawaharlal Nehru (*Fay, 1995*). The primary objective of this league was to foster Indian nationalism and gain Japanese support for the Indian Independence Movement. To achieve this, they created numerous propaganda materials to be used on various war fronts across Southeast Asia, where both British and Japanese forces, including Indian soldiers, were engaged in combat. These posters featured the texts "STOP" and "JOIN US TO STRIKE THE BRITISH" in Hindi, English, Urdu, Tamil, and Bengali, accompanied by symbolic representations of Mahatma Gandhi and soldiers. These symbols aimed to "emphasize the principles of nonviolence and civil disobedience as powerful tools for challenging the oppressive forces of colonialism" (*Philatelic Incarnation, 2014*). Furthermore, the posters sought to encourage Indian soldiers, who were fighting alongside the British army, to switch sides and unite in their fight against the British as one nation.

In FIGURES 5 and 6, the same event is depicted from a German perspective. Subhas Chandra Bose, a freedom fighter who led the League, took advantage of the outbreak of the Second World War to travel to the Soviet Union, Germany, and Japan. He aimed to ally with these countries to attack the British in India. As the Head of State of the Provisional Government of Azad Hind, Bose participated in the Greater East Asia Conference held in Tokyo in November 1943 as an "observer," as India was still under British rule. This allowed him to gain new allies along the way (*Fay, 1995*).

One of the posters written during this time aimed to counter British propaganda by stating that the Germans do not imprison but kill, emphasizing the false nature of such claims. These posters were created to persuade Indians who were part of the British forces to switch sides and lay down their arms for the Germans or Japanese. The emergence of these posters can be attributed to the growing nationalist sentiment and the need for a mass medium that could effectively disseminate political ideas and rally public support for the freedom struggle.

The political references found in Indian modern art played a significant role in sparking social change and a cultural renaissance. These references encouraged dialogue and introspection among the artistic community and the broader public following India's independence. Artists challenged traditional artistic conventions and questioned the prevailing ideologies and power structures that influenced the nation's trajectory. Satyajit Ray, a prominent artist, is known for his cinematic narratives deeply rooted in Bengal's cultural ethos. His films, such as *Pather Panchali* and *Charulata* captured the "essence of everyday life" while subtly critiquing the social and political structures that shaped his characters' experiences (FIGURES 7, 8). Ray's film posters, which translated the contents of his films, utilized indigenous artistic motifs like Madhubani and incorporated intricate patterns, hand-painted strokes, typography, and vibrant hues that celebrated India's cultural diversity and artistic richness (FIGURES 9, 10). Although Ray was not directly involved in the avant-garde movement, his artistic sensibilities and narrative style aligned with the movement's broader ethos, emphasizing the importance of artistic innovation and social commentary within the Indian cultural context.

The genesis of Indian modern art can be traced back to a time of civil unrest and ambiguity. The fusion of Western techniques with indigenous art forms represented a blending of cultural influences. It embodied the resilience and adaptability of Indian artists in the face of changing socio-political landscapes. This movement revitalized traditional art forms and folktales while also reflecting the bold stances and uncensored aspects of the freedom struggle. Furthermore, these artworks emphasized the importance of art as a tool for social transformation, providing a platform for marginalized voices and fostering a sense of collective consciousness and national pride. As we continue to examine the historical significance of art styles, it is crucial to acknowledge the lasting impact of these artistic movements in shaping contemporary discourse and gaining a deeper understanding of the intricate interplay between art, history, and socio-political dynamics. Doing so will help to promote a more inclusive and comprehensive narrative of India's rich artistic heritage and cultural evolution.

BIBLIOGRAPHY

1. FAY, PETER WARD. "The Forgotten Army: India's Armed Struggle for Independence, 1942-1945." University of Michigan Press, 1995.

2. KANTAWALA, AMI. "Art Education in Colonial India: Implementation and Imposition" Studies in Art Education 53, no. 3 (Spring 2012): 208-222.

3. MITTER, PARTHA. "Rabindranath Tagore and Okakura Tenshin in Calcutta: The Creation of a Regional Asian Avant-garde Art." In Arrival Cities: Migrating Artists and New Metropolitan Topographies in the 20th Century, 147-158. 2020.

4. MITTER, PARTHA. "The Triumph of Modernism: India's Artists and the Avant-Garde, 1922-1947." London: Reaktion Books, 2007.

5. "Philatelic Incarnation." Saturday, April 26, 2014." Blogger. https://www.blogger.com/profile/13605071807022814918

6. PURI, HARISH K. "Revolutionary Organization: A Study of the Ghadar Movement." Social Scientist 9, no. 2/3 (Sep. - Oct., 1980): 53-66. https://doi.org/10.2307/3516925.

7. SINGH, SUNIT. "Ghadar Conspiracy." In 1914-1918-online: International Encyclopedia of the First World War, edited by Ute Daniel, Peter Gatrell, Oliver Janz, Heather Jones, Jennifer Keene, Alan Kramer, and Bill Nasson. Issued by Freie Universität Berlin. Berlin, 2015-10-29. https://encyclopedia.1914-1918-online.net/article/ghadar_conspiracy/2015-10-29

8. SIVA KUMAR, R. "Modern Indian Art: A Brief Overview." Art Journal 58, no. 3 (Autumn 1999): 14-21. https://doi.org/10.2307/777856.

9. STOCKWELL, A. J. "Changing Visions of East Asia, 1943–93: Transformations and Continuities." Edited by Chad J. Mitcham. Abingdon: Routledge, 2007. Published online by Cambridge University Press, 17 July 2008.

1.

2.

3.

FIGURES

1. Jamini Roy, *Three Women*, 1889-1972. Credit: Indian Museum, Kolkhata.

2. Yugantar Ashram, *Hindustan Ghadar* article detailing arrest of Lala Hardayal, 1914. PD, US/EU copyright expired.

3. Yugantar Ashram, Book cover of *Ghadar di Gunj*, 1913. PD, US/EU copyright expired.

4.

5.

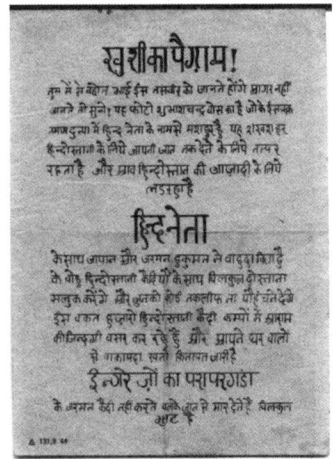

6.

4. Indian Independence League, *Mahatma Gandhi urging Indian troops to united against Britain*, 1941-44. Credit: Jyotirmay Bareria.

5. *German WW II leaflet depicting Netaji Subhas Chandra Bose* (front), 1944. Credit: Jyotirmay Bareria.

6. *German WW II leaflet depicting Netaji Subhas Chandra Bose* (front), 1944. Credit: Jyotirmay Bareria.

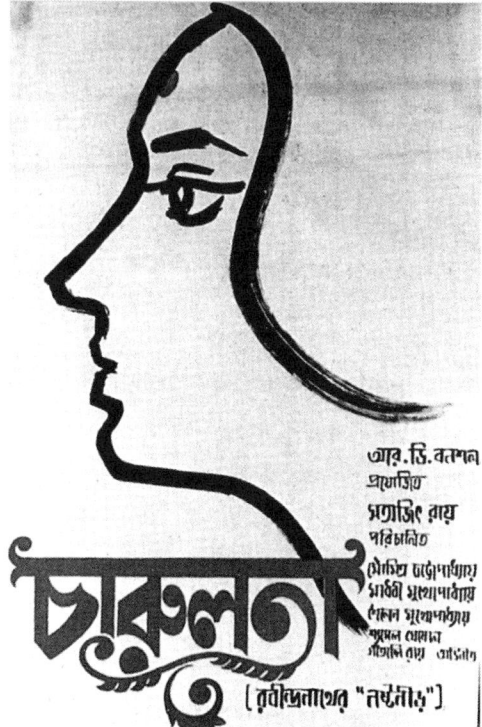

7.

8.

7. Satyajit Ray, *Pather Panchali*, poster, 1955. Source:
PD eBay image.

8. Satyajit Ray, *Charulata*, 1964. Source: PD eBay image.

9.

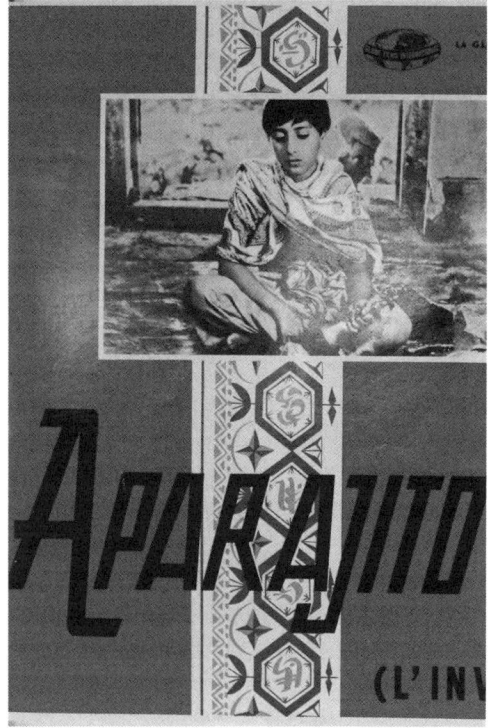

10.

9. Satyajit Ray, *Jana Aranya*, 1976. Source: PD eBay image.

10. Satyajit Ray, *Aparajito, The Apu Trilogy*, 1959. Credit: Benito Medela Internacional Movie Poster.

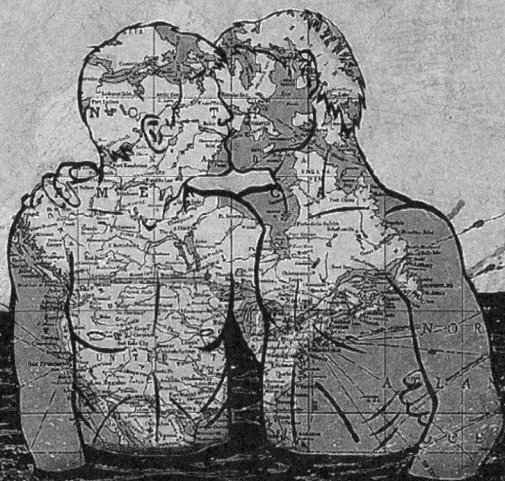

Rage and Resilience: The Artistic Legacy of David Wojnarowicz

"To make the private into something public is an action that has terrific ramifications" *(Kerr, 2021)*.

These words by the late David Wojnarowicz capture the power of visibility. Born in Red Bank, New Jersey, Wojnarowicz made his name in 1980s New York, a city reeling from the AIDS crisis that had already claimed thousands of lives. Amid this tragedy, stigma intensified around queer culture, with gay men particularly targeted as scapegoats for the so-called "gay disease." In the 1980s, being gay was already challenging, but the shadow of an incurable disease made queer life in New York feel nearly unbearable.

Ciaran Freeman, writing for *America Magazine*, captures this sentiment: "He seeks to find his place in a world that is not designed for him" *(Freeman, 2018)*. During the AIDS crisis, Wojnarowicz's work became infused with urgency as he documented the lives of those affected and fought against the stigma and discrimination surrounding the LGBTQ+ community. He personally lost many to AIDS while also battling the disease himself, gaining firsthand insight into the injustice facing both the gay community and AIDS victims. The epidemic, branded a "gay disease," grew as government support faltered, with funding for interest groups and researchers falling drastically short. This failure to act ignited a movement, giving Wojnarowicz a platform to channel his frustration over the politicization of human suffering into art.

FIGURES 1 and 2 provide striking examples of his work: in FIGURE 1, the contrast between sterile text and a playful photo stuns the viewer, while FIGURE 2 takes a more somber tone with a darker image. Elaine Velie's article unpacks the depth of these works: "Wojnarowicz smiles at the viewer through a photograph of himself as a schoolboy. Surrounding the photo—a classic Americana image of boyhood—a foreboding text warns of what the subject will experience throughout his life because of his sexual orientation" *(Velie, 2022)*. Wojnarowicz's pieces, rooted in personal experience, were raw, confrontational, and emotionally charged, blending gritty visuals with poetic texts to create powerful, immersive experiences for his viewers.

David Wojnarowicz emerged as a pioneering figure whose work pushed the boundaries of art and design, challenged dominant cultural narratives, and was a powerful tool for political activism and social justice. Nicole-Ann Lobo observes in

Wojnarowicz an acute level of awareness. Wojnarowicz knew the AIDS crisis was greater than him and his art, but he nonetheless felt compelled to use his art as a platform to communicate the reality of the AIDS experience. "It wasn't important that you liked his art, he insisted: merely that it did something to you, that it provoked" *(Lobo, 2018)*. FIGURE 5 manifests this idea.

Wojnarowicz used collage as a show of force, evoking in viewers the hatred and stigma that queer people experienced since the beginning of the AIDS crisis. The contrast in imagery halts viewers, urging them to read news clippings documenting hate crimes against gay men. In doing so, Wojnarowicz highlighted the absurdity of the stereotypes that fueled this hatred. However, Wojnarowicz's work remains largely excluded from the Western design history canon despite his contributions. David Wojnarowicz deserves to be recognized as an important contributor to the field of design history — he pushed the boundaries of art-making. He revealed dark truths about the state of society during the AIDS epidemic.

Wojnarowicz's artistic career was deeply shaped by personal tragedy and political struggle. In the early 1980s, he met Peter Hujar, a fellow artist and his romantic partner. In *The New Yorker*, provides important insight into Wojnarowicz and Hujar's relationship, "Twenty years Wojnarowicz's senior, Hujar had been a lover, a teacher, and a father figure. Hujar had first taken Wojnarowicz's art seriously" *(Donegan, 2018)*. Hujar supported Wojnarowicz's artistic journey. When Hujar died of AIDS-related complications in 1987, Wojnarowicz was devastated. He felt angry and helpless, trapped in a culture that both refused to acknowledge the crisis and marginalized people who were actually living with AIDS. Fueled by loss and injustice, Wojnarowicz channeled his grief and rage into explicit, confrontational, and deeply personal art.

Although he was confrontational through his art, he did it in a way that allowed multiple layers of meaning and interpretation. FIGURE 3 combines bold typography and other stunning imagery in classic "layers as meaning" Wojnarowicz style. The detailed graphics evoke the harsh judgment thrust upon the AIDS community, underscoring the lack of understanding and empathy they felt. He documented the realities of life with AIDS, challenged the complacency of those in power, and asserted the dignity and humanity of those who were suffering. His work was a powerful testament to the need for empathy, compassion, and activism in the face of adversity.

Wojnarowicz's response to Hujar's death was not unique. Artists and activists in the LGBTQ+ community depended on art and advocacy to cope with indescribable loss, expressing their anger and grief, and fighting for change. However, Wojnarowicz's work stood out for its rawness, honesty, and urgency. FIGURE 4 evokes Wojnarowicz's graphic and confrontational aesthetic ethos. Moreover, Andrew Edmonson's article acknowledges the significance of Wojnarowicz's choice of a vulgar title "in which he took a homophobic slur and transformed it into a sensual, homoerotic image of two men kissing" *(Edmonson, 2021)*. Wojnarowicz knew no other way; including the derogatory slur widely used to critique gay men and gay culture in the title shocked the viewer and brought attention. The image is striking and provocative, but it also reveals the anger and frustration that Wojnarowicz felt during the AIDS crisis. The piece is intentionally graphic and confrontational. The toy soldier, which is a symbol of childhood innocence and playfulness, is being used violently and sexually. The mouth is also a sexual symbol, but here it is transformed into a grotesque object, reflecting the negative stereotypes and stigmatization of gay men during the AIDS crisis.

Wojnarowicz was unafraid to show the graphic details of the disease and its impact on individuals and communities. He used various media, including painting, photography, and writing, to create a multifaceted portrait of the crisis. He refused to compromise his vision or tone down his message, even in the face of censorship and opposition from conservative politicians and religious groups. For Wojnarowicz, art was not just a means of self-expression or entertainment but a vital tool for social critique and transformation.

BIBLIOGRAPHY

1. KERR, EVAN. "A Gay Artist's Brilliant Fury." Outsmart Magazine, April 2021. https://www.outsmart-magazine.com/2021/04/a-gay-artists-brilliant-fury/.

2. KERR, EVAN. "Project Commemorates the 30th Anniversary of David Wojnarowicz's Death." Hyperallergic, July 2021. https://hyperallergic.com/750758/project-commemorates-the-30th-anniversary-of-davidwojnarowiczs-death/.

3. MORRISON, KERRY. "Review: Finding Hope in Anger in David Wojnarowicz." America Magazine, September 2018. https://www.americamagazine.org/arts-culture/2018/09/21/review-finding-hope-anger-david-wojnarowicz.

4. Philadelphia Museum of Art. "Untitled (Train)." Philadelphia Museum of Art. https://philamuseum.org/collection/object/310198

5. SANTE, LUC. "David Wojnarowicz's Still-Burning Rage." The New Yorker, May 2021. https://www.newyorker.com/culture/photo-booth/david-wojnarowiczs-still-burning-rage.

6. SCHNEIDER, THOMAS. "Standing Up for the Little Guy." Commonweal Magazine, September 2021. https://www.commonwealmagazine.org/standing-little-guy.

7. The Art Institute of Chicago. "Queer Basher/Icarus Falling." Art Institute of Chicago. https://www.artic.edu/artworks/184212/queer-basher-icarus-falling.

8. The Art Institute of Chicago. "Untitled (One Day This Kid…)." Art Institute of Chicago. https://www.artic.edu/artworks/159822/untitled-one-day-this-kid.

9. The Art Institute of Chicago. "When I Put My Hands on Your Body." Art Institute of Chicago. https://www.artic.edu/artworks/222004/when-i-put-my-hands-on-your-body.

10. Whitney Museum of American Art. "David Wojnarowicz: History Keeps Me Awake at Night." Whitney Museum of American Art. https://whitney.org/exhibitions/david-wojnarowicz?section=2&subsection=8#exhibiti on-artworks.

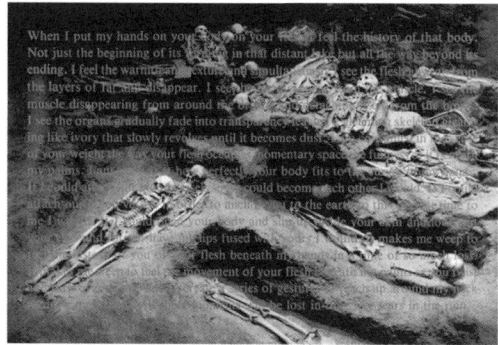

2.

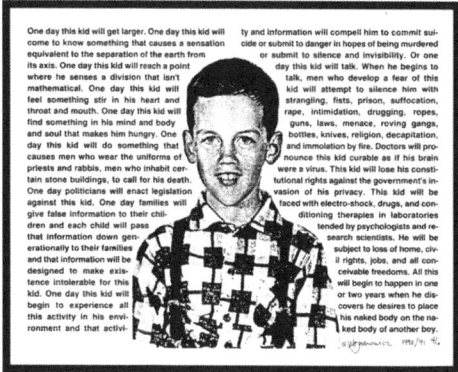

1.

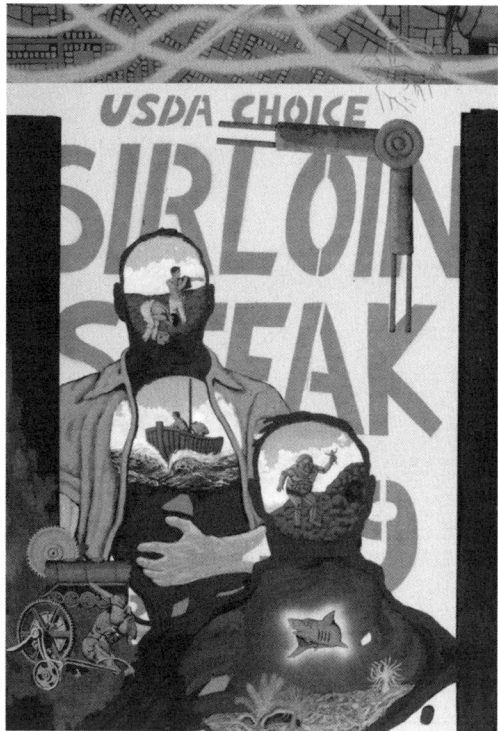

3.

FIGURES

1. David Wojnarowicz, *Untitled (One Day This Kid...)* 1990. Credit: The David Wojnarowicz Foundation.

2. David Wojnarowicz, *When I Put My Hands on Your Body*, 1990. Credit: The David Wojnarowicz Foundation.

3. David Wojnarowicz, *Queer Basher/Icarus Falling*, 1986. Credit: The David Wojnarowicz Foundation.

4.

5.

4. David Wojnarowicz, *Fuck You Faggot Fucker*, 1984.
Credit: The David Wojnarowicz Foundation.

5. David Wojnarowicz, *Untitled (Train)*, 1988-1989.
Credit: The David Wojnarowicz Foundation.

RUXIAN WANG

Chinese Fashion Traditions Projected Through a Western Lens

As the fashion industry continues to evolve, stereotypes within haute couture often go unnoticed. These biases extend beyond race, influencing how different clothing styles are viewed and embraced by Western culture. Chinese fashion occupies a complex space, where it is both appreciated and exploited. While it has become part of mainstream fashion discourse, it continues to face critique from the West.

Traditional Chinese clothing leans into a rich cultural history, but Westerners often misunderstand and unfairly characterize it. These stereotypes relegate Chinese styles as outdated and mundane, with the clichéd image of a big red flower adorning puffy sweaters. This limited and misguided representation does not accurately reflect Chinese styles' diverse and sophisticated range. These misconceptions stem from initial encounters with Chinese culture, leaving Western consumers with fixed impressions that fail to capture the whole essence of China's clothing traditions. As a result, many Western consumers reject Chinese traditions and their accompanying historical and cultural baggage despite the depth of those traditions as a source for avant-garde innovation.

It is essential to distinguish authentic Chinese fashion, which beautifully reflects the country's rich cultural heritage, from the appropriated versions co-opted by Western consumers who lack a full understanding of its significance. Appropriating Chinese clothing dilutes its cultural gravity and commodifies forms to such an extent that those very forms lack recognizability to their founding contexts.

By raising awareness about these stereotypes and encouraging respect and admiration toward authentic cultural symbols, we can move towards a more inclusive and judicious fashion landscape. Universally embracing the vast expressions of authentic beauty in clothing fosters a meaningful and enriching fashion experience on a global scale. "Made in China" labels are a hallmark of modern manufacturing. What do those three words even mean? According to fashion designer Huishan Zhang, "I feel that the product is more important than the concept — it's not something you stand for but something you can show, and people can experience, touch and feel, and then appreciate. So for me, I don't come to that big ambition of wanting to change people's perspective. I just really want to make clothes and something beautifully made in my hometown for people to actually appreciate" *(Asri, 2022)*. The phrase "Made in China" carries more significance for Chinese makers; it symbolizes pride and artistry.

Huishan Zhang and other Chinese designers rely on Chinese traditions to create their modern fashion lines, all while ensuring the visibility of the Chinese influence. Fashion designer Grace Chen combines hundreds of thousands of "Chinese Knots" woven with embroidered flowers popular in ancient China into modern silhouettes (FIGURE 1). The subtleness of these traditions is completely lost when Western portrayals of Chinese motifs reduce the historical symbols to mere cliches (FIGURE 2). The misappropriation of these ancient symbols, like the dragon, only perpetuates naive stereotypes.

Ma Ke similarly uses traditional manufacturing techniques in her designs, noting that "All stages of production are done in-house, including the spinning, weaving, dyeing, and sewing; even using traditional equipment such as a Chinese loom dating from the 19th century" (Zhang, 2016). Ma's aesthetic vision is rooted in tradition, sustainability, and simplicity. According to Eco Fashion Talk, "Ma Ke is an advocate for luxury as simplicity and austerity, and her work is full of powerful, sculpted forms, referencing China's rich history" (Zhang, 2016). Ma Ke situated herself among the Western elite in a fashion scene dominated by foreign labels through her minimalist "Made in China" contours.

There are distinctiveness differences between Chinese clothing and Western clothing. According to Jiwen Zhang's article "An Exploration of the Differences between Chinese and Western Costumes in the Archaeological Archaeology of Clothing Culture in Different Periods of Agriculture," "Chinese [aesthetics] emphasize beauty and elegance, and the complexity of life [...] Settling down, returning to the heart, experiencing all things, connecting with heaven and earth, integrating self and all things as one, and obtaining the soul." The result is a more complex and harder-to-decode aesthetic intended for Chinese audiences. Westerners, on the other hand, "advocate freedom and dreams [where] clothing reflects an exaggerated, distinctive characteristic, often through the mix of hip hop, rock and roll, and even a peculiar Gothic style [...] however, daily clothing choices reflect a lust towards comfort" (Zhang, 2022). Western clothes are universally admired and understood and align to mainstream tastes more easily.

While Western styles appeal to broader audiences, they continue to fetishize Chinese traditions to naive consumers who need to be made aware of the provenance of their fashion choices. The most notable recent example of Western designers appropriating Chinese looks without proper acknowledgment is when Christian Dior released a pleated skirt in 2019. Chinese social media users were outraged to see Dior portray the skirt in a new light without any credit given to the ancient tradition. Dior's skirt is an exact replica of the Chinese horse-faced skirt (FIGURE 4). While Dior refused to acknowledge the similarities to the Chinese horse-face skirt — claiming that the skirt was theirs — the company eventually removed it from their catalog (Cheung, 2022). Dior continued to borrow from Chinese traditions despite the uproar over the skit. Their 2022 autumn and winter ready-to-wear series, "Dior Jardin d'Hiver," includes several pieces that showcase traditional Chinese painting elements, including the 花鸟图 bird-and-flower paintings created by Ming dynasty artist Lu Zhi in 1575 (FIGURE 5).

Defining traditional Chinese fashion can only be done internally. Chinese designers like Ma Ke, Grace Chen, and Huishan Zhang intrinsically know traditional Chinese values, culture, and aesthetics, which allows their application of historical styles to feel authentic. Western consumers could focus on understanding this authenticity, rather than viewing Chinese aesthetics as a stylistic maneuver that can be borrowed and relocated. Doing so cheapens the aesthetic value and masks authentic Chinese traditions. To fully understand these Chinese aesthetics requires an engagement in Chinese history and culture.

BIBLIOGRAPHY

1. AHUJA, SHILPA. "Inspiration China- Moving beyond Dynasties & Dragons." University of Fashion Blog , 1 Nov. 2019, https://www.universityoffashion.com/blog/inspiration-china-moving-beyond-dynasties-dragons/.

2. ASRI, JASMAN. "Fashion Designer Huishan Zhang on Staying True to His Roots." Buro , 10 Jan. 2022, https://www.buro247.sg/huishan-zhang-interview-fashion-designer-shangri-la-from-asia-with-he art/.

3. CHEN, GRACE. "Craftsmanship | Grace Chen," n.d. https://www.gracechen.cn/craftsmanship.

4. CHEN, PEILIN. "When Cultural Appreciation Becomes Appropriation: Lei Ping on Chinese Imagery in Western Fashion." US , 19 Dec. 2019, https://uschinatoday.org/qa/2019/12/19/when-cultural-appreciation-becomes-appropriation-lei-pi ng-on-chinese-imagery-in-western-fashion/.

5. CHEUNG, RACHEL. "$3,800 Dior Skirt Accused of Appropriating Chinese Culture." VICE , 18 July 2022, https://www.vice.com/en/article/wxndqn/dior-skirt-china-cultural-appropriation.

6. "Yoho!" Yoho!Now , 27 Aug. 2019, http://www.yohoboys.com/news/index-84681-0-0.html.

7. "Ma Ke, One of China's Most Successful Designers." Ma Ke, One of China's Most Successful Designers | , 12 Apr. 2015, https://agnautacouture.com/2015/04/12/ma-ke-one-of-chinas-most-successful-designers/.

8. "Ma Ke" Eco Fashion Talk , 23 Dec. 2012, https://www.ecofashiontalk.com/2012/12/ma-ke/ . "Ma Ke: Designer of Peng Liyuan Style." Soochow Univeristy , http://eng.suda.edu.cn/eng/News/People/201712/b19f7439-18d5-4472-8e99-8948498ad3f3.html.

9. "Trench Coat Beige Cotton Gabardine with Dior Jardin D'Hiver Motif." DIOR , https://www.dior.com/en_us/fashion/products/257M56A3961_X1810-trench-coat-beige-cotton-g abardine-with-dior-jardin-d-hiv er-motif?objectID=257M56A3961_X1810&query=Dior%20Jardi n%20 d%27HiverDior%20Jardin%20 d%27Hiver%20jacket&query-ID=995016b1f9aa4f9a666a2b dba87f58a0.

9. ZHANG, JIWEN. "An Exploration of the Differences between Chinese and Western Costumes in the Archaeological Archaeology of Clothing Culture in Different Periods of Agriculture." Journal of Environmental and Public Health , U.S. National Library of Medicine, 15 June 2022, https://www.ncbi.nlm.nih.gov/pmc/articles/PMC9217584/.

9. ZHANG, MENGYI. "Designer Ma Ke: Exception to the Rule." Designer Ma Ke: Exception to the Rule - Lifestyle - Chinadaily.com.cn , https://www.chinadaily.com.cn/fashion/2016-11/10/content_27335779.html.

1.

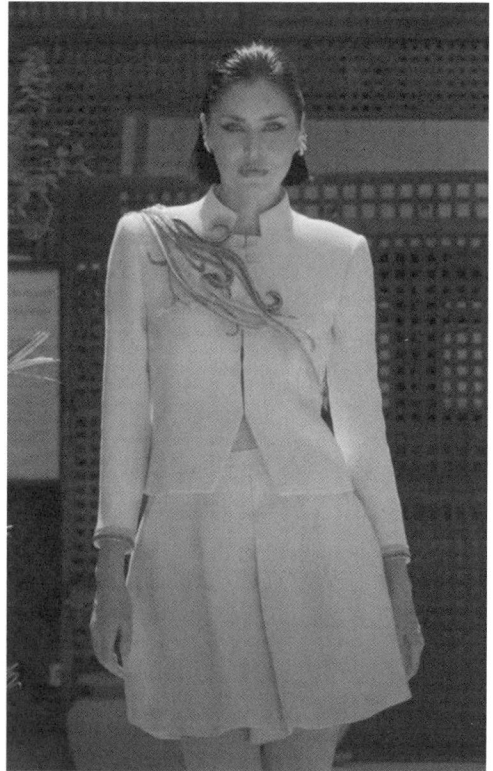

2.

FIGURES

1. Grace Chen, *Spring/Summer Collection*, knotted detail, 2024. Source: YouTube video screenshot, "GRACE CHEN 2024 Spring/Summer collection "Soul for Eternity - Egypt," fair use for educational use.

2. Grace Chen, *Spring/Summer Collection*, embroidered detail, 2024. Source: YouTube video screenshot, "GRACE CHEN 2024 Spring/Summer collection "Soul for Eternity - Egypt," fair use for educational use.

3.

4.

5.

6.

3. Versace, *Met Gala dress for Jennifer Lopez*, 2015. Source: YouTube video screenshot, Clevver News, "Jennifer Lopez vs Kim Kardashian SHEER Dresses at Met Gala 2015," fair use for educational use.

4. Dior, *Pleated wool skirt*, 2022. Source: YouTube video screenshot, AvenueX, "Dior and Its Cultural Appropriation of Chinese Ma Mian Skirt," fair use for educational use.

5. Chinese, *Man and Woman in Horse Face Skirt*, Boxer Codex, 1590. Source: Tieba.badu.com, PD Chinese copyright expired.

6. Ma Ke, fashion designer; Zhou Mi, photographer, *The Earth*, 2007. Credit: Ma Ke Wuyong.

7.

7. Lu Zhi, *Peach Blossom bamboo & Golden Pheasant Scroll Painting*, Ming Dynasty, 1575. PD US/EU copyright expired.

人間の星社

蔵　票

SHERYL PENG

The Impact of Colonization on Taiwanese Graphic Design

Taiwanese graphic design has yet to receive the attention it deserves on the global stage. Professor Wendy S. Wong of York University, an expert in Chinese graphic design history, noted in her article "Design History and Study in East Asia: Part 2 Greater China" that "writings on the design history and design studies of the Greater China region (The People's Republic of China, Taiwan, and Hong Kong) have not emerged yet" (Wong, 2011). While multiple factors contribute to this oversight, Taiwan's absence from the graphic design narrative and its delayed entry into the field can primarily be traced to its lack of political autonomy. Taiwan's ongoing political struggles have impeded its development in this domain. Although colonization expedited the rise of the graphic design industry, it also left a complex legacy — simultaneously limiting and shaping Taiwan's design language and industry.

Specifically, Japanese and Chinese influences have become integral pillars of Taiwanese design. The bustling graphic design world in current-day Taiwan would not exist without these influences. This essay analyzes how Chinese occupation stunted design and how the Japanese occupation of Taiwan shaped the development of design and its visual language as a field in Taiwan.

For most of modern history, the development of Taiwan has been controlled by whichever power staked a claim over the island. From 1683 to 1895, Taiwan was under Chinese rule and followed China's timeline *(Myers, 1996)*. The Western concept of contemporary design was introduced to China during the First Opium War in 1839 but didn't gain traction. Unlike the West, China did not consider design or design history "a legitimate discipline or a discipline in which one could make a living" *(Wong, 2011)*. Not only was the discipline of design not taken seriously, it didn't even exist linguistically. For centuries, the vocabulary to describe art had only consisted of "gongyi," which meant craftsmanship and skill. This term was used to describe items made "to satisfy the needs of everyday life." New terms began to emerge as the East met the West, like "zhuangshi yishu" (decorative arts), "meishu" (art), "tuan" (drawing), and finally, "sheji" (design) *(Wong, 2011)*. Taiwan and China both use Mandarin, so this development of language on the mainland also made its way to Taiwan. Interestingly enough, "tuan" (drawing) and "sheji" (design) originated from Japan's writing system, Kanji, which has many similarities with written Chinese (*Wong, 2011*). This is the tip of the iceberg regarding Japan's influence on Taiwanese design.

After ending 265 years of isolation, Japan was in a hurry to modernize, industrialize, and catch up with the world's international powers. This manifested an aggressive desire to understand Western civilization and disseminate these Western trends into Japanese society (*Kublin, 1959*). They also sought overseas expansion and acquired Taiwan from Qing dynasty China in 1895 through the *Treaty of Shimonoseki* (*Yao, Sun, and Lin, 2013*). Upon the island's annexation, Japan began using its newfound knowledge of the West to change Taiwan's cultural and artistic landscape. Wong noted that "Japanese occupiers were eager to colonize the island with assimilation strategies and quickly installed the infrastructure for modernization in all areas of life, including the growth of art and design education and activities" (*Wong, 2011*). Japanese colonialism in Taiwan was unique in that Japan considered Taiwan "an extension" of themselves because they "shared a common script and race" (*Hui, 2006*). Unlike most cases of occupation where the natives are discriminated against for differences in "race, color, religion, and so on, Japanese colonizers in Taiwan often invoked their common cultural roots, highlighting the fact that the Japanese and Taiwanese shared the same language and ethnicity" (*Hui, 2006*). This relationship meant that Japan poured a lot of time and effort into the development of Taiwan, and to them, the colony served as a place to experiment with art and design. Ultimately, Japan's efforts during this period finally introduced modern design to Taiwan.

Japan did two major things that brought modern design to Taiwan. They industrialized Taiwan quickly, creating a demand for commercial art design, and they implemented colonial education, which introduced Western culture to the Taiwanese. The rapid industrialization Japan forced Taiwan to undergo resulted in the birth of commercial markets on the island. As a result, mass-produced content, advertising, and product packaging (all of which require design) were suddenly needed. An unprecedented number of design jobs were created to satisfy the uptick in advertising (*Yao, Sun, and Lin, 2013*). On the other hand, colonial education under Japan established Taiwan's first art curriculum, where students learned illustration and drawing, foundational skills for graphic design. Taiwanese students could receive an art education and continue to learn through extracurricular art activities, which were growing increasingly popular. Many instructors were Japanese artists trained in the West and brought modern art movements like post-impressionism, cubism, fauvism, etc., back to Japan and Taiwan (FIGURE 1). For example, Ishikawa Kinichiro studied in England and then returned to Taiwan later in life to teach and bring fauvism to Taipei Normal College and Taipei Provincial First High School (*Yao, Sun, and Lin, 2013*). Tateishi Tetsuomi was another teacher during this period who is now memorialized for his book cover designs. He designed over 160 covers during his career and "is considered by many the greatest book cover design artist of the Japanese colonial period" (*Yao, Sun, and Lin, 2013*). Fascinated by Taiwanese folk culture, he created bookplate engravings that marry his overseas training with the existing, native visual language. His standout piece is the cover he designed for the poetry collection *Ode to Taiwan*, which combines geometric landscape imagery with delicate, elegant typography (FIGURE 2). Tetsuomi's work is representative of the first stage of Taiwanese graphic design.

Most other Japanese designers went abroad to study with the Bauhaus and returned to Japan and Taiwan to popularize these design ideologies. The influence of the Bauhaus was so pervasive that despite Taiwan having no official curriculum teaching it, Bauhaus's ideas still "clearly influenced the expression and development of Taiwanese design as it combined with the dissemination of Japanese culture [...] in Taiwan" (*Yao, Sun, and Lin, 2013*). The principles of composition and simplicity can be seen as early as in textbooks used in public school illustration classes in the early 1920s. Moreover, colonial Japan emphasized the idea of "pragmatic academics," which placed a focus on craft and handiwork, another "practice [...] of Bauhaus design education" (*Yao, Sun, and Lin, 2013*). The dissemination of Western design trends usually presented itself as imitation. The Taiwanese publication *Modern Style* was a prime example of this. Their content was about Western learning and ideologies, and their cover art showed incredible likeness to the Western trends of the time. 1920s Bauhaus aesthetics "were influenced by the Collage Art of the Cubists, and this influence made its way to Taiwan" (*Yao, Sun, and Lin, 2013*). Therefore, the covers of *Modern Style* had obvious nods to cubism, reducing forms to their basic shapes and dividing their compositions in a very "rational manner" (FIGURES 4, 5).

Through these imported designers, teachers, and ideas, Taiwan got its first taste of graphic design. The work from the colonial Japan period is the foundation of modern Taiwanese design as we know it today. This essay has traced the journey of Western graphic design concepts from their place of origin to Taiwan, specifically through the lens of the Japanese intermediaries. Professor Kikuchi Yuko, expert in craft history, calls this "refracted easternism" (*Wong, 2013*). The fact that the Japanese first touched Western trends and ideas taught to the Taiwanese differentiates Taiwanese graphic design. Wong explains this perfectly, "The foreign culture that Japan brought to Taiwan possessed a Western visual form, but in the process of dissemination and in response to environmental changes, different vocabularies and materials were added [...] to the most basic form of modern design" (*Wong 2013*). Taiwanese graphic design is a unique blend of native, Western, and Japanese ideas that exists nowhere else in the world — this is why it is important to amplify Taiwanese design. Its visual language represents the adaptability of the Taiwanese people and their ability to thrive under occupation. Taiwan's design culture and industry will always be a reminder of its history, the good and the bad.

BIBLIOGRAPHY

1. KUBLIN, HYMAN. "The Evolution of Japanese Colonialism." Comparative Studies in Society and History 2, no. 1 (1959): 67–84. http://www.jstor.org/stable/177547.

2. MYERS, RAMON H. "A New Chinese Civilization: The Evolution of the Republic of China on Taiwan." The China Quarterly, no. 148 (1996): 1072–90. http://www.jstor.org/stable/655517.

3. PING-HUI, LIAO. "Taiwan Under Japanese Colonial Rule, 1895–1945: History, Culture, Memory." In Taiwan Under Japanese Colonial Rule, 1895-1945: History, Culture, Memory, edited by LIAO PING-HUI and DAVID DER-WEI WANG, 1–16. Columbia University Press, 2006. http://www.jstor.org/stable/10.7312/liao13798.6.

4. WONG, WENDY S. "Design History and Study in East Asia: Part 2 Greater China: People's Republic of China/Hong Kong/Taiwan." Journal of Design History 24, no. 4 (2011): 375–95. http://www.jstor.org/stable/41419644.

5. YAO, TSUN-HSIUNG, CHU-YU SUN, AND PIN-CHANG LIN. "Modern Design in Taiwan: The Japanese Period, 1895-1945." Design Issues 29, no. 3 (2013): 38–51. http://www.jstor.org/stable/24267088.

1.

2.

3.

FIGURES

1. Ishikawa Kinichir, *Imperial Life Insurance Building in Taihoku*, 1910-1930. PD Taiwan copyright expired.

2. Tateishi Tetsuomi (illustrator), Mitsuru Nishikawa, *Ode to Taiwan*, 1940. Credit: National Museum of Taiwan LIterature. PD Taiwan copyright expired.

3. Tateishi Tetsuomi, *"Fuhu" Engraved Bookplate*, 1935. Credit: National Museum of Taiwan LIterature. PD Taiwan copyright expired.

4.

5.

4. *Modern Style*, 1928. Credit: Creative Commons, MIT Press. *Design Issues*, 29, no.3.

5. *Modern Style*, 1929. Credit: Creative Commons, MIT Press. *Design Issues*, 29, no.3.

DEMOCRACY ON DEMAND

To say technology revolutionizes the way ideas flow is a cliche. But "printing on demand"—an increasingly affordable low-run option—unleashed a massive opportunity for mass communication and distribution. Printing on demand emerged with a fleeting casualness but simultaneously imprinted itself on a collective consciousness, capturing the zeitgeist and positioning inconspicuous attitudes into the forefront of public awareness.

The zines, flyers, and prints included here demonstrate how technology gave rise to an idea—whether acting as a mouthpiece for a marginalized community, providing a platform for dialogue, or even publicizing underground events. The work here isn't just about expression; it is about the power of immediacy and how that immediacy nurtured community, connection, and a spirit of activism.

twenty five cents   MARCH, 1972

GiDRA

MONTHLY OF THE ASIAN AMERICAN EXPERIENCE

Gidra, Inc.
P.O. Box 18046
Los Angeles, Calif. 90018

Gidra:
The Rise of Asian American Student Activism

The year was 1969, Richard Nixon was president, the first man landed on the moon, Woodstock happened, and the Beatles released their first album. It was the last year of the turbulent sixties, filled with political and social upheaval. An era defined by counterculture, civil rights movements, and the ongoing Vietnam War. Coasting underneath all these historical events, five students of the University of California in Los Angeles — Mike Murase, Dinora Gil, Laura Ho, Colin Watanabe, and Tracy Okida — founded and published a revolutionary zine titled Gidra: The Monthly of the Asian American Experience (Kawashima 2012).

Like the self-titled Japanese monster, *Gidra* grew and expanded into a revolutionary zine representing an entire generation of young Asian Americans. It set a precedent for student-made activist editorials that should be more appreciated. *Gidra's* creators were not just students, journalists, artists, or even writers but young activists. The silencing of minorities, students, and the younger generation has historically excluded these crucial voices. *Gidra* helped build upon a culturally rich Asian American community and became an emotional expression and voice for young activists.

The zine became a spearhead for the underrepresented Asian American Movement and communicated political perspectives such as ending the war in Southeast Asia and women's rights. This paper will further emphasize that *Gidra: The Monthly of the Asian American Experience* needs to be seen, heard, and included in the Western design history canon by examining the countless poems, political cartoons, editorials, and illustrations created for *Gidra*.

The UCLA Asian American students were frustrated with the lack of historical representation of their culture in their education. In retaliation for the anti-Asian sentiment on campus and in Los Angeles, they sought recognition from the administration to start an Asian American community newspaper. The university denied their request, so each of the five students provided a hundred dollars of their own money to produce their paper independently. These activists demanded to be seen and heard, insisting that institutions reconcile gaps between universities and their local communities *(Rowan, 2017)*. As *Gidra* became more resonant for local Asian Americans, the art form and content evolved. According to co-founder Mike Murase, "Gidra gradually changed its focus from the campus to the community, from Asian identity to Asian unity, and from 'what happened' to 'what can we do'" *(Ishizuka, 2015)*. Works like *Gidra* deserve to be represented in today's culture because they draw attention to the minorities once silenced. The designs were works of a generation historically overlooked because they were students and young. The fresh voices with the courage to speak out demonstrate that *Gidra* deserves attention.

Through illustration, political cartoons, and information, *Gidra's* designers helped grow, cultivate, and unite the already culturally rich Asian American community that surrounded them. Specifically, the zine employed various aesthetic strategies pertaining to controversies around corporate development and community immobilization. The redevelopment of Little Tokyo concerned the local community because it was once a source of commerce for Japanese Americans. *Gidra* spotlighted the disparity in urban development and the lack of affordable housing in Asian American communities *(Honma, 2016)*. *Gidra's* cover illustration by David Monkawa depicts a futuristic dystopian Little Tokyo, populated by big corporate businesses, technology, and an overcrowded atmosphere. The caption "Little Tokyo 1984?" refers to the novel by George Orwell (FIGURE 1). The magazine brought together Asian student communities who shared feelings of discrimination and marginalization in their own local cultures. The zine utilized the rhetorical power of political cartoons. In one issue of *Gidra*, the zine depicted the different patronizing and racially targeted notions often associated with Asian Americans. The caption "Discovering the American Dream (or being Asian in America) means" uses a satirical tone combined with a more realistic visual drawing (FIGURE 2). In the political cartoon, irony is a source of knowledge and a way of understanding *(Ishizuka, 2015)*. When *Gidra's* designers dealt with serious issues such as stereotyping, they captured images with humor relatable to the Asian American community.

The Asian American Movement (AAM) was one of the many social movements during the "cultural revolution of the long sixties." *Gidra* communicated while vetting similar ideals and goals to this new Asian American consciousness *(Ishizuka, 2015)*. Soon, the zine became the leading voice for the movement. Evelyn Yoshimura, a member of the zine since 1971, stated that the most effective way to convey an idea is not necessarily a long article delivering a message in a palpable manner but in a way that people relate to it *(Japanese American National Museum, 2011)*. As a result, *Gidra* embedded numerous graphics and illustrations rather than just texts. Faces were a repeated element that graced the covers of *Gidra* because of the eye-catching and emotional depiction, eliciting an equally stirring response. Since the *Gidra* team was diverse and had numerous activists, each spread was uniquely stylized and fit the artist's voice. Some artworks reflected similar Asian artistic styles and characteristics. In one cover that depicted a woman's face, the artist used harsh black lines, stripes, and negative space contrasted with one bright, solid color (FIGURE 3). *Gidra's* use of similar cultural styles and techniques of the past visually aligned readers.

Gidra continually engaged with radical political perspectives to explore historical and current events such as the Vietnam War and women's rights. The artistic presentations were bold, prominent, and striking. The cover designs enveloped the reader, using symbolically daring colors such as red with harrowing icons. An example of *Gidra's* creative use of information and emotion was in the commemoration of Hiroshima/Nagasaki, published on a front cover *(Ishizuka, 2015)*. The back cover was stylistically similar, with a grainy image of a woman's face in bright red, but from the

Vietnam War (FIGURE 4). The point was to connect the emotional and political similarities between past and present realities. *Gidra* defined the voice of Asian American youths who needed an outlet to express their own vitriol against racism and historically charged events.

In conclusion, the zine *Gidra: The Monthly of the Asian American Experience*, led by young activists, was a revolutionary exploration of the Asian American voice during civil distress and uncertainty. It became an emotional expression for a generation combating harmful stereotypes while connecting with a vibrant but racially targeted community. The zine guided the sixties through the Asian American Movement and the Vietnam War with powerful conviction. The voices and written word echoed in the bold design choices as *Gidra* strived for uncensored truth (FIGURE 6). Although *Gidra* published its last issue in 1974, it continued to have a far-reaching impact and legacy. In 2019, a new group of Asian Americans announced the return of *Gidra* (*Tagami, 2021*). An exemplary collision of the past with the present with the intention of reinvention and renewal. The design characteristics feel organic and authentic in the covers, poems, layout, and editorials because they reflect the young activist voice. As a result, *Gidra's* presence in the past, present, and future reminds us to examine the things around us and think beyond gender and skin color (*Huang, 2020*). Perhaps *Gidra's* visual legacy lies in the fearlessness of actively participating with society and the world. The daring concepts, coupled with the bold designs, inform the importance of activism. Like the young designers who started the zine more than fifty years ago, designers and society should not merely abide by the world as it is but actively engage with the vision for change.

BIBLIOGRAPHY

1. GLICK, JOSHUA. "The Rise of Minority Storytelling: Network News, Public Television, and Independent Collectives." In Los Angeles Documentary and the Production of Public History, 1958-1977, 1st ed., 69–106. University of California Press, 2018. http://www.jstor.org/stable/10.1525/j.ctt1x3s3sd.8.

2. HONMA, TODD. "From Archives to Action: Zines, Participatory Culture, and Community Engagement in Asian America." The Radical Teacher, no. 105 (2016): 33–43. https://www.jstor.org/stable/48694788.

3. HUANG, YANCHI. "A Many-Headed ." Futuress. Futuress, December 9, 2020. https://futuress.org/stories/a-many-headed-monster/.

4. ISHIZUKA, KAREN LEE. "'Gidra', the Dissident Press and the Asian American Movement: 1969 - 1974." Order No. 3715745, University of California, Los Angeles, 2015. https://ezproxy.bu.edu/.

5. Japanese American National Museum. "Drawing the Line—GIDRA". YouTube. YouTube, 2011. https://www.youtube.com/watch?v=OYwPTNtuhhc.

6. KAWASHIMA, YOSHIMI. "Gidra: The Voice of the Asian American Movement." Discover Nikkei, January 12, 2012. https://discovernikkei.org/en/journal/2012/1/12/gidra/

7. LOPEZ, LORI KIDO. "The Yellow Press: Asian American Radicalism and Conflict in 'Gidra.'." The Journal of Communication Inquiry 35, no. 1 (2011): 235.

1.

2.

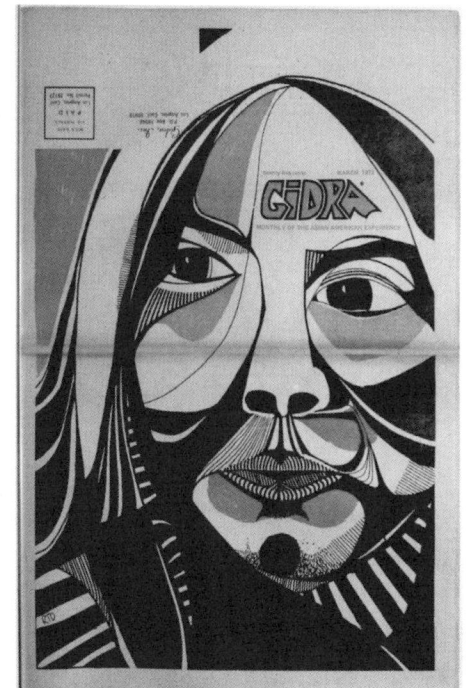

3.

FIGURES

1. David Monkawa, *Gidra, Vol. V, No. 8*, 1973. Credit: GIDRA.

2. Alan Ota, Alan Takemoto, and Evelyn Yoshimura, *Gidra, Vol. V, No. 4*, 1973. Credit: GIDRA.

3. Richard Tokunaga, *Gidra, Vol. IV, No. 3*, 1972. Credit: GIDRA.

4.

5.

4. Mike Murase, Gidra, *Vol. IV, No. 8*, 1972. Credit: GIDRA.

5. Mike Murase, Gidra, *Vol. I, No. 1*, 1969. Credit: GIDRA.

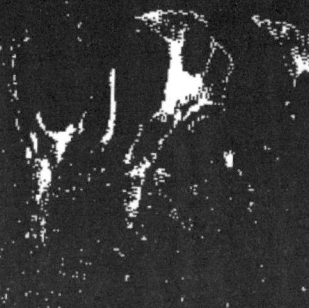

feminine

marvelous

and

tough

feminine, marvelous, and tough:
An Ode to the Mimeograph

Poetry elicits a sense of immediacy. Poets of the New York School used the mimeograph to self-publish quickly, economically, and abundantly. Formal considerations for these black-and-white saddle stitch booklets were necessarily inherited from their function. Maintaining a constant exchange of ideas with poets elsewhere was the foremost consideration, so crude reproductions or misprints could be overlooked in favor of expediency.

Of the mimeograph, Ron Loewinson remarked in 1970: "Having them, we could see what we were doing, as it came, hot off the griddle [...] & we could respond instantly to what the guy across town or across the country had written last week" (Mayer, 2009). Poets of this mindset were concerned with positioning their work in proximity to an ongoing dialogue. Mimeo culture was a precursor to the explosion of fanzines in DIY punk scenes across New York, Los Angeles, and the United Kingdom in the 1980s. The New York School's embrace of the indie press rewrites commercialized 1960s and 1970s design narratives.

Members of the first and second generations of the New York School readily embarked on collaborations exploring an interplay between poetry and visual art. Between 1957 and 1959, Frank O'Hara and pop artist Larry Rivers produced a series of twelve lithographic prints entitled *Stones* (FIGURE 4). The purity of the collaboration — in which both men worked side-by-side, using the same writing utensil and responding to the same prompt — allowed O'Hara's words and Rivers' drawings to coexist in harmony (FIGURE 2). O'Hara and Rivers, who were lovers, offer a collaborative model imbued with intimacy which the next generation of New York School poets chose to follow in both platonic and romantic working relationships.

Joe Brainard lies at the heart of second-generation New York School collaborations. In an introduction to the 2000 edition of Ted Berrigan's *The Sonnets*, poet Alice Notley recalls: "'Joe's lettering is getting really good,' Andy Warhol once said admiringly to Ted, lettering being a prized skill in the Pop Art sixties" (Jennings, 2016). Brainard's line work had the precision one would expect of a cartoonist or commercial artist (FIGURE 8, 11–12). His kitschy, sometimes crass hand renderings formed a distinctive visual language for the New York School (FIGURE 7). When poets collaborated with artists within their inner circle — such as the cover designs and illustrations Brainard created — the creative direction was no longer sequestered to an extrinsic realm. Brainard's editorial style contrasts with the cold detachment of commercialized attempts (FIGURE 12). An underlying author-illustrator relationship enriches the publications, particularly looking towards work he created with the "soi-disant Tulsa School" — coined by Ashbery about Brainard, Berrigan, Ron Padgett, and Dick Gallup, who initially met in Tulsa, Oklahoma in 1960 and subsequently moved to New York together — and Kenward Elmslie, who was Brainard's life partner. A letter from Berrigan to Brainard about their publication *C Comics*, dated October 1969, makes explicit the symbiotic relationship between their mutual group of friends and forthcoming work (FIGURE 10):

> We can get together and I can see what you are doing, and have done, with others, and show you my new poems, and maybe we can figure something out. Maybe something 'about' all our friends, maybe something about Frank [O'Hara]. Or Edwin [Denby]. Something about Anne Waldman. (Jennings, 2016).

The mimeograph dismantled traditional publishing house models and enabled a greater capacity for authorial control with the poet as publisher.

The contemporary focus tends to land on a male-dominant New York School. Still, Alice Notley, Bernadette Mayer, and Anne Waldman contributed significantly to its tradition as poets and publishers (FIGURE 9). Notley's foray into literary magazines began with *CHICAGO*, a legal-sized mimeo that ran for nine issues with cover illustrations by George Schneeman. Notley's radical editorial vision for *CHICAGO* encouraged poets to contribute collections of poems rather than standalone and considered how pieces interacted with the large trim size. *0 to 9*, published by Bernadette Mayer and Vito Acconci, was a highly experimental publication that unravels language and form. Though it ran for only six issues, Mayer and Acconci enabled obscure writings to be recontextualized for new audiences. Waldman's press Angel Hair included a six-issue serialized run and a catalog of 72 titles from poets of the New York School. The mimeograph elicited a range of strong reactions in its time as an active form from those in the surrounding literary community. Ed Sanders, the editor of *Fuck You: A Magazine of the Arts* who vowed "I'll print anything," generated perhaps the most explosive reception and subsequent consequences. He founded *Fuck You* shortly after being released from jail for protesting nuclear submarine launches in 1960, and an antiauthoritarian vein runs from its title throughout each publication. The press's place of publication is listed as "a secret location on the Lower East Side," referring to Peace Eye Book Store, which gathered books and people in equal measure (FIGURE 1). Police raided Peace Eye in January of 1966, and Sanders was slapped with obscenity charges. The charges were later unanimously dismissed, with the help of the ACLU, which came to his defense.

Sanders continued to enrage when he acquired an unpublished manuscript of Ezra Pound's *Drafts & Fragments of Cantos CX-CXVI* and quickly sent it off to press. Pound sent the manuscript to an editor of *The Paris Review*, who then gave a copy to Tom Clark as he was working on an honors thesis on The Cantos. Clark, a friend of Sanders', offered up the poems when asked for anything he could "instantly freak into print" *(Worden, 2016)*. Featuring a cover design by Joe Brainard depicting a disembodied male torso, mimeograph copies of *Drafts & Fragments* were circulating within a matter of days (FIGURE 5). James Laughlin, poet and founder of New Directions

Publishing, slammed the unauthorized publication in a letter to Pound, "This all comes out of the dope culture of the Lower East Side. They are all high on one drug or another and don't care what they do" *(Worden, 2016)*. New Directions had been after Pound to publish another volume of his cantos for years, so his anger was partly directed towards Sanders getting to it first by a stroke of luck. However, Laughlin also objects to Brainard's "hideous, semi-obscene cover," which marks a total disconnect between his generation of poets and the mimeograph revolution. A more nuanced debate on the mimeograph as a form occurred in the pages of the *Poetry Project News-letter*, which was itself a mimeographed publication. In the March 1982 edition, Eileen Myles, a poet closely associated with the New York School, published the article "Opus Mimeo," reviewing two mimeograph titles by Lenny Goldstein and Cliff Fyman. Myles opens with the declaration, "I've never liked Mimeo" *(Katz, 2017)*. He remarks how she has two Mimeo books in print and poems published in Mimeo journals but can only appreciate its function over form. She writes, "I like to see them breathe beyond my typewriter, though I'm much happier when their type-set" *(Mayer, 2009)*. Bernadette Mayer responded directly in a subsequent newsletter, condemning Myles' celebration of glossy covers over the modest mimeo wrappers. Whereas Myles viewed the mimeographs as obstructing fame and success as a poet, Mayer refutes any such notion of commercializing her work. She writes, "The cheaper and slightly more instantaneous reproduction of poetry for those who can use it is not a bourgeoisie value; the craving for a book with a binding is" *(Mayer, 2009)*. She relates her argument back to the form of the newsletter — staple-bound, monospaced, and quickly able to spread information to a wide audience. Mayer sees her role as a poet "at an angle slightly askew to any desire for fame," which contradicts the impetus of books with a high production value *(Mayer, 2009)*. Observing opposing sides of the argument from two poets of the same school is significant.

In his elegy For Ted, Sanders recalls his first encounter with Berrigan while using the same mimeo machine at Phoenix Bookshop in 1963, Berrigan for *C: A Journal of Poetry* and Sanders for *Fuck You*. Sanders writes, "It was obvious / we were slaves / to the lyre and the bee", underscoring how their roles as publishers stemmed from a mutual devotion to poetry and its surrounding community. He goes on to say, "We pranced around / our mimeo machines / like Bassarids / the benzene dripping / from our fingers" *(Berrigan, 1969)*. His lyrical expansion on the process of mimeo-making constructs it as a ritualistic activity that venerates its source material. Since the mimeograph implies a process of rewriting through transcription of the original manuscript, the printer engaging in this analog activity penetrates the poet's psyche. In his note "On The Sonnets," published in the 1991 Coffee House Press anthology *Nice To See You: Homage to Ted Berrigan*, Ron Padgett speaks of his experience editing the first edition of *The Sonnets* for Berrigan in 1964 (FIGURE 13). He writes, "I remember typing the mimeograph stencils and marveling at the poems and marveling at how I was seeing them in a way you can't see them unless you actually sit down and type them, almost as though you were writing them yourself" *(Padgett, 2012)*. The slow art of the mimeograph pays each word its due respect.

BIBLIOGRAPHY

1. BERKSON, BILL. Bomb 15. Sept. 2016, https://bombmagazine.org/articles/spoleto-65/.

2. BERRIGAN, TED. "Letter to James Schuyler." 19 Oct. 1969, Folder 2, Box 47, Ted Berrigan Papers, Mandeville Special Collections Library, UCSD.

3. HELWIG, MAGDELYN HAMMOND. "Scratching the Surface: Frank O'Hara's and Larry Rivers's Integrated Collaboration on 'Stones.'" The Journal of the Midwest Modern Language Association 43, no. 2 (2010): 59–73. http://www.jstor.org/stable/41960527.

4. JENNINGS, CHELSEA. "Pirating Pound: Drafts & Fragments in 1960s Mimeograph Culture." Journal of Modern Literature 40, no. 1 (2016): 88-108. muse.jhu.edu/article/643363.

5. KATZ, VINCENT. "Collaborating with Poets: An Interview with Rudy Burckhardt." The Art of Collaboration, edited by Katz, Hatje Cantz, 2017, pp. 87-93.

6. KERNAN, NATHAN. "Remembering Joe Brainard." Joe Brainard: All Possible Colors, University of California Press, 2020, pp. 1-14.

7. MAYER, BERNADETTE. "The Ethics of Sleep." Mimeo's Argument: Seventeen Years of Poesy and Politics from the Pages of Mimeograph Revolution, edited by Michael Ruby, City Lights Books, 2009, pp. 153-156.

8. NELSON, MAGGIE. "A Note on Women and the New York School." Women's Studies Quarterly, vol. 36, no. 3/4, 2008, pp. 68-78.

9. PADGETT, RON. "Sonnets and the Placebo Effect." On the Sonnets, University of Michigan Press, 2012, pp. 23-38.

10. WORDEN, DANIEL. "Joe Brainard's Grid." Journal of Modern Literature, vol. 39, no. 4, 2016, pp. 1-17.

1.

2.

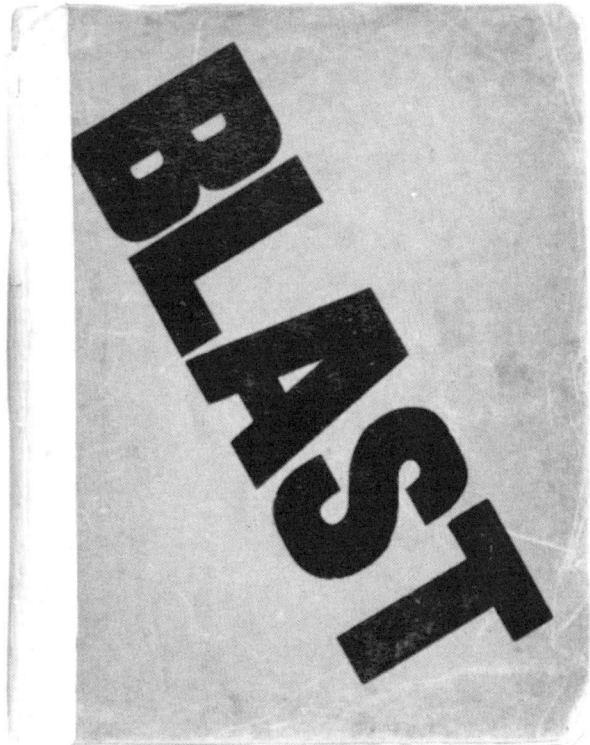

3.

FIGURES

1. Ed Sanders, *Peace Eye Mimeo*. Credit: Ed Sanders.

2. Larry Rivers (Illustrator), Frank O'Hara, "For the Chinese New Year & For Bill Berkson" from *In Memory of My Feelings*, 1967. Source: eBay photo.

3. Wyndham Lewis, Ed. *Blast: Review of the Great English Vortex. No. 1*, 1914. Credit: Wyndham Lewis and the Estate of Mrs G A Wyndham Lewis by kind permission of the Wyndham Lewis Memorial Trust.

4.

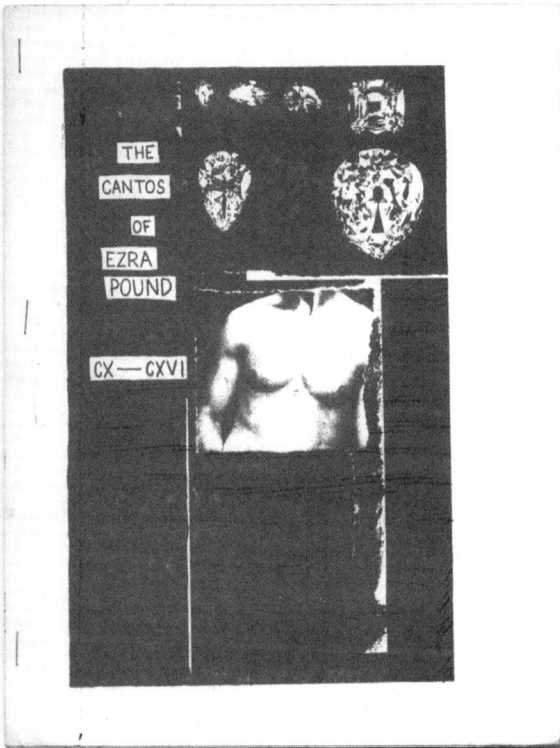

5.

4. Larry Rivers, *Us from Stones*, 1957. Credit: Artist's Rights Society.

5. Ezra Pound, *Cantos 110-116*, 1967. Credit: Tibor de Nagy Gallery.

6.

7.

8.

9.

6. Robin Chandler Duke, *Isamu Noguchi, Buckminster Fuller, and Ezra Pound*, Spoleto, Italy, 1971. Credit: INFGM and ARS.

7. Joe Brainard (artist), Ted Berrigan and Ron Padgett (authors), *Bean Spasms*, 1967. Credit: Tibor de Nagy Gallery.

8. Joe Brainard (artist), Ted Berrigan and Ron Padgett (authors), *The Nancy Book*. 1963-1978. Credit: Tibor de Nagy Gallery.

9. Bernadette Mayer, *Schauplatz*, 1981. Credit: The Poetry Project.

10.

11.

12.

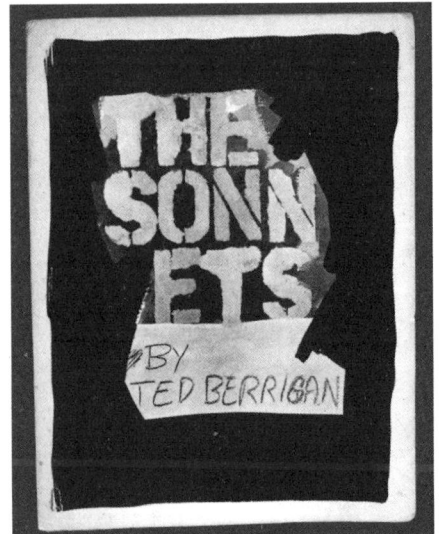

13.

10. Joe Brainard, *Cover of C Comics No. 2*, 1965. PD, originally published without valid copyright.

11. Ted Berrigan (author), Joe Brainard (illustrator), *Living With Chris*, New York: Boke Press, 1968. Credit: Tibor de Nagy Gallery.

12. Joe Brainard, *If Nancy Was Art Nouveau*, 1972. Credit: Tibor de Nagy Gallery.

13. Joe Brainard, *The Sonnets*, 1964. Credit: Tibor de Nagy Gallery.

The Early Hip-Hop Flyer: PHASE 2 and Buddy Esquire

Hip-hop is one of the most popular musical genres of our time. In 2020, half of the top ten global recording artists fell under the R&B/hip-hop category, and over 30 percent of all on-demand audio streams in the US were of R&B and hip-hop tracks, followed by only 16 percent for rock and 13 percent for pop (Ingham, 2021). Hip-hop has become such an integral part of contemporary mainstream culture that it is sometimes easy to forget its humble roots as an underground urban movement in the South Bronx of New York City.

In the late 1970s, hip-hop emerged from an economic paralysis affecting the predominantly Black and Latino community. The movement was centered around DJing and rapping, but it also included graffiti and breakdancing and acted as a meaningful expression for disenfranchised and marginalized youth.

Early DJ parties in community centers and row house basements spread hip-hop culture throughout the borough and beyond. To attract crowds, promoters relied on party flyers to spread the word; the flyers quickly became an essential part of early hip-hop culture. PHASE 2 and Buddy Esquire, two young Black creatives and Bronx natives, were among the most prolific and innovative designers working behind the scenes to cultivate a visual hip-hop language through their flyer designs. Today, these flyers have transcended their ephemeral nature and are some of the few remaining artifacts of the Bronx's live hip-hop culture. However, PHASE 2 and Buddy Esquire are rarely mentioned in the traditional canon of graphic design history. I believe this canon should be expanded to include their impressive work, which played a key role in shaping the visual aesthetics of hip-hop and promoting the movement so that it could grow into the influential global phenomenon it is today.

Michael Lawrence Marrow, known as PHASE 2, was born in Manhattan in 1955. He was raised primarily in the Bronx and attended DeWitt Clinton High School, which was rapidly becoming a graffiti hotbed in the early 1970s. This influenced him to start his career as a subway graffiti writer, pioneering bubble-style letters called "softies" and using loops and arrows. In September of 1973, his work was featured at the first gallery show of graffiti, a United Graffiti Artists presentation at the Razor Gallery in SoHo. PHASE 2 was also fully immersed in hip-hop as a talented DJ, dancer, and rapper.

In the late 1970s, after recognizing a lack of promotional materials for hip-hop events, PHASE 2 turned to a new medium: party flyers. He went on to create hundreds of flyers throughout his career for a variety of events, often involving some of hip-hop's biggest names. PHASE 2 handcrafted beautifully modern and dense compositions that pushed legibility and broke the grid using primarily sans serif Letraset adhesives, markers, cut-out photographs, and glue. Geometric shapes and dynamic lines fused with collages of the performing artists to create energy and excitement for each event.

PHASE 2's ability to implement an array of styles gave him a versatility that set him apart from his competitors. In an interview with Jerome Harris for *AIGA Eye on Design*, PHASE 2 said he drew inspiration from Art Deco, Jack Kirby comic books, Romare Bearden collages and paintings, and manga, and he described his eclectic style as "funky nous deco" *(Harris, 2019)*. PHASE 2 also originated a unique, compositional technique of symmetrical stars, circles, squares, and silhouettes within his flyers that has become a staple in hip-hop aesthetics. The artwork for Dave Chapelle's *Block Party* and *The Get Down* Netflix series is clear, recent examples of this appropriated style. When asked about his thoughts on this, PHASE 2 responded: "I saw the Block Party poster on the street and thought it was something of mine. It's a style that is recognized as and spells 'hip-hop.' I'd say the proof is right there. Then and even to this day, if you see a chronology of flyers in this type of style, you'd find it pretty evident that I implemented it" *(Harris, 2019)*. PHASE 2's methods can also be found in Nike and Adidas campaigns, VH1 Hip Hop Honors graphics, and other promotional materials.

PHASE 2 promoted hip-hop culture through other design formats as well. He created logos for Mike & Dave Records, Tuff City Records, and Crash Crew and designed the Europe One NYC Rap Tour poster. He also created covers for Mike & Dave's Fast Money LP and the Boogie Boys' *Romeo Knight* LP. PHASE 2 later became the art director and co-editor of the international street writing and subway art publication, *International Graffiti Times*. He recently collaborated with the popular skate brand Supreme and designed album covers for the Rawkus and Definitive Jux labels. Until his death in 2019, he worked as a fine artist, selling his work privately and occasionally in galleries.

One of PHASE 2's contemporaries was the self-proclaimed but widely acknowledged "Flyer King" Buddy Esquire, born Lemoin Thompson in 1958. Like PHASE 2, Buddy Esquire started as a graffiti artist but considered the medium a stepping-stone in his artistic development. At the age of twenty, he designed his first hip-hop flyer, and between 1978 and 1984, he created over three hundred more. Within his flyer designs, Buddy Esquire developed a unique style that he referred to as "neo-deco," which involved merging Art Deco-inspired borders and Letraset fonts from the Deco era with neutralized graffiti and disco motifs to create a lively mixture of old and new *(Lalonde, 2014)*.

While some graffiti features like stars, arrows, cloud-like borders, and spray-paint textures remain in his designs, Buddy Esquire offered a fresh and clean interpretation of them. He suppressed and transformed familiar graffiti-style imagery to achieve greater legibility and neatness; crisp lines of pre-made Letraset symbols replaced the bleed, blur, and splatter that might occur from a felt pen or can of spray paint *(Lalonde, 2014)*. Buddy Esquire's flyers also have clear references to disco, most notably in their content. The term "disco" is commonly found in the names of venues, performers, and groups, and extravagant wording is used to describe events. Disco typefaces and sunburst imagery are drawn upon as well.

While graffiti features like stars, arrows, cloud-like borders, and spray-paint textures remain in his designs, Buddy Esquire offers a fresh and clean interpretation. He suppressed and transformed familiar graffiti-style imagery to achieve greater legibility and neatness; crisp lines of pre-made Letraset symbols replaced the bleed, blur, and splatter that might occur from a felt pen or can of spray paint (*Lalonde, 2014*). Buddy Esquire's flyers also clearly reference disco, most notably in their content. The term "disco" is commonly found in the names of venues, performers, and groups, and extravagant wording is used to describe events. Disco typefaces and sunburst imagery are drawn upon as well.

The combination of lavish Art Deco elements, graffiti symbols detached from notions of "vandalism," and references to the stylish aura of disco that was fundamental to Buddy Esquire's "neo-deco" style reflected hip-hop's aspiration to sophistication and professionalism (*Lalonde, 2014*). The intended effect of the style within his flyers was to elevate the status of the promoted events while staying true to the core nature of hip-hop. As Buddy Esquire explained in a 2011 interview with Amanda Lalonde: "That's what I tried for, you know: give it a level of class even though it was just a ghetto jam" (*Lalonde, 2014*). Buddy Esquire's design became a matter of prestige for hip-hop artists and promoters; having a flyer designed by him was eventually the gold standard for promoting a live event. But interestingly, he never made a living from his work.

Looking at their body of work, it is evident that PHASE 2 and Buddy Esquire were skilled designers and craftsmen. Their flyer designs went well beyond their promotional purpose, demonstrating clear attention to detail and thoughtful consideration of materials, composition, and references to both the past and present. They are sophisticated and informative yet lively and intricate and act as important historical mementos in the development of Black culture. So, why are PHASE 2 and Buddy Esquire excluded from our design history books? There are several possible factors. For one, minority designers seldom receive the attention and recognition they deserve in traditional, white-washed narratives of graphic design history, especially if they are designing for minority audiences. In her 1968 article, "The Black Experience in Graphic Design," Dorothy Jackson interviewed several Black designers who expressed frustration over the lack of representation and respect they experienced in both academic and professional settings. Unfortunately, not much has changed. According to the 2019 design census created by AIGA and Google, Black men and women comprise just 3 percent of the design industry (*"Black," 2020*).

Furthermore, hip-hop has historically suffered from a negative reputation due to its associations with violence, vandalism, and drug use. After all, the movement's infancy coincided with the war on drugs, which villainized and disproportionately imprisoned Black men. The music and culture of hip-hop became, in part, an expression of Black male anger toward a nation that pinned them as monsters. It is possible that PHASE 2 and Buddy Esquire's work wasn't taken seriously because of the negative stereotypes and prejudices surrounding hip-hop as well as its underground "amateur" status at the time. Party flyers are also transient by nature and inexpensively reproduced, which could have minimized their perceived legitimacy. Jerome Harris' experience when applying to art school reflects this possibility. When he sent his party flyers to the Tyler School of Art at Temple University, the administrative chair indicated that his work did not constitute graphic design. Harris said in an interview, "I don't remember the exact message, but it was something along the lines of, 'This is not graphic design. You don't have the skills to take classes in this program. You need to apply with a proper portfolio.' And I remember being confused because I was like, but this is graphic design" *(Fuller, 2019)*.

Contrary to conventional accounts of design history, I believe it is important to elevate the work and voices of Black designers like PHASE 2 and Buddy Esquire. Their flyers are worth studying and sharing because they were critical to the development of hip-hop, which has blossomed into a ubiquitous and vibrant culture with far-reaching influences in fashion, art, politics, and media. They offer a unique glimpse into the birth of hip-hop style and continue to inspire current design trends. To ignore this work is to dismiss a major cultural influence originating from the Black community.

BIBLIOGRAPHY

1. "The Black Experience in Graphic Design: 1968 and 2020." Letterform Archive, Letterform Archive, 8 July 2020, https://letterformarchive. org/news/view/the-black-experience-in-graphic-design-1968- and-2020.

2. CARAMANICA, JON. "Phase 2, an Aerosol Art Innovator, Is Dead at 64." The New York Times, The New York Times Company, 20 Dec. 2019, https://www.nytimes. com/2019/12/20/arts/phase-2- dead.html.

3. FULLER, JARRETT. "Episode 127: Jerome Harris." Scratching the Surface, 10 July, 2019, https://scratchingthesurface. fm/post/186179980475/127-je- rome-harris.

4. HARRIS, JEROME. "In the Late '70s in the Bronx, PHASE 2's Party Flyers Created a Visual Language for Hip-Hop." AIGA Eye on Design, The Professional Association for Design, 16 July 2019, https:// eyeondesign.aiga.org/in-the-late- 70s-in-the-bronx-phase-2s-party- flyers-created-a-visual-language- for-hip-hop/.

5. INGHAM, TIM. "Nearly a Third of All Streams in the US Last Year Were of Hip-Hop and R&B Artists (as Rock Beat Pop to Second Most Popular Streaming Genre)." Music Business Worldwide, 7 Jan. 2021, https://www.musicbusinessworld- wide.com/nearly-a-third-of-all- streams-in-the-us-last-year-were- of-hip-hop-and-rb-music/.

6. LALONDE, AMANDA. "Buddy Esquire and the Early Hip Hop Flyer." Popular Music, vol. 33, no. 1, Feb. 2014, pp. 19–38., https://doi. org/10.1017/s0261143013000512.

7. Cornell Hip-Hop Collection: https://rmc.library.cornell.edu/ hiphop/flyers.php.

1.

FIGURES

1. Lonny Wood (PHASE 2), *Earth's Edge*, 1983. Credit:
Cornell University.

2.

3.

4.

5.

2. Lonny Wood (PHASE 2), *Ecstasy Garage Disco*, 1980. Credit: Cornell University.

3. Lonny Wood (PHASE 2), *Harlem World*, 1981. Credit: Cornell University.

4. Lonny Wood (PHASE 2), *Evander Childs High School*, 1978. Credit: Cornell University.

5. Buddy Esquire, *Stardust Ballroom*, 1982. Credit: Cornell University.

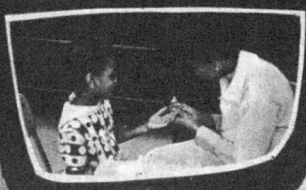

Emory Douglas and the Black Panther Party

"No artist can remain aloof; the artist must be engaged with the world, attuned to its sounds, its cries, its suffering, and its laughter," Emory Douglas expresses in *The Black Panther Party: Service to the People Programs* by David Hilliard (Hilliard, 2008). In this powerful statement, Douglas, an American graphic artist, underscores the essential role of art in communicating messages and raising awareness about the diverse struggles of people. He firmly believed that Black artists have a responsibility to expose the injustices faced by marginalized communities. Douglas remains an activist, continuing to collaborate with fellow artists and organizations to amplify voices and address the ongoing trauma and injustice experienced by minorities.

With a life spanning various eras and roles, from the Black Panther Party to his current activism, Douglas stands out as an intriguing figure to discuss due to his unwavering commitment to advocating for justice. In this paper, I will delve into the evolution of his work and how he has consistently upheld the same mission and message over the years.

In a video interview titled *Emory Douglas: The Black Panther Artist*, published by KCET, Douglas recounts his childhood experiences, sharing instances of discrimination he faced as a Black individual. These encounters with discrimination led him to the California Youth Authority, where he found an opportunity to work in the print shop. It was in this environment that he developed a passion for graphic design. Later, he pursued studies in commercial art at City College, driven by encouragement from black revolutionary movements to create "revolutionary art" to advocate for Black individuals' rights. Subsequently, Douglas became a member of the Black Panther Party in 1967, an organization dedicated to combating police brutality and the unjust killings of Black people *(Hilliard, 2008)*.

In addition to championing the rights of Black individuals, the Black Panther Party extended its efforts to combat discrimination and offered social programs to address tangible needs. Among these programs was the free breakfast program, as described by Mary Potorti in her article "Feeding the Revolution: The Black Panther Party, Hunger, and Community Survival." Potorti characterized this initiative as "necessary measures to ensure the physical survival of poor communities" *(Potorti, 2017)*. This program focused on food survival, addressing hunger issues and fostering physical and political empowerment. While providing assistance and nourishment to underprivileged communities couldn't eliminate racism and discrimination, the Party believed that fortifying individuals physically would bolster the broader movement *(Potorti, 2017)*.

In 2008, Douglas unveiled a painting titled *They Should Be Paying My Rent* (FIGURE 1). Within this artwork, Douglas portrays a woman cradling a rifle while holding a child, accompanied by the statement, "Listen to them pigs banging on my door, asking for some rent money; they should be paying my rent." Colette Gaiter, in her work *The Art of Liberation: Emory Douglas the Black Panther Artist in 1968*, points out that Douglas employs the term "pigs" to refer to the police force and politicians, "The pig was Douglas's signature image and the panthers' term for the killer police force" *(Gaiter, 2020)*. The reference to "pigs," therefore, alludes to the police demanding rent payment from the woman.

Likewise, the painting vividly conveys the unjust system of police brutality against Black individuals. The depiction presents an intensely angry Black woman who asserts that the authorities are the ones who should be covering her rent expenses. The deliberate choice to feature the woman and child also holds profound symbolism within the design. Gaiter elaborates in their article that Douglas's designs "depicted women as active participants in the armed self-defense actions, portraying them with children and firearms"*(Gaiter, 2020)*. This imagery conveys inclusivity, underscoring the shared burdens and struggles experienced by all Black individuals.

Following the dissolution of the Black Panther Party in 1982, Douglas persevered as an advocate for Black people's rights. He remained dedicated to his beliefs and ideals, producing designs that aligned with his convictions. In 2018, he unveiled a painting titled *We Shall Survive. Without a Doubt* (FIGURE 2). This artwork embodies Douglas's hopeful perspective on the destiny and prospects of people of color.

The painting portrays numerous children, with one child notably wearing glasses that reflect two images from the Free Breakfast Program initiated by the Black Panther Party in 1969. This visual element symbolizes Douglas's optimistic outlook, emphasizing the enduring positive impact of the Black Panther Party's efforts. The inclusion of the smiling child underscores the success of the Party's commitment to the well-being of the Black community. Although the Party disbanded in 1982, Douglas's belief in the enduring influence of their work reflects his unwavering loyalty to the Party's cause and vision for a brighter future.

FIGURES 1 and 2 reveal the evolution of elements and materials over time. FIGURE 1 demonstrates a simpler approach, utilizing limited technology with black ink prints layered with colors. In contrast, FIGURE 2 showcases more sophisticated techniques like collage and advanced printing on higher-quality paper. Despite living in an era of advanced technology, Douglas remains committed to his mission of conveying messages about the Black community's experiences and aspirations, remaining loyal to his original stance from his time with the Party.

During his time with the Party, Douglas's art celebrated Blackness, capturing their essence by emphasizing their facial features and identities *(Gaiter, 2020)*. This signature style endures, as seen in FIGURE 2. Remarkably, despite his journey from 1967 to today, his design style became synonymous with himself and the Black Panther Party.

While time and periods influenced Douglas's materials and production processes, his work consistently conveys the same message of hope and the reality of the Black community.

BIBLIOGRAPHY

1. "EMORY DOUGLAS: The Black Panther Artist | Artbound | KCET." Youtube, uploaded by KCET, 22 June. 2021, https://www.youtube.com/watch?v=oMZBq-2X9TA

2. GAITER, COLETTE. The Art of Liberation: Emory Douglas and the Black Panther Artists in 1968. South Atlantic Quarterly 1 July 2020; 119 (3): 567–586. doi: https://doi- org.ezproxy.bu.edu/10.1215/00382876-8601422

3. POTORTI, MARY. "'Feeding the Revolution': The Black Panther Party, Hunger, and Community Survival." Journal of African American Studies, vol. 21, no. 1, 2017, pp. 85–110. JSTOR, http://www.jstor.org/stable/44508193. Accessed 9 Jun. 2022.

4. HUEY P. Newton Foundation, The. The Black Panther Party : Service to the People Programs, edited by David Hilliard, University of New Mexico Press, 2008. ProQuest Ebook Central, https://ebookcentral.proquest.com/lib/bu/detail.action?docID=1105279.

5. "THEY SHOULD be Paying my Rent." Artsy, 2009, https://www.artsy.net/artwork/emory-douglas- they-should-be-paying-my-rent-1

6. "WE SHALL Survive. Without a Doubt." Artbook, 2 Mar. 2018, https://www.artbook.com/blog-black-panther-soul-of-a-nation.html

LISTEN TO THEM PIGS BANGING ON MY DOOR
ASKING FOR SOME RENT MONEY...
THEY SHOULD BE PAYING MY RENT

1.

FIGURES

1. Emory Douglas, *They Should be Paying my Rent*, 1971.
Source: Internet Archive. Credit: Sam Durant, Ed. *Black Panther: The Revolutionary Art Of Emory Douglas.*

2.

2. Emory Douglas, We Shall Survive Without A Doubt,
1971. Source: Internet Archive. Credit: Sam Durant, Ed.
Black Panther: The Revolutionary Art Of Emory Douglas.

3.

4.

5.

6.

3. Los Angeles Times, *Huey Newton leader of the Black Panther Party*, 1977. Credit: UCLA Library, Los Angeles Times Photographic Collection, PD CC-BY 4.0 license.

4. Black Panther Party, *Free Breakfast Program for Children*, 1970. PD, originally published without a copyright notice.

5. *Bobby Seale at John Sinclair Freedom Rally*, Ann Arbor, Michigan, University of Michigan yearbook, 1971. PD, originally published without a copyright notice.

6. *The Black Panther newspaper, vol. 4, No. 2*, December 13, 1969. Source: Internet Archive, fair use for educational use.

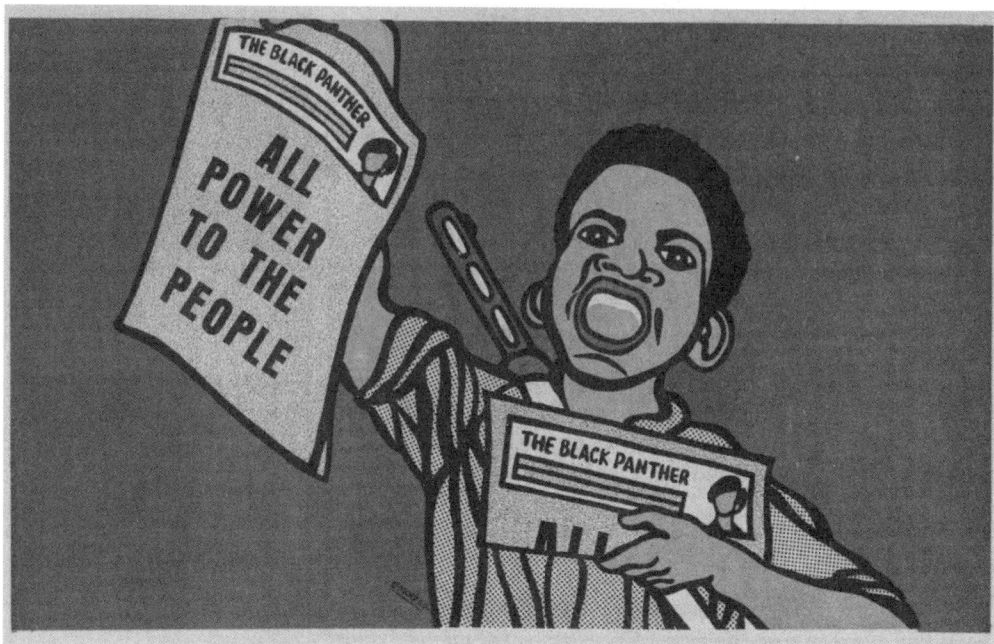

7.

7. Emory Douglas, *All Power to The People*, 1969. Source:
Internet Archive. Credit: Sam Durant, Ed. *Black Panther:
The Revolutionary Art Of Emory Douglas*.

8.

9.

10.

11.

8. Emory Douglas, *The Black Panther*, 1970. Source: Internet Archive. Credit: Sam Durant, Ed. *Black Panther: The Revolutionary Art Of Emory Douglas.*

9. Emory Douglas, *The Black Panther*, 1971. Source: Internet Archive. Credit: Sam Durant, Ed. *Black Panther: The Revolutionary Art Of Emory Douglas.*

10. Emory Douglas, *You Can Murder a Revolutionary, But You Can't Murder a Revolution*, 1970. Source: Internet Archive. Credit: Sam Durant, Ed. *Black Panther: The Revolutionary Art Of Emory Douglas.*

11. Emory Douglas, *Revolution in Our Lifetime*, 1969. Source: Internet Archive. Credit: Sam Durant, Ed. *Black Panther: The Revolutionary Art Of Emory Douglas.*

SPECTACULAR GIMMICKS

The allure of "cute" emanates charm, embraces clichés, and indulges in guilty pleasures. Designed for consumption, these spectacular gimmicks evoke no shame — they are flamboyant, if not garish, and attention-seeking. The designs featured here blur idealism with desire, practicality with personality, sincerity with camp, progress with tradition, and audacity with elegance — all while unapologetically delivering striking imagery that exudes an air of aloof elitism.

A Depiction of Modern Japan: The Superflat Movement

Takashi Murakami, one of the most prominent Japanese contemporary artists of the 1990s, introduced the Superflat movement to the global stage in 2000. His Superflat exhibition gained international acclaim, and he went on to establish his own studio, Kaikai Kiki. Murakami's design style draws from traditional Japanese Ukiyo-e art, with its emphasis on simplicity and two-dimensional layout. It also incorporates influences from Japanese anime and manga, creating a surreal, joyful impression through its spaceless, comic-inspired design (Favell, 2014). While Superflat has achieved worldwide popularity, the core values of the movement—deeply rooted in Japanese culture—are often overlooked in Western design history.

Superflat reflects the attitude of Japanese people toward the decadent period after the burst of the Japanese economic bubble and comprises the Japanese subcultures Otaku (geek) and Kawaii (cuteness) (Favell, 2014). This essay explores the development of the Superflat movement through a Japanese historical background, a combination of traditional Japanese aesthetics with the newly emerged Otaku and Kawaii aesthetics, and the social values behind this movement.

The Superflat movement began when Japan was in a period of great prosperity after World War II. Japan experienced rapid economic growth due to investment from the United States. In the early 1990s, Japan entered a "lost decade" due to the asset price bubble. Insufficient government regulation did not solve the economic crises but posed a series of new problems: social inequality, an aging population, exploitation of labor, and uneven modernization (Adriasola, 2016). People were depressed about the future of Japan. Meanwhile, the Kawaii aesthetics in commercial culture, which stands for "cuteness" culture in Japanese, became a comfort for helpless people. Kawaii objects arouse pity and the desire to protect from the Japanese audience. According to Kumiko Sato's article "From Hello Kitty to Cod Roe Kewpie," Kawaii culture "mirrored Japan's shift from political idealism to post-industrial consumerism, from men's ambition to women's fancy, from the dream of progress to the desire for difference, and from consumption of things to consumption of images" (Sato, n.d.). The obsession with Kawaii objects is a fantasy for Japanese people to escape from the reality of social-economic depression. They pretend to be childish and resist taking adult social responsibility *(Sato, n.d.)*. Women started to dress in cute styles. Kawaii design became mainstream in Japan, especially among the adolescent population.

Another subculture derived from the social-economic downfall is Otaku, translated as an unattractive man addicted to computers and anime and isolated from any social activity, or in a simple word: geek *(Kaichiro, 2013)*. The Otaku culture is often endowed with negative meanings. This led to a uniquely Japanese style of art, Otaku art, a style of character design depicting the pure and idealized beauty of anime girls *(Kaichiro, 2013)*. Otaku collects manga and Kawaii-style girl figures to fulfill their sexual desires and serves as a retreat into the fantasy realm *(Darling, 2001)*. The Otaku living style reflects the dissipated Japanese attitude toward the corrupted economy of the early 1990s, which is an unhealthy living style according to Michael Darling's "Plumbing the Depth of Superflatness" *(Darling, 2001)*. Along with the Kawaii aesthetics, both design styles create ideal paradises that attract male and female populations and make up mainstream pop culture in Japan.

Takashi Murakami uses the Superflat movement as a metaphor to depict the overall structure of modern Japanese society — the mixing of "high" and "low" art. In 2000, Murakami published his book *Superflat* which is based on his theory of superflatness. He describes Japan as a flat image: "At the center of the image is the thick trunk of Japan's eccentric, secular, grotesque 'sub-culture.' Moving up the truck [...] you see a small bird representing a meaningless 'hierarchy' [...] along a horizontal path to the right are 'celebrations' and 'media frenzies'" *(Murakami, 2000)*. Murakami expresses the social issues of modern Japan through his theory, including social inequality, over-westernization, the addiction of the young generation to technology and social media, and their evasive attitude toward problems that came to place after the befell of the bubble economy. He points out that the pop culture of Kawaii and Otaku is an abnormal phenomenon in Japanese society. The two-dimensionality of his works indicates people's "flatness," superficialness, or the lack of insightful thoughts on objects in a fast-paced world. The fact that the two-dimensional feature of his Superflat style originates from Ukiyo-e is a symbol of the blending of "high" and "low" art, where "high" art stands for the traditional art, and "low" art represents pop and subcultures design styles *(Looser, 2006)*. The combination of premodern and postmodern style also signifies his appeal to conserving traditional Japanese art and culture from the over-westernized Japan.

One of Murakami's typical artworks, *Lots, Lots of Kaikai and Kiki,* shows the underlying Superflat values (FIGURE 1). He utilizes repetitive anime characters to fill out the entire space. Although the happy faces give most audiences the first impression of joy and amusement, Murakami mentions that he includes several tears and disappointed faces in his art *(Museum of Fine Arts)*. Moreover, Kaikai and Kiki are anime versions of two traditional Japanese monsters portrayed in a Kawaii style *(Museum of Fine Arts)*. Murakami leaves a space for the observers to contemplate the meaning of this drawing other than the easy first impression. Referring back to his book *Superflat*, it can be seen that the overflow of anime characters represents the "'celebration' of 'media frenzies'" *(Murakami, 2000)*. The sorrowful faces he hides from a group of delighted faces stand for superficiality, and the observers must carefully look at the different looks.

Lastly, Kawaii's depictions of two traditional Japanese monsters are a fusion of popular Japanese subcultures and his inclusive attitude toward Japanese conventional art.

While Murakami is one of the most visible Japanese artists today in the West, the original concept of Superflat theory was lost when it transformed to the world stage. Although Western audiences are familiar with Kawaii and Otaku cultures, they are categorized as "subcultures." However, Kawaii and Otaku belong to mainstream culture in Japan because they are products derived from a distinct Japanese historical background. According to an interview with Murakami, he points out the fundamental disparity between Japanese and American social values, "The American mindset is a product of the culture of success, whereas the Japanese psyche is a product of the culture of defeat" *(Nakamura, 2005)*. The defeat of World War II, the downfall of the bubble economy in the 1900s, and the unsolved social issues in Japanese society today are all driving forces that made Kawaii and Otaku become mainstream culture in Japan.

Furthermore, Superflat seems to lose its significance when Murakami's works are associated with consumerism and capitalism. Murakami debuted in the West market with a successful collaboration with Louis Vuitton. He incorporated his iconoclastic design style with the classic Louis Vuitton monogram in the *Eye Love Superflat* 2003 screenprint.[1] The handbag with his Louis Vuitton monogram print design is sold for limited availability, and this "hunger marketing" strategy attracted many consumers worldwide *(Lisica, 2010)*. Yet, the core values of Superflat disappeared, and Murakami's design became part of Louis Vuitton's branding *(Darling, 2001)*. Today, Murakami's design style and studio, Kaikai and Kiki also became a luxury brand. He made his limited-edition merchandise in collaboration with other famous brands. A Kaikai figure can cost more than $7000 online (FIGURE 2), and even a T-shirt from his collaboration with Uniqlo now costs more than a hundred dollars, where the original price is only $14.99 *(Cohen, 2020)* (FIGURE 3). Like the Louis Vuitton bag, Murakami's collectible merchandise became a status symbol. Ironically, the commercialization of Murakami's art is a process of superflattening. Consumers pursue the fame of a luxury brand more than the design style and ignore the message that Superflat wants to deliver. Do people today appreciate Murakami's design style or the fame of his brand? It seems that Superflat is moving in an opposite direction from the initial motif of this movement, which is to critique people's superficialness and in-depth social issues.

---

1 *Eye Love Superflat* is a striking screenprint design featuring Murakami's trademark anime eye motif interspersed with the Louis Vuitton monogram logo and classic four-pointed flower in dazzling colors for a brilliant statement on art and capitalism.

BIBLIOGRAPHY

1. ADRIASOLA, IGNACIO. "Design and Society in Modern Japan: An Introduction." Review of Japanese Culture and Society, vol. 28, [Josai University Educational Corporation, University of Hawai'i Press], 2016, pp. 1–50, http://www.jstor.org/stable/44649883.

2. COHEN, ALINA. "Breaking Down Takashi Murakami's Wildly Popular, Expansive Art." Artsy, 13 May 2020, https://www.artsy.net/article/artsy-editorial-breaking-takashi-murakamis wildly-popular-expansive-art.

3. DARLING, MICHAEL. "Plumbing the Depths of Superflatness." Art Journal, vol. 60, no. 3, [Taylor & Francis, Ltd., CAA], 2001, pp. 76–89, https://doi.org/10.2307/778139.

4. FAVELL, ADRIAN. "Visions of Tokyo in Japanese Contemporary Art." Impressions, no. 35, Japanese Art Society of America, 2014, pp. 68–83, http://www.jstor.org/stable/24869101.

5. KAICHIRO, MORIKAWA, AND DENNIS WASHBURN. " Otaku/Geek." Review of Japanese Culture and Society, vol. 25, [Josai University Educational Corporation, University of Hawai'i Press], 2013, pp. 56–66, http://www.jstor.org/stable/43945382.

6. LISICA, CINDY. Beyond Consumption: The Art, Merchandise and Global Impact of Takashi Murakami. University of the Arts London, 2010, https://ualresearchonline.arts.ac.uk/id/eprint/5210/1/THESIS_LISICA.pdf.

7. LOOSER, THOMAS. "Superflat and the Layers of Image and History in 1990s Japan." Mechademia, vol. 1, University of Minnesota Press, 2006, pp. 92–109, http://www.jstor.org/stable/41510881.

8. MURAKAMI, TAKASHI. "Lots, Lots of Kaikai and Kiki." Museum of Fine Arts, Boston, 2009, https://www.mfa.org/exhibitions/takashi-murakami/mfa-mobile.

9. MURAKAMI, TAKASHI. "The Superflat Manifesto." Superflat, Madra, Tokyo, 2000.

10. NAKAMURA, RYOKO M. "Vision of a 'Superflat' Future." The Japan Times, 13 Apr. 2005, https://www.japantimes.co.jp/culture/2005/04/13/arts/vision-of-a-superflat-future/.

11. SATO, K. (n.d.). "From hello Kitty to Cod Roe Kewpie: A Postwar Cultural History of Cuteness in Japan." Asian Studies. Retrieved from https://www.asianstudies.org/wp-content/uploads/from-hello-kitty-to-cod-roe-kewpie-a-pstwar-cultural-history-of-cuteness-in-japanA.pdf.

12. TAKASHI MURAKAMI. Eye Love Superflat. p. 1, https://jstor.org/stable/community.14279028.

13. TAKASHI MURAKAMI/KAIKAI Kiki Co.,. Takashi Murakami: Lineage of Eccentrics. Museum of Fine Arts, Boston.

14. "Uniqlo Doraemon UT by Takashi Murakami." Grailed.com, https://www.grailed.com/listings/23395834-takashi-murakami-x-uniqlo-doraemon-ut-by takashi-murakami.

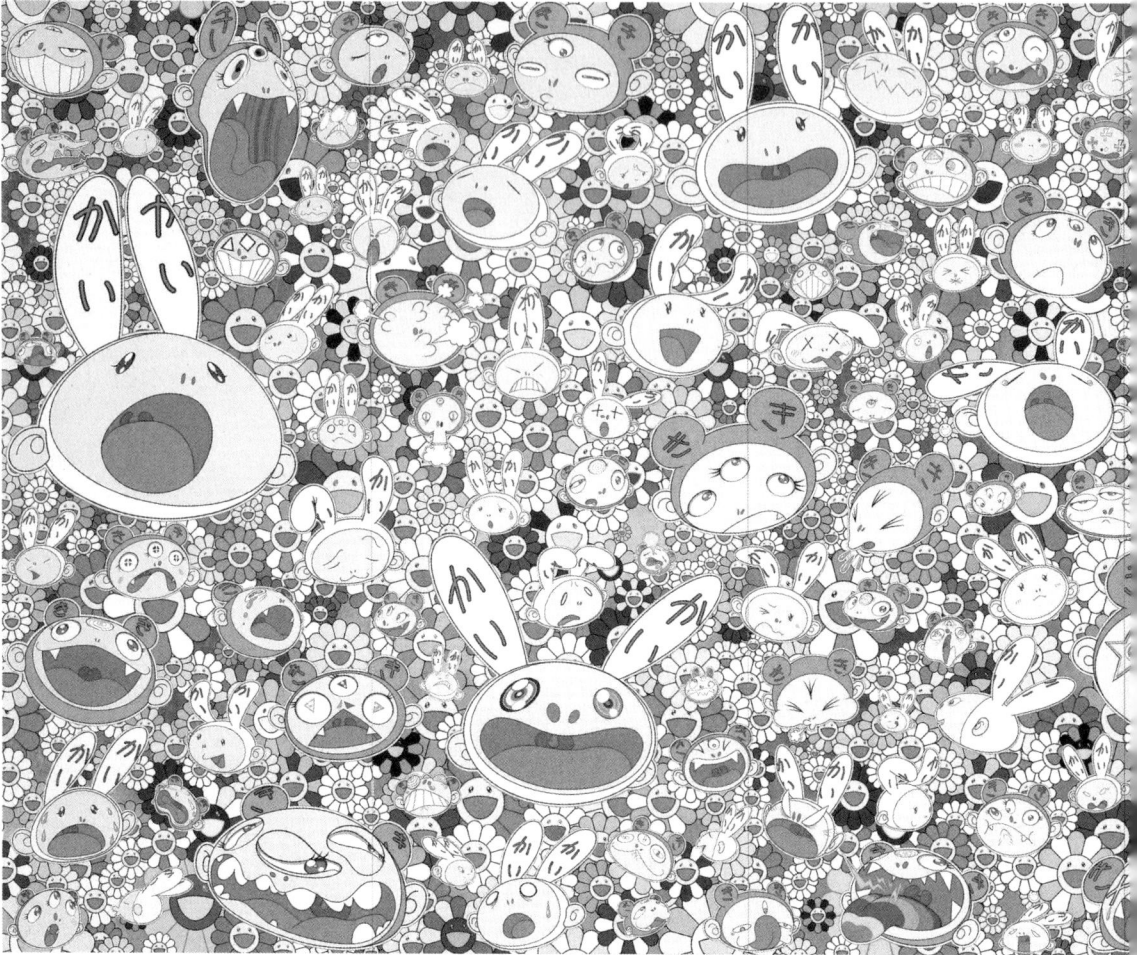

1.

2.

3.

2. Takashi Murakami, Kaikai plush doll, 2019. PD eBay photo.

3. Takashi Murakami & Uniqlo, *Doraemon UT*, 2010-2019. PD eBay photo.

Baby Consuelo
Morais Moreira
e os Novos Baianos

Tropicália: A Resistance to the Brazilian Military Dictatorship

In 1964, an established coup organized by the political military party in Brazil led to a twenty-year hiatus of democratic rule in the country. During this period, cultural and artistic expression were heavily controlled, and there was a push for the unification of Brazilian identity, which was followed by the adoption of an international capitalist attitude. Left-wing communities, especially artists and musicians, opposed the ideas and structures imposed by this new and more restrictive regime (Napolitano, 2018). To escape oppression — in the form of imprisonment or even murder — a mass exodus ensued. Yet, a group of strident artists and musicians revolted by developing a new aesthetic, Tropicália, to celebrate the diversity within Brazilian culture that the conservative government aimed to stifle.

Concrete artist Hélio Oiticica first introduced the concept of Tropicália in 1967 with his experiential art piece of the same name. Oiticica depicted how Brazilian "tropical" culture was co-opted as a stereotype used to silence the chaos and struggles that marginalized groups experienced (Canejo, 2004). The concept Tropicália first appeared in the poet Oswald de Andrade's *Anthropophagic Manifesto* (1928), where he emphasized how appropriating European styles and resituating them into a Brazilian context served as a form of resistance against the increasing Northern domination in Brazil (Dunn, 2001). Oiticica, along with various other Brazilian artists and musicians, expanded on Andrade's concept, acknowledging the influence of American and European cultures on Brazil. But Oiticica went further by highlighting unique and diverse voices native to the Brazilian identity. Tropicália ultimately encompassed the multinational movement for freedom, peace, and spiritual exploration and celebrated the dramatic and ironic displays of an idiosyncratic Brazilian culture. Tropicália played an influential role in the redevelopment of Brazilian and Afro-Brazilian culture, leading to a strong opposition and eventual revolution against the cultural and democratic restrictions implemented under the Brazilian military dictatorship

Oiticica's revolutionary work preceded Brazil's military coup — he used spatial and interactive art to represent hidden aspects of Brazilian identity (FIGURE 1). He and several other artists, including Lygia Clark (FIGURE 2) and Lygia Pape, established the Neo-Concrete group in response to the Concrete movement. The Neo-Concretes sought "the sensorial experience of erstwhile 'viewers' turned 'participants'" (Dunn,

2013). This served as a form of expansion of the pictorial frame, inviting the audience to collaborate on the artistic message. Oiticica visited the *favelas* in Rio de Janeiro to learn more about the impoverished lives suffered by a majority of the Brazilian population, focusing specifically on the presence of *favela* culture in modern-day society.[1] His art called on marginality as an increasing phenomenon leading to urban violence and criminalization. "Poverty was itself criminalized as large segments of the population were excluded from the formal economy [...] For Oiticica, marginality was an ethical stance rebuffing state violence against *favelados*" *(Dunn, 2013).* His Tropicália piece consisted of two structures, denominated "Penetrables," which invited the audience to enter the art, evoking sensorial and emotional reactions (FIGURES 3, 4). "Sand, palm plants, parrots, and colorful makeshift structures suggest a tropical stereotype of Brazil. But this fake, fun world also has a radical political undercurrent. The favelas inspired the structures [...]. Oiticica advocated for the radical potential of simply hanging out" *(Tate, n.d.).* The piece serves as a commentary on the societal exclusions favela residents were experiencing, along with exposing the realities of the violence behind the stereotypically tropical Brazilian culture. The scale of this work compelled participants, who ranged in age, language, and background, to explore their sensorial responses to the art without explicitly defining the intentions behind it. Oiticica spoke to the hidden reality that many impoverished Brazilians endured but also invited the public to take time to play with their own senses and experience emotion about that reality — all while the military dictatorship steadily increased the industrial and capitalist agenda that ultimately erased the favela culture from mainstream consciousness.

Over time, the violence and military control increased. Oiticica's piece continued to inspire Brazilians who were suffering under this new form of government. "This way of alluding indirectly, rather than explicitly confronting issues, becomes the trademark of Tropicalist artists, including musicians, directors, and poets" *(Canejo, 2004).* The use of symbolic and stereotypical imagery, sound, and style emerged to attract the public into seeing and taking control over the ingrained issues within Brazilian society. Music soon became the largest conduit for Tropicália expression when two young musicians, Caetano Veloso and Gilberto Gil, joined the movement. Both musicians came from Bahia, a state further north from the industrial and cultural capitals of São Paulo and Rio de Janeiro, where Afro-Brazilian culture dominates. In 1968, Veloso and Gil released the monumental song "Tropicália," which served as a manifestation of the Brazilian reality, speaking to the country's general public and listeners internationally (FIGURE 5). The song is produced using various Brazilian instruments, and the lyrics are quite illustrative, evoking a narrative. In Veloso's words, the song points to "the gap between the country's intellectual and artistic development on the one hand, and the backwardness of a great part of the population due to poverty, on the other" *(Veloso and Dunn, 1996).* Veloso and Gil highlighted how the increasing thirst for capital gain failed to acknowledge the extreme poverty and lack of widely accessible public infrastructures present in the

---

1 Favelas are dense, self-produced areas of extreme poverty surrounding urban centers in Brazil (Aguiar, 2006).

country. Their song was meant to shock the Brazilian audience into recognizing the reality around them, serving as a threat toward a military party that relied on public control. It was a declaration of Brazilian culture, reminding people of their country's own identity. In a time when international forces collided with a dominant North, looking beyond the stereotypical imagery of Brazil was a form of resistance toward the dictatorship but also a crucial step that underscored public support for an authentic and inclusive culture.

The album cover art for *Tropicália* was created by Rogério Duarte, whom Veloso met when he relocated to São Paulo. Duarte and Veloso introduced a contempo-rary psychedelic aesthetic to the cover, fitting with the ongoing "hippie" movement (*Almeida, Fuchs & Kaminski, 2018*).[2] The cover displays various Brazilian symbols and bright tropical colors surrounding an image of Veloso's serious face, his eyes veering directly forward, looking toward the viewer (FIGURE 6). Perhaps Veloso's face serves as a declaration of the rising strictness in Brazilian culture. At the same time, the naked woman's embrace of the portrait holds two purposes: a stereotypical symbol of the Brazilian woman and the embrace representing the public's indulgence of this new "serious" identity. Veloso and Gil induced cultural outrage throughout the country, with those in favor joining the movement while those siding with the gov-ernment felt threatened. Opposition was growing, but with the military's strength, the left had to increase forces for the revolution while ensuring their beliefs in peace and freedom persisted.

The official Tropicália movement lasted little more than a year, ending in De-cember of 1968. However, the foundational ideas persisted in leftist culture through-out the dictatorship, serving as hope that one day, Brazilian democracy and freedom of expression would return. As the dictatorship carried on and oppositional voices were increasingly banned, "many members of the opposition voluntarily went into exile to escape ever-increasing suppression by the regime's authorities" (Cruz, 2011). The resolve of the leftist resistance weakened as international and underground forces entrenched themselves in power positions. Oiticica and Veloso spent time in the UK and the US (FIGURES 7, 8), gaining public recognition overseas which allowed for the connection of Tropicália with other social movements that shared similar propositions.

Artists and musicians who remained in Brazil continued aligning with the Trop-icália style, with colorful and psychedelic designs reminiscent of the "hippie" move-ment (FIGURE 9). An affinity for dynamic motifs, gridded compositions, and obscure object alignment typified the work of Tropicália designers (*Oliveira, 2011*). In terms of anonymity, "newly founded underground magazines took over the important role of offering a local platform to the voices of those who were abroad" (*Cruz, 2011*). These publications advocated for ideas and messages that otherwise contradicted the party line. At this inflection point, the Tropicália movement took on new meaning as an alternate form that could endure the social and cultural restrictions imposed by the dictatorship. Even in 1985, when the dictatorship finally collapsed, democracy was

---

2 Paraphrased because the original article is in Portuguese.

restored, and formerly exiled musicians and artists returned. Tropicália culture was a symbolic voice acknowledging twenty years of political and cultural oppression.

Although relatively misunderstood, the Tropicália movement permeates international consciousness. What manifested as stereotypical representations of tropical art evokes deeper themes of resistance and hope. Furthermore, Tropicália suggests that expanding the Western design history canon can honor underknown stories of lost cultures, communities, and attitudes. It also serves as a beacon for resistant movements who suffer from oppression, encouraging members to be unafraid to voice and express beliefs amid global and international turmoil.

BIBLIOGRAPHY

1. ALMEIDA, FERNANDO dos Santos, Fuchs, Isabela Marques and Rosane Kaminski. 2018. "A Tropicália de Rogério Duarte em 'Caetano Veloso' e 'Gilberto Gil'(1968)". Projética 9, no. 1: 69-86. DOI: 0.5433/2236-2207.2018v9n1p69. Brown University Library. n.d. "O Pasquim (1969-1991)". Brasiliana Collection. Accessed November 6, 2023. https://library.brown.edu/create/brasiliana/pasquim-2/.

2. CANEJO CYNTHIA. 2004. "The Resurgence of Anthropophagy". Third Text 18, no. 1 (August): 61-68. https://doi.org/10.1080/095288 2032000182712.

3. CRUZ, MAX JORGE. 2011. "Tropicamp: Pre- and Post-Tropicália at Once: Some Contextual Notes on Hélio Oiticica's 1971 Text". Afterall: A Journal of Art, Context and Enquiry 28 (Winter): 4-15. https://doi.org/10.1086/662966.

4. DUNN, CHRISTOPHER. 2013. " 'Experimentar o Experimental': Avant-garde, Cultural Marginal, and Counterculture in Brazil, 1968-72". Luso-Brazilian Review 50, no. 1 (June): 229-52. https://doi.org/10.1353/lbr.2013.0013.

5. DUNN, CHRISTOPHER. 2001. "Tropicália and the Emergence of a Brazilian Counterculture". In Brutality Garden, 122-59. Chapel Hill: University of North Carolina Press.

6. NAPOLITANO, MARCUS. 2018. "The Brazilian Military Regime, 1964 – 1985". Oxford Research Encyclopedia of Latin American History. (April): 1-24. https://doi.org/10.1093/acrefore/9780199366439.013.413.

7. OLIVEIRA, CAUHANA Tafarelo. 2011. "The Tropicalist Rupture in Graphic Design". Universidade Tecnológica Federal do Paraná, 10-72. http://repositorio.utfpr.edu.br/jspui/bitstream/1/13874/2/CT_CODEG_2011_2_07.pdf.

8. Tate. n.d. "The story of Hélio Oiticica and the Tropicália movement". Accessed November 6, 2023. https://www.tate.org.uk/art/artists/helio-oiticica-7730/story-helio-oiticica-and-tropicalia-movement.

9. Tate. n.d. "Tropicália, Penetrables PN2 ' Purity is a myth' and PN3 'Imagetical'". Accessed November 6, 2023. https://www.tate.org.uk/art/artworks/oiticica-tropicalia-penetrables-pn-2-purity-is-a-myth-and-pn-3-imagetical-t12414.

10. VELOSO, CAETANO and Christopher Dunn. 1996. "The Tropicalist Rebellion". Transition, no. 70: 116-38. https://doi.org/10.2307/2935353.

1.

2.

FIGURES

1. Hélio Oiticica, *P15 Parangolé Cape 11, I Embody Revolt,* worn by Nildo of Mangueira, 1967. Credit: Cesar Oiticica.

2. Lygia Clark, *Máscaras sensoriais*, 1967. Source: Wikiart, PD for educational use.

3.

4.

3. Tropicália, *Penetrables PN 2 'Purity is a myth' and PN 3 'Imagetical'*, 1966-7. Credit: Cesar Oiticica.

4. Tropicália, *PN2 e PN3, "Nova objetividade brasileira"*, 1967. Credit: Cesar Oiticica.

from "Tropicália" (1968)

Caetano Veloso

Eu organizo o movimento
Eu oriento o carnaval
Eu inauguro o monumento
No Planalto Central do país

Viva bossa - sa - sa
Viva a palhoça - ça - ça - ça - ça

O monumento é de papel crepom e
  prata
Os olhos verdes da mulata
A cabaleira esconde atrás da verde mata
O luar do sertão
O monumento não tem porta
A entrada de uma rua antiga estreita e
  torta
E no joelho uma criança sorridente feia
  e morta
Estende a mão

Viva mata - ta - ta
Viva a mulata - ta - ta - ta

O monumento é bom moderno
Não disse nada do modelo do meu
  terno
Que tudo mais vá pro inferno
Meu bem

Viva banda - da - da
Carmem Miranda - da - da - da - da

translation "Tropicália"

I organize the movement
I direct the carnival
I inaugurate the monument
on the central high plains
of the country

Long live the bossa
Long live the straw hut

The monument of *papier-maché* and
  silver
The green eyes of the *mulata*
Her long hair hides behind the green
  forest
The moonlight over the plains
The monument has no door
The entrance is an old street, narrow
  and winding
On his knees a smiling, ugly dead child
Extends his hand

Long live the forest
Long live the *mulata*

The monument is quite modern
You said nothing of my fashionable
  suit
To hell with everything else
My love

Long live the band
Long live Carmen Miranda

5.

---

5. Caetano Veloso & Gilberto Gil, *Tropicália* lyrics. PD for educational use.

6.

7.

6. David Drew Zingg (photography), Rogerio Duarte
(project director), Liana d'Urso (Illustrator, artist), Paulo
Oliveira (typography), *Caetano Veloso*, album cover,
1968. Source: Wikipedia, PD for educational use.

7. Hélio Oiticica, *Eden*, 1969. Credit: Cesar Oiticica.

8.

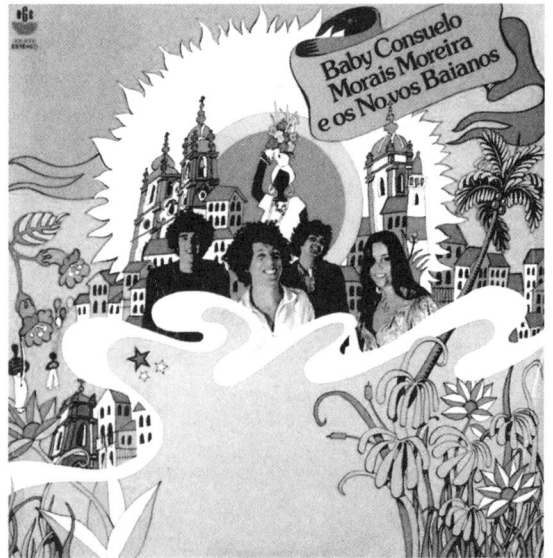

9.

8. Hélio Oiticica, *Parangolé Cape 30 in the New York City Subway*, 1972. Credit: Cesar Oiticica.

9. Unknown artist, *Os Novos Baianos* album cover, 1981. Source: Discogs, fair use for educational use.

Yoshitomo Nara's Influence on Mainstreaming Japanese Superflat

Yoshitomo Nara's artwork diverges from the fine art typically found in blue chip museums, yet that is exactly where Nara's work resides (FIGURE 1). Nara trades formal mark-making innovations for flat, cartoon-like girls that feel like illustrations found in children's books (FIGURE 2). These girls share common features — large, round eyes and distorted proportions — that create an impression of cuteness and approachability, breaking ground with high art stoicism.

Over the past few decades, Takashi Murakami has ushered in the Superflat movement *(Looser, 2006)* (FIGURE 3). Superflat injects contemporary art into commercial environments — and, therein lies its power. This way, art becomes more accessible and consumable to broader audiences. Yoshitomo Nara stands out as one of the artists who have blurred the boundaries between high art and low art, infusing the aesthetics of pop culture into fine arts and evoking emotional responses from viewers through the intimacy of his artwork.

Nara's style draws heavily on his youth, when he was immersed in a world of pop culture. Born in Japan in 1959, he spent much of his childhood engrossed in solitary play while his affinity for rock and punk music solidified. These influences remain palpable throughout his body of work.

During the 1990s, Nara traveled to Germany and attended the renowned Kunstakademie Düsseldorf. This transformative period gave birth to his iconic girl figures, which he describes as a reflection of his own self and the loneliness of his youth *(Marino, 2020)* (FIGURE 4). Manifested in the familiar pop style reminiscent of comics and cartoons, these enigmatic girls evoke feelings of nostalgia.

Nara's viewers discover fragments of themselves and others in his paintings through an exploration of shared exuberance, rebellion, petulance, and serenity *(Vanderweide, 2021)*. Viewers discover an intensity of expression, forging a connection to shared memories of bygone childhoods *(Ivy, 2010)*. His approach adeptly combines mainstream pop generalities with introspective localities, a paradox Nara balances with unmitigated precision. Beyond mere depictions of adorable children, characters with unyielding gazes and defiant attitudes elicit visceral emotional responses (FIGURES 5, 6). In conflating innocence and audacity, Nara captures the essence of a child's heart while subtly critiquing contemporary culture. Nara charms both artist and viewer through his girls' unrelenting cuteness.

His work also reminds us of Japanese traditional painting, ukiyo-e, because of its flattened artistic style. Ukiyo-e, or two-dimensional woodblock prints and paintings developed during Japan's Edo period from the 17th–19th century, is best known for democratizing access to art. High art became available to a broader public by disseminating less expensive and more easily reproducible ukiyo-e — collapsing the gulf between high and low art *(Farago, 2023)*. Hokusai Katsushika, the virtuoso of ukiyo-e, renowned for his iconic print *The Great Wave*, positioned what was once an Eastern rarity into the global consciousness (FIGURE 7). Hokusai's influence can be seen in the flatness Nara incorporates in his own work, further underscoring the value of Japanese tradition in the pop art landscape *(Yoshitomo Nara, n.d.)*. We see this in Nara's *The Floating World* (1999) (FIGURE 8), where he combines the ukiyo-e aesthetic with his iconic girl figures. Nara and fellow Superflat artists who actively and purposefully integrate Japanese flat images into contemporary art are redefining Japan's modern art landscape. As Vollmer, the author of *Mokuhanga International*, explains, "Ukiyo-e — or flat and pop image — retained a significant link to the past while recreating itself as a vital medium for expressive thought today" *(Vollmer, 2012)*.

Nara uses specific materials to highlight his own lived experiences to evoke feelings of empathy and familiarity. For example, scratch paper drawings on envelopes, flyers, and cardboard stifle feelings of stuffiness or obtuseness for the general public engaging with high art *(Yoshitomo Nara, n.d.)* (FIGURES 9, 10). Despite its casualness and sketchy quality reminiscent of childhood doodles, Nara's work resides at the pinnacle of Japanese contemporary art — his market value is only reinforced by the attention bestowed by museums and galleries worldwide.

Nara's foray into multimedia painting, drawing, three-dimensional wood, FRP, ceramic, and bronze sculptures, and large installations forecasts the future of Japanese contemporary art. His newer paintings and sculptures appear as street murals at the park and the station (FIGURES 11, 12). Like Murakami, Nara governs the market around his work. He trademarked his now iconic girls, which can be found across a range of commercial products, including clothes and books *(Your Dog, n.d.)*. He is a boundary breaker who made art more approachable by breaking new ground in the high art field with warmer and friendlier materials and painting styles.

Nara figures prominently in the Japanese contemporary art world, yet his work often finds itself the target of skepticism from those who harbor biases against pop culture or commercial art. This bias persists throughout design history and has relegated comics and cartoons to the periphery, undermining their value in established institutional discourses. Consequently, some critics may find themselves bewildered by the aesthetics of Nara's distinctive girl paintings, as they defy conventional expectations of traditional fine art.

Nara's paintings reveal a fascinating exchange between fine art and pop culture, drawing viewers in with undeniable relatability and unabashed attitude. Nara emerges as a pivotal figure who showcases ukiyo-e-inspired Superflat aesthetics in contemporary art settings. Nara's work dismantles artificial barriers erected between different art forms, effortlessly bridging high and pop culture. His contribution to design history is marked by championing the inclusion of pop culture, proving that it is a force that deserves attention.

BIBLIOGRAPHY

1. FARAGO, JASON. "How Hokusai's Art Crashed over the Modern World." The New York Times, June 22, 2023. https://www.nytimes.com/2023/06/22/arts/design/hokusai-boston-museum-fine-arts-review.html.

2. IVY, MARILYN. "The Art of Cute Little Things: Nara Yoshitomo's Parapolitics." Mechademia 5 (2010): 3–29. http://www.jstor.org/stable/41510955.

3. LOOSER, THOMAS. "Superflat and the Layers of Image and History in 1990s Japan." Mechademia 1 (2006): 92–109. http://www.jstor.org/stable/41510881.

4. MARINO, NICK. "Yoshitomo Nara Paints What He Hears." The New York Times, July 24, 2020. https://www.nytimes.com/2020/07/24/t-magazine/yoshitomo-nara.html.

5. YOSHITOMO NARA. "Your Dog." 2002. Global Contemporary Art. Not on View. Dimensions: 72 x 51 x 108 in. (182.88 x 129.54 x 274.32 cm). Japanese.

6. VANDERWEIDE, ZOË. "Nara's 'big-Headed Girls' as Unsparing Self Portrait." Sothebys.com, April 9, 2021. https://www.sothebys.com/en/articles/naras-big-headed-girls-as-unsparing-self-portrait.

7. VOLLMER, APRIL. "Mokuhanga International." Art in Print 2, no. 2 (2012): 4–13. http://www.jstor.org/stable/43045387.

8. "Yoshitomo Nara. All My Little Words." The albertina Museum Vienna. Accessed June 26, 2023. https://www.albertina.at/en/albertina-modern/exhibitions/yoshitomo-nara/.

9. "Yoshitomo Nara." Pace Gallery. Accessed June 26, 2023. https://www.pacegallery.com/artists/yoshitomo-nara/.

10. "Yoshitomo Nara: 'My Works' Roots Are in Fairytales, Not Comics'." The Guardian, January 7, 2022. https://www.theguardian.com/artanddesign/2022/jan/07/yoshitomo-nara-my-works-rootsare-in-fairytales-not-comics.

1.

FIGURES

1. Yoshitomo Nara, *TOBIU*, 2019. Credit: Yoshitomo Nara.

2.

3.

2. Yoshitomo Nara, *Through the Break in the Rain*, 2020.
Credit: Yoshitomo Nara.

3. Takashi Murakami, *And Then, And Then, And Then And Then, And Then (Red)*, 1996. PD for educational use.

4.

5.

6.

4. Yoshitomo Nara, *The Girl with the Knife in Her Hand*, 1991. Credit: Yoshitomo Nara.

5. Yoshitomo Nara, *Knife Behind Back*, 2000. Credit: Yoshitomo Nara.

6. Yoshitomo Nara, *The Little Judge*, 2001. Credit: Yoshitomo Nara.

7.

8.

7. Hokusai, *The Great Wave*, 1831. PD, Japanese
copyright expired.

8. Yoshitomo Nara, *No Nukes!*, "In the Floating World",
1999. Credit: Yoshitomo Nara, *Strike for Climate*, 2019.

9.

10.

9. Yoshitomo Nara, *Strike for Climate*, 2019. Credit: Yoshitomo Nara.

10. Yoshitomo Nara, *Bye Bye*, 2019. Credit: Yoshitomo Nara.

11.

12.

11. Yoshitomo Nara, *Traveling Yamako*, 2019. Credit:
Yoshitomo Nara.

12. Yisris (photographer), *A to Z Memorial Dog* by
Yoshitomo Nara, 2006. Creative Commons Attribution
2.0 Generic CC by 2.0.

13.

14.

13. Yoshitomo Nara, *Stop the Bombs*, 2019.
Credit: Yoshitomo Nara.

14. Yoshitomo Nara, *No War*, 2019.
Credit: Yoshitomo Nara.

Beyond the Brush: Exploring the Evolution of Korean Typography

China's strong political and cultural influence in the East manifested in the development of writing systems throughout Asia. In fact, Korean writing systems and calligraphic techniques were heavily influenced by China. Koreans adopted the Chinese character, Hanja, from the 2nd century BCE to make exchange between governments more seamless (Sejong Taewang Kinyom Saophoe, 1970). However, the dissonance between the Korean writing system and the phonetics of the Korean spoken language created a division for those seeking to be literate. The general population struggled while educated elites succeeded. To promote widespread literacy, nationalism, and independence from China during the 15th-century Joseon dynasty, King Sejong led a project to create a new writing system, Hangul (Tips, 2020).

Influenced by China's adoption of the calligraphic brush, King Sejong encouraged a new printing device, which is believed to have driven the current style of Korean typography. This essay examines the emergence of Hangul and its modern typographic variations. With the rise in popularity of Korean culture and typography, the context and its history should be recognized.

The Korean Hangul alphabet represented upward mobility for the Korean people, symbolizing a path toward literacy and education. From a multitude of iterations — including Hunmin Chong Um and Idu, which were alphabets inspired by Chinese ideographs — some 50,000 Hanja characters were reduced to just 24 Hangul letters that include 14 consonants and 10 vowels. The alphabet drew attention for its remarkably innovative and scientific design decisions (Sejong Taewang Kinyom Saophoe, 1970) (FIGURE 1). The design of the alphabet follows a system inspired by the human body and nature to encourage easy adoption and comprehension. Consonants are simplified organs of speech produced by combinations of the tongue touching the palate, the shape of the mouth, the teeth, and the form of the throat. The vowels fall into one of three groups — heaven, earth, and man — with combinations of the principle of duality (yin and yang), the five elements (wood, fire, earth, metal, water), the musical scales, and Confucianism (Cawley, 2021).

Confucianist ideas are built on a collectivist mindset. Confucianist ideals are universally recognized and drive social standards throughout Korean culture, regardless of any individual religious affiliation. As it related to typography, Hangul was heavily influenced by Chinese Confucianism (FIGURE 2). The straightforward and logical principles in the Korean alphabet and typography manifest as visually harmonious and simplified forms. The logic of this system is visible, with characters appearing "stacked in character blocks with 2–5 characters" per set (Cawley, 2021). Efforts to simplify the organs of speech meant Hangul was sans serif, and the arms of the vowels were expressed as dots. Serifs informed by traditional calligraphy and stone chiseling were also available. That early Hangul alphabets carried both serif and sans serif characters was actually a radical advancement for Korean typography. Serif or sans serif forms distinguish Korean typography from any neighboring language, giving it an unrivaled timelessness.

King Sejong wanted more than just universal literacy and education for Koreans — he also promoted Korean literature, art, and science to national and international audiences. With a growing literate population in Korea, Sejong envisioned a system that allowed mass communication quickly. He enlisted the local type foundry to improve the metallic type in order to print books for mass distribution. Laypeople planted papyrus to meet Sejong's demand for mulberry paper, military families switched to civil careers, and artisans cast new types for the foundry. Through a collaboration between mathematicians and Jade Hall Palace of Scholars, Yi Ch On tightened the type sets and created the world's first movable bronze metal printing device. The new printer doubled the production capacity and eliminated the zig-zagging printing patterns seen in less sophisticated machines (Cawley, 2021).

The influence of technology on the development of Hangul can be traced from its calligraphy origins to modern-day printing machines. As 20th-century Korean culture draws universal mass appeal across the East and the West through pop phenomena like K-pop music, the cosmetic industry, fashion, and film — Hallyu has established a rightful position in mainstream consciousness (Adams, 2022).[1] With the growth and globalization of Korean culture, more Western influence can be seen. As the Hallyu movement became even more mainstream, it ushered in new Korean slang, fashion, art, and typefaces. Rather than Korean typography becoming Westernized, it seems to have taken a similar trend to the early stages of Hangul typography. The Hallyu movement brought out two trends in Korean typography: an exaggerated reinterpretation of calligraphy serifs and a contemporary "modular form" of sans serif (Fu, 2020). Standard Korean typography comprises thick, bold lines inspired by the Confucian principle of strength and solidity; modern Korean typography suggests Western influence, manifesting as progressive, flexible forms.

Contemporary Korean typography embraces the original systems of Hangul with a spirit of experimentation. Read left to right; newer typefaces challenge Hangul's traditionally stacked structure and purposeful spacing. The elements of calligraphy and linear strokes remain, but the target audience shifted from Korean traditionalists to Western admirers (FIGURES 3-8). The typography is hardly legible and viewed as a compositional ornament, while it is paired with a secondary language/alphabet

---

1 Hallyu, also known as the Koren Wave, refers to the global mainstreaming of Korean pop culture.

that holds more information. English texts interspersed throughout contemporary Korean posters suggest that the Korean language is designed to amuse and decorate compositions intended for Western readers. In the spirit of King Sejong, modern Korean typography demands attention. More than a tool for mass communication and literacy, it transcends mass media and pop culture today.

BIBLIOGRAPHY

1. ADAMS, TIM. "K-everything:the rise and rise of Korean culture." The Guardian, September 4, 2022. https://www.theguardian.com/world/2022/sep/04/korea-culture-k-pop-music-film-tv-hallyu-v-and-a.

2. "A Guide to Typography with Character." inform.design.calarts.edu. December 2017. Accessed March 12, 2023. https://inform.design.calarts.edu/2017/12/a-guide-to-typography-with-character/.

3. CAWLEY, KEVIN N. "Korean Confucianism." Stanford Encyclopedia of Philosophy. Stanford University, November 24, 2021. https://plato.stanford.edu/entries/korean-confucianism/.

4. FU, FLORENCE. "This Just in: Contemporary Design of South Korea." Letterform Archive, September 14, 2020. https://letterformarchive.org/news/contemporary-design-of-south-korea/.

5. SEJONG TAEWANG KINYM SAPHOE. King Seijong the Great: A Biography of Korea's Most Famous King. King Seijong Memorial Society, 1970. Original from the University of Michigan. Digitized Sep 10, 2008. 194 pages.

7. TIPS, DIANA LPUNEANU. "A Quick Guide to Hangul, the Korean Alphabet - Pronunciation and Rules." Mondly Blog, October 7, 2020. https://www.mondly.com/blog/hangul-korean-alphabet-pronunciation/.

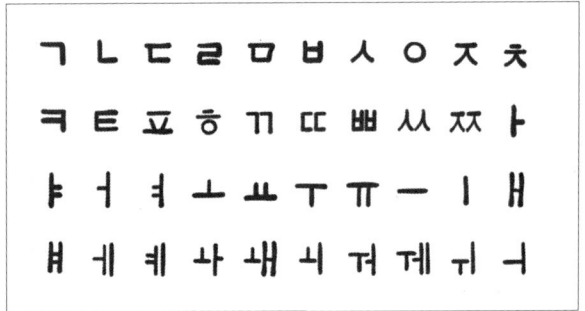

1.

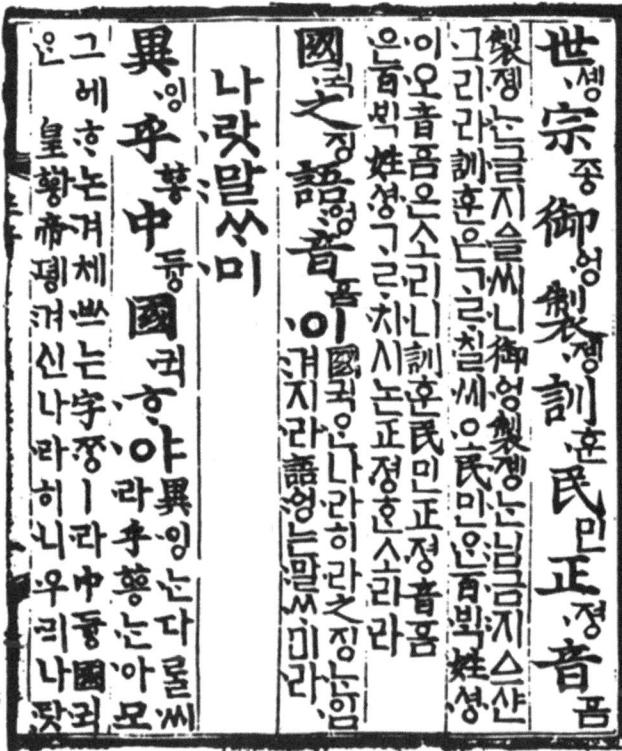

2.

FIGURES

1. Hanguel Chart. Source: Wikimedia, Creative Commons Attribution-Share Alike 4.0.

2. Khukuklub, *Hunminjeongeum1*. Source: Wikimedia, Creative Commons Attribution-Share Alike 3.0 Unported.

3.

4.

5.

6.

3. An Mano, *Breakdown*, posters for Jeonju International Film Festival, 2019. Credit: An Mano.

4. Jaeho Shin, *Junha's Planet*, Jeonju International Film Festival, 2019. Credit: Jaeho Shin.

5. An Mano, *Spring is Coming*, 2019. Credit: An Mano.

6. DDBBMM, *Noryang Battle*, 2019. Credit: DDBBMM.

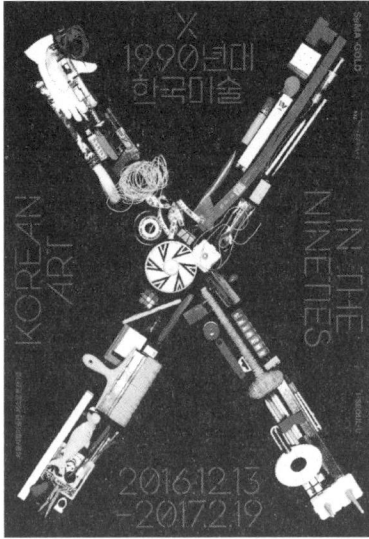

7.

8.

9.

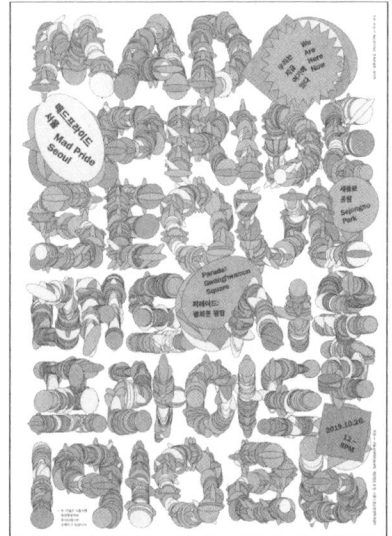

10.

7. Everyday Practice, *Korean Art in the Nineties*, 2019. Credit: Everyday Practice.

8. Sera Yong, *We Want Soul*, 2012. Credit: Sera Yong.

9. Sera Yong, *East Village NY*, 2018. Credit: Sera Yong.

10. Eunjoo Hong and Hyungjae Kim, *Mad Pride Seoul* posters, 2019. Credit: Eunjoo Hong and Hyungjae Kim.

APPRECIATION v. APPROPRIATION

The question of authenticity comes into sharp focus
when original forms and philosophies cross cultural
boundaries and adopt new meanings and materialities.
This chapter highlights the issue of cultural appropriation.
The designs included here became glamorized for mass-
market consumption, creating ambiguity around cultural
admiration, which led to instances of fetishization
and discrimination. In this labyrinthine landscape,
the question of appropriation v. appreciation arises.
To distinguish between the two, fostering awareness
and respectful exploration that goes beyond superficial
curiosity is necessary.

Chinese Arts
in a Western Frame

In the 1st century BCE, ancient Romans wore silks exported from China through overland trade routes. The Silk Road (Figure 1) flourished until maritime trade replaced land routes in the 16th and 17th centuries. Merchants continued to import silk from east to west while demands for porcelain, tea, spices, and lacquerware grew exponentially across Europe. Since then, the eastern and western hemispheres have operated as economic and cultural co-dependents. Buddhist ideology spread to the West, while people in the East encountered the gospels in churches, hearing the teachings of God. Two distinct cultures initiated a lengthy period of mutual appreciation and integration, which had a widespread impact on all cultural sectors. This essay analyzes the influence of Eastern art on Western art and highlights the challenges associated with integrating Western art with Chinese art.

By the 1st century CE, British and Spanish merchants, diplomats, and travelers brought treasures to the East. They traded for porcelains, lacquerware, silks in China, and spices in Southeast Asia. The Chinese commodities held such value and quickly pervaded aesthetic culture across Europe. François Boucher's 1739 painting *Le Déjeuner* (FIGURE 2), showcases blue and white teacups, tableware, and ebony tables used by the host believed to be imported from China. Entrepreneurs in the West tried to mimic Chinese porcelains (FIGURES 3, 4) but failed. Europe lacked the essential mineral, kaolin, a unique soil capable of withstanding high temperatures and achieving a translucent, glass-like effect. It was only when the French Jesuit François Xavier d'Entrecolles discovered the art of making porcelain that Europeans gained sufficient knowledge in this craft. Before his discovery, the quality and craftsmanship of Chinese replica porcelain lagged behind the original.

The Chinese impact extended to Chinoiserie, influencing interior design, furniture, pottery, textiles, and garden design. Rococo designers of the 18th century crafted a mysterious and exotic Asian style inspired by their perceptions of the East. They incorporated imitations and adaptations of Chinese, Southeast Asian, Japanese, and Indian styles, integrating oriental patterns and ornaments into various objects. For example, a Japanese pinewood cabinet decorated with Chinese landscapes and figures, designed by John Linnell and made by William Linnell, showcases this fusion of styles (FIGURE 5). Noteworthy examples of Chinoiserie also include an overmantel and a wall bracket designed by Thomas Chippendale (FIGURE 6), as well as Catherine the Great's Chinese Palace (FIGURE 7). Critics called the Chinoiserie style irrational and claimed its aesthetic motifs distorted authentic Chinese art and architecture. Nonetheless, it experienced a period of popularity until the 18th century and the first Opium War, after which China implemented a closed-door policy and ceased foreign trade. Chinoiserie became a thing of the past and gradually disappeared from view.

Domestically, China experienced years of war and chaos throughout the 18th century, destabilizing its political, economic, and cultural identity. To restore and recover, China relinquished historic traditions in place of new schools of thought modeled in the West. After the 1911 Revolution and under the leadership of Kang Youwei, Chinese art followed suit, embarking on a process of Westernization. As traditional Chinese art declined, Chinese artists contemplated styles beyond the familiar Eastern references and themes, integrating Western ideas, resulting in a strange new hybrid aesthetic. University of Chicago professor and a prolific historian of Chinese art, Wu Hung, argues, "All the concepts we use to study Chinese art are derived from Western art history [...] In China, there were, of course, traditional discourses on art, even from as early as the ninth century. But they only dealt with calligraphy and painting. Sculpture and architecture were not considered art. So it was a very narrow art history" (Hung, 2019). Preserving authentic Chinese qualities while gaining acceptance in Western art to establish a distinctive Chinese art system remains a crucial direction for contemporary Chinese artists.

Contemporary society is built on exchange and defined by globalization. However, dominance exists. The West drives aesthetic standards, defining a universal language of what is valuable and appreciated in the art world. Although Asian aesthetics indeed influenced Western culture for thousands of years, Asian art is consistently devalued in Western art historical discourses. Instead, Asian arts evoke a sense of exoticism and are excluded from mainstream art for non-Asian viewers. In contrast to Western art, David Clarke argues, "Rather than forcing a reorganization of the system of conceptual pigeonholes, Asian contemporary art may still be placed as a further temporary novelty for Western palates or viewed as comforting evidence that the non-Western world is becoming more like the West, is learning to speak its (artistic) language" (Michel-Schertges, 2019). Among all Asian arts, the public's knowledge of Chinese art is even less than Japan, for example. This dominance persists in the widely circulated US-American college art textbook Art Through the Ages, where the author provides zero introductions to Chinese arts in the eight versions of the textbook to date. Only in the ninth version does Chinese arts eventually have their only little chapter. Simply including Chinese art in the historical narrative would provide enormous benefits toward acknowledging its vast impact.

Like many artists from non-Western countries, Chinese artists confront a culture of othering and alienation. Artists Cai Yixuan and Wu Yue share that "the identity of Chinese contemporary artists will bring them some opportunities in Western society, but it will also become a label that traps them, making their works racialized and niche to viewers" *(Conversazione, 2020)*. The "Chinese" label, in fact, exacerbates their "otherness." Adding to this paradox, the Chinese style has been overused across select international markets, reducing authentic references into to mere symbolic commodities. Too often, designers and artists superficially use the banner of a Chinese style to incorporate "exotic" elements: Dior's cultural appropriation of Mannequin, a centuries-old Chinese skirt (FIGURE 8); Dolce and Gabbana's naive celebration of Chinese New Year with exaggerated Chinese cliches that elicited racist backlash (FIGURE 9). When Western designers shallowly incorporate Eastern elements into their work, and those outcomes are evaluated within Western frameworks and by Western standards, viewers are left with an ill-informed impression of Chinese art that reflects a content creator's naive and generalist perspective.

Eastern and Western art have complemented each other for centuries. Integration and exchange are a byproduct of globalization — when two separate and distinct art forms come together, a prolonged period of acclimatization is inevitable. As more Eastern artists emerge and seek recognition in the Western world, they face a considerable journey ahead in de-othering non-Western art.

BIBLIOGRAPHY

1. AMES, VAN METER. "Aesthetic Values in the East and West." The Journal of Aesthetics and Art Criticism, vol. 19, no. 1, 1960, pp. 3–16. JSTOR, https://doi.org/10.2307/427407. Accessed 12 Oct. 2023.

2. "Asian Americans Then and Now." Asia Society, asiasociety.org/education/asian-americans-then-and-now. Accessed 11 Oct. 2023.

3. CARTER, CURTIS L. "Globalization and Chinese Contemporary Art: West … - Marquette

4. CHUMLEY, LILY. "Seeing Strange: Chinese Aesthetics in a Foreign World." Anthropological Quarterly, vol. 89, no. 1, 2016, pp. 93–122. JSTOR, http://www.jstor.org/stable/43955516. Accessed 12 Oct. 2023.

5. Conversazione. "The Dilemma of Chinese Contemporary Art: CVSZ Issue 39." Medium, Medium, 25 Sept. 2020, cvsz.medium.com/the-dilemma-of-chinese-contemporary-art-cvsz-issue-39-98d65fb3fc9

6. HUNG, WU. "Wu Hung Explains How Western Concepts Have Drastically Shaped the History of Chinese Art." Artnet News. April 25, 2019.

7. MICHEL-SCHERTGES, DIRK. "Contemporary Asian Art and Western Societies: Cultural 'Universalism' or 'Uniqueness' in Asian Modern Art - Asian Journal of German and European Studies." SpringerOpen, Springer Singapore, 30 Oct. 2019, ajges.springeropen.com/articles/10.1186/s40856-019-0042-4.

8. POHL, KARL-HEINZ. "Chinese and Western Aesthetics Some Comparative Considerations - Uni Trier." "Chinese and Western Aesthetics — Some Comparative Considerations," Trier University, Germany, www.uni-trier.de/fileadmin/fb2/SIN/Pohl_Publikation/Chinese_and_Western_Aesthetics_E.pdf. Accessed 12 Oct. 2023.

1.

2.

FIGURES

1. Abraham Cresques, *"Caravane sur la Route de la soie,"* Catalan Atlas, 1375. Source: Wikimedia, PD, US/EU copyright expired.

2. Francois Boucher, *Le déjeuner*, 1739. Source: Wikimedia, PD, US/EU copyright expired.

3.

4.

3. Jean-Claude-Thomas Duplessis, *Covered tureen and underplate*, 1754-1755. Credit: Minneapolis Institute of Art.

4. *Chinese dish for the European market*, late 17th century. Credit: The Metropolitan Museum of Art.

5.

6.

7.

5. William Linnell, *Standing Shelf*, 1753-54. Credit: The Metropolitan Museum of Art.

6. Thomas Chippendale, *Chinese Sofa*, 1754. Source: Wikimedia, Creative Commons CC0 1.0 Universal Public Domain Dedication.

7. *Oranienbaum*, Chinese Room, 18th century. Source: Wikimedia, Creative Commons Attribution 4.0 International.

8.

9.

8. Dior, *Flared wool skirt*, 2022. Source: YouTube video screenshot, AvenueX, "Dior and Its Cultural Appropriation of Chinese Ma Mian Skirt," fair use for educational use.

9. Dolce & Gabbana, *DG Loves China promotional video*, 2018. Source: YouTube video screenshot, DW News, "Dolce & Gabbana under fire over racism accusations," fair use for educational use.

RHEA JAUHAR

Reclaiming India's Design Identity

The term graphic design originated in 1922 when book designer William Addison Dwiggins' used it in his essay "New Kind of Printing Calls for New Design." Although Dwiggins is often credited with introducing graphic design, design history existed 38,000 years ago, when cave paintings and glyphs captured stories documenting lived experiences. Even though graphic design is integral to world history, the narrative of graphic design history reflects only a small part of its long and lasting impact, one that historically prioritized Europe and the United States of America above all else.

Researching the history of Indian graphic design presented one roadblock after another, as it's been hindered by a lack of extensive documentation. However, Indian art boasts a deep-rooted heritage dating back to the Vedic period (1500 BCE), characterized by its religious, spiritual, and mythological significance. Painting, architecture, fashion, and sculpture transcended global consciousness through a rich visual culture encompassing iconic spaces and objects, including the Taj Mahal, South Indian Temples, paisley pattern designs, block printing, religious art, and traditional henna design.

Despite this rich design legacy, the scarcity of historical records has left India's design identity somewhat undefined and unclaimed, limiting opportunities for cultural appreciation while inadvertently fostering paths toward cultural appropriation. Numerous Indian design traditions, concepts, and techniques have gained global popularity. They are embraced in high and pop art settings, including fashion, interior design, architecture, typography, and graphic design. However, drawing a clear line between cultural appreciation and appropriation can be complex and ambiguous. It is essential to recognize India's authentic cultural heritage, transcending the world's artistic and design landscape to the point of ubiquity. As these cultural elements continue to find widespread acceptance, preserving their integrity and acknowledging their origins to protect against potential vulnerabilities to cultural appropriation is vital.

WHERE IT ALL BEGAN

India's design history is a rich tapestry dating back over 7,000 years, evident in cave carvings and paintings that served as early examples of artistic expression. Notably, the Bhimbetka petroglyphs in Central India significantly introduced art and sculpture to the Indus Valley and Mughal Empires. However, with the advent of British colonial rule, European attitudes began to influence and ultimately dominate Indian art. However, with the advent of British colonial rule, European attitudes began to influence and ultimately dominate Indian art.

In 1947, India gained its independence from Great Britain and faced the grueling task of rebuilding their nation from the ground up. The government was eager to restore and renew the country's culture, traditions, education, and economy. This period of industrialization also paralleled the increased need for design. In 1957, the Indian government requested that internationally celebrated designers Charles and Ray Eames visit India to help the country define a system for design education. The Eames visit resulted in The India Report, a founding pedagogy that led to the establishment of the Bauhaus-inspired National Design Institute in 1961.

This pivotal moment in India's history marked the country's embrace of design and design education, ushering in a new era of creativity and innovation. Knowing that for the past sixty years, India legitimized its own design narrative through an institutional discourse raises curiosity about how iconic elements of its visual history are perceived both internally and by a non-Indian audience. This essay focuses on two key areas where appropriation has subsumed iconic Indian forms into a larger global dialogue. Examining the formal and conceptual origins of prints and patterns and religion and mythology is an important step in building India's design identity.

PRINTS AND PATTERNS

Paisley and block printing are two of the most widely used and widely appropriated Indian prints and patterns, deeply ingrained in India's design history. These designs appear across a range of visual applications, from fashion to interior design, ornamenting apparel, accessories, furniture, home linens, and more.

The paisley pattern, resembling a teardrop shape, originated in Kashmir, where it was known as "kalga" or "kalanga." While its shape has Persian origins, the paisley pattern holds significant symbolism in Hinduism, representing fertility. It is prominently used in depictions of Indian royalty and Hindu deities. Its popularity spread from Kashmir to Europe, where it gained its modern name from the Scottish city of Paisley. Art Nouveau designers appreciated paisley for its ornamental characteristics, and soon, paisley became associated with hippie culture, rebellion, counterculture, and psychedelia — straying far from its religious origin. Influential figures, including Oscar Wilde, The Beatles, The Rolling Stones, and Jimi Hendrix, wore paisley patterns to express their association with a "bohemian" counterculture. Companies including Vera Bradley, Ralph Lauren, and Tommy Hilfiger embellish bags, clothing items, and accessories with a seeming naivete toward the historical connotations. These examples of appropriation underscore the need to acknowledge paisley's Indian origin and religious significance.

Block printing, a concept likewise seemingly divorced from its originating context, originated in Jaipur, as a method for creating textiles in fashion and interior design. This traditional technique involves using hand-carved wooden blocks as stamps to print exquisite textiles with natural dyes. Marginalized communities in India predominantly uphold this practice, passing it down through generations and relying on it to support their livelihoods.

However, the rise of mass production allows large multinational companies to use techniques on an industrial scale. Exact block printing designs are copied and sold without providing any credit to its Indian creators. Fashion labels such as Louis Vuitton, Zara, and Christian Dior face criticism for using traditional Indian block-printed patterns without acknowledgment. Most recently, Dior plagiarized block printing designs from People Tree, a small art collective in Rajasthan, devaluing the original work, negatively impacting the livelihoods of local artisans, and marginalizing women and children who make up the collective. While People Tree creates garments to sell at fair prices, it can't compete with the scale of Dior's brand recognition or manufacturing operations. When Dior appropriated People Tree's aesthetics for their luxury-priced Dior label, the People Tree collective realized the shortfall.

It is imperative to recognize the efforts of local and marginalized Indian artists and designers who skillfully create designs, patterns, prints, and fabrics using the ancient Indian block printing process and techniques of Jaipur. India's prints and patterns have had a profound influence and impact on design, fashion, and textile industries worldwide. They deserve respect and recognition for their rich history and cultural significance to Indians.

RELIGION AND MYTHOLOGY

The appropriation of Hindu religion, mythology, and Indian culture pervades global trends. It manifests in pop culture, fashion, graphic and product design, corporate branding, advertising, accessories, and tattoos depicting Hindu deities and religious symbols such as Om and the lotus flower.

Religion and mythology profoundly influence distinct aspects of Indian visual culture. The visualizations of deities and religious symbols significantly shaped India's design history. However, when outsiders incorporate religious relics in their work, they often lack an understanding of the history and significance behind these visuals. For example, Jimi Hendrix's 1967 *Axis: Bold as Love* album cover replaced the head of a Hindu deity from a historical, devotional Indian painting — Lord Vishnu, the protector, destroyer and regenerator of the universe and all life — with that of his own. Given its association with psychedelia and proximity to counterculture, the album cover design detracts from and disrespects the Hindu religion. More recently, Reebok used a depiction of Durga — the goddess of war and strength — in a collaborative advertisement with rapper Cardi B. The advertisement portrays Cardi B as Durga, with her many arms, dressed provocatively, and holding a Reebok sneaker. Although the advertisement may have had good intentions, Reebok's brand suffered backlash for its insensitivity toward the Hindu religion.

In Hinduism, wearing shoes and not covering one's head and shoulders when in the presence of deities is considered disrespectful. Yet, consumer-oriented companies continue to cross this line. American Eagle sells "Ganesha Sandals." Urban Outfitters sells socks with the Hindu Lord Ganesha printed on them. While Ganesha is deified for many important cultural contributions, such as being the remover of obstacles, the deva (supernatural being) of wisdom and intelligence, and a patron of arts and sciences, cladding American Eagle or Urban Outfitters hipsters is not one of them. With the rise of yoga culture in the West, thoughtfully designed religious symbols like Aum (Om) and the lotus are widely appropriated in many different forms without consideration of their history and cultural meaning and value.

Further exploration of cultural appropriation reveals the significant impact historical Indian design has had on multiple design histories and industries worldwide. Additional examples of popular focal points of cultural appropriation of Indian design involve using traditions such as bindis and henna across pop culture.

Design, as a form of visual expression and communication, is deeply intertwined with the history of a culture, its social fabric, its politics…its personality. A more inclusive design history culture can better reflect unique cultural identities that have been otherwise dominated by external forces. India's diverse landscape, encompassing various languages, cultures, religions, and traditions, coupled with the lasting impact of European influence from British colonization, presents challenges in constructing a unified design identity, mainly due to the absence of comprehensive documentation of its design evolution.

A comprehensive exploration of the history of art in India, coupled with an examination of contemporary artifacts derived from Indian culture, can provide valuable insights into the country's rich and diverse design history. By delving into the artistic legacy of India, dating back thousands of years, we can uncover the influences, techniques, and aesthetics that have shaped the nation's design identity and appreciate its impact on contemporary culture at large.

BIBLIOGRAPHY

1. ARYA, RINA. "Cultural Appropriation: Analysing the Use of Hindu Symbols within Consumerism." Https://Blogs.lse.ac.uk/, London School of Economics, 7 Sept. 2017, blogs.lse.ac.uk/south-asia/2017/09/07/cultural-appropriation-analysing-the-use-of-hindu- symbols-within-consumerism/.

2. BARKATAKI, SUSSANA. "Om Tattoos & Cultural Appropriation (4 Min Read)." OmStars, 12 Oct. 2020, omstars.com/blog/yoga-philosophy-insight/om-tattoos-cultural-appropriation-4-min-read/.

3. BENAVIDES, DANI. "Cultural Appropriation Defined." NA Eye, 6 May 2020, naeye.net/13082/opinion/cultural-appropriation-defined/.

4. BEUSMAN, CALLIE. "Urban Outfitters, Ever Insensitive, Pulls Offensive Ganesh Socks." Jezebel, Jezebel, 17 Dec. 2013, jezebel.com/1485197751.

5. "A Brief History of Paisley." Elements, 27 Feb. 2019, blog.culturalelements.com/a-brief-history-of-paisley/.

6. CABALLERO, PEDRO. "Eastern Religion in Psychedelic Rock Culture." AR 120 Seeing and Writing, web.colby.edu/ar120/2014/04/24/eastern-religion-in-psychedelic-rock-culture/.

7. COVELL, NOA. "The Beautiful History & Culture Behind Bindi." Jetset Times, 29 Sept. 2020, jetsettimes.com/countries/india/the-history-culture-behind-bindi/.

8. DEVA, SANSKRITI. "The Modern Appropriation and White-Washing of Hinduism." Medium, Medium, 30 July 2020, medium.com/@sanskriti.deva/the-modern-appropriation-and-white-washing-of-hinduism-6566f31dec55.

9. MEHTA, FORAM. "Being Indian Wasn't Cool for Me. Now White People Are Profiting From It." Medium, The Bold Italic, 6 May 2020, thebolditalic.com/being-indian-wasnt-cool-for-me-now-white-people-are-profiting-from-it-c16c7e93853.

10. FARHA, FATIMA. "Why 'Bindis' Should Not Be a Fashion Trend." Niles West News, 22 Apr. 2013, nileswestnews.org/31336/west-word/bindis-are-not-a-fashion-trend/.

11. GUHA, SREYOSHI. "People Tree v. Dior: IP Infringement, Cultural Appropriation or Both?" SpicyIP, 1 Feb. 2018, spicyip.com/2018/02/people-tree-v-dior-ip-infringement-cultural-appropriation-or-both.html.

12. MAVERICKBIRD. "Understanding Cultural Appropriation on My Jaipur Handicrafts Tour." Maverickbird, 25 Aug. 2019, www.maverickbird.com/india/west/rajasthan-india-3/understanding-cultural-appropriation-on-a-jaipur-handicrafts-tour/.

13. OBERLENDER, ISABEL. "Henna: Cultural Appreciation or Cultural Appropriation?" Her Culture, Her Culture, 3 May 2016, www.herculture.org/blog/2016/5/3/henna-cultural-appreciation-or-cultural-appropriation.

14. REGAN, SARAH. "Here's What The Om Symbol Really Means & How To Use It." Mindbodygreen, Mindbodygreen, 15 July 2020, www.mindbodygreen.com/articles/what-does-the-om-symbol-mean.

15. Registry of Sarees. "The Registry of Sarees." The Paisley - an Iconic Motif in India... - The Registry of Sarees, 24 Sept. 2017, www.facebook.com/registryofsarees/posts/the-paisley-an-iconic-motif-in-india-has-deep-rooted-origins-ancient-babylon-in-/173370853239307/.

16. RUSTAGI, SUCHETA. "The Sensible Symbolism of the Lotus Flower in Hinduism and Buddhism." ChakraNews.com, 30 July 2015, www.chakranews.com/the-sensible-symbolism-of-the-lotus-flower-in-hinduism-and-buddhism/5000/.

17. WAHI, ROHINI. "10 Indian Graphic Designers." Design Sponge, www.designsponge.com/2016/06/10-indian-graphic-designers.html.

1.

2.

FIGURES

1. Scotland, *wool and cotton Paisley shawl*, 1860-69.
Credit: The Metropolitan Museum of Art.

2. edvvc (photographer), *John Lennon's 1965 Rolls-Royce Phantom V*, 2004. Source: Wikimedia, Creative Commons Attribution 2.0 Generic.

3.

4.

5.

3. ImGz (photographer), Vera Bradley, *Paisley Pattern Bag*, 2007. Source: Wikimedia, Creative Commons Attribution-Share Alike 3.0 Unported.

4. Sallyboy's Knowledge (photogeapher), *Paisley Bandanna,* 2023. Source: Wikimedia, Creative Commons CC0 1.0 Universal Public Domain Dedication.

5. Jorge Mejía Peralta (photographer), Paisley dress, 2010. Source: Wikimedia, Creative Commons Attribution 2.0 Generic.2010.

6.

7.

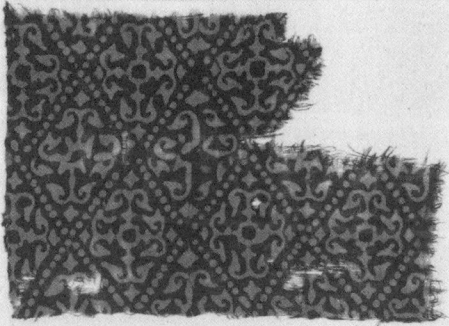

8.

9.

6. Kutch, Gujarat, India, *Carved block for alum paste*, 2016. Credit: The Metropolitan Museum of Art.

7. Eric2753 (photographer), Mohammed Khatri, *Traditional block printing*, 2017. Source: Wikimedia, Creative Commons Attribution-ShareAlike 4.0.

8. Gujarat, India, *Block-printed textile*, 13th-14th century. Credit: The Metropolitan Museum of Art.

9. Guler School, *Goddess Durga*, fighting Mahishasura, the buffalo-demon, early 18th century. Source: Wikimedia, Creative Commons Attribution-ShareAlike 4.0.

10.

11.

13.

14.

12.

10. *Goddess Lakshmi tee shirt*, 2024. Fair use eBay photo.

11. *Tapestry*, Goddess Lakshmi, 2024. Fair use eBay photo.

12. Heidi Klum, *Halloween Party Costume*, Indian Goddess Kali, 2008. Credit: *Page Six*, fair use for educational use.

13. Jivanjor, *Goddess Lakshmi calendar*, 20th century. Fair use eBay photo.

14. Roger Law and Karl Ferris (cover art), The Jimi Hendrix Experience, *Axis: Bold as Love album cover*, 1967. Source: Wikipedia, fair use for educational use.

17.

15.

16.

18.

19.

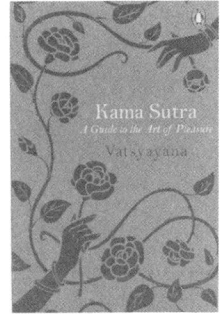

20.

15. Rihanna, *henna-inspired hand tattoo*, 2018. Source: Wikimedia. SIGMA, Vimeo: *Fenty Beauty* by Rihanna, Creative Commons Attribution 3.0 Unported.

16. *Gwen Stefani wearing a bindi*, MTV Music Awards, 1998. Source: Pinterest, fair use for educational use.

17. Vivek Solanki (photographer), *Statuette of Ganesha*, 2022. Credit: Vivek Solanki, Pexels.

18. Studio Kohl, Illustration inspired by Indian block-printing and architecture, 2019. Credit: Studio Kohl.

19, 20. Studio Kohl (Illustrator), *I, Lalla: The Poems of Lal Ded* and *Kama Sutra: A Guide to the Art of Pleasure*, inspired by traditional Indian block-printing, 2011. Credit: Studio Kohl.

Overcoming "Indo-Chic" Fetishization in Henna Artistry

Most people would not recognize the name Lawsonia Inermis. However, the more common name for this is the henna plant. This plant is best suited for dry and hot climates and is primarily found in northern India (Jain, 2020). When the henna plant is ground into a fine paste, it can be applied to the skin to create a stain. This paste is used for Mehndi, also called henna body art. Today, artists from around the world create intricate henna designs that adorn the bodies of their gracious customers. There is no question that henna body art is beautiful and worth celebrating. But, when Western audiences commercialize henna body art as something trendy, questions of cultural appropriation come into focus.

The term "Indo-chic" has been used to describe the way "Indianness" has become a "fashionable mode of representing exoticized cool and commodifiable difference" (Mannur, 2011). Understanding the cultural significance of henna body art and other Indian traditions is essential to counteract the hollow and exploitative nature of the "Indo-chic" market.

In Western society, the word henna is well known because of the recent popularity of henna tattoos. However, the cultural significance and rich history of henna artistry are poorly understood. Jessica Jain studied henna art in Jaipur, the capital of the Rajasthan state in India (Jain, 2020). While reading Jain's manuscript, it becomes clear that henna artists take great pride in their work and have unique styles. Each artist cultivated paste and an application method that they fine-tuned over many years. It is an art form that requires a lot of attention and detail. Jain notes that "the weather conditions as the henna plant [is] growing, the freshness of the leaves or powder used to make the paste [...], the thickness of the skin on which the paste is applied" and many other factors can potentially change the intensity of the henna stain (Jain, 2020). The intensity of the stain is tied to religious practices in India. It is extremely common for brides in India to decorate their arms with Henna before or during the wedding. There is even "a common saying in India that the deeper the stain, the deeper the love between a woman and her husband" (Jain, 2020). This artistry is lost in the "Indo-chic" movement in the West. Commercialized henna becomes less about the thoughtful design process and more about quick fun. Like yoga and other "New Age Orientalism" trends, henna falls into the category of cultural expression that Westerners see as exotic and, therefore, exploitable (Mannur, 2011).

This marketability could potentially be a benefit to Indian artists if racist tropes and stereotypes were not woven into the narrative. Defining "Indo-chic" allows the conversation about this exploitation to occur. Sunaina Maira defines Indo-chic as the mass-marketed "consumption" of "commodified Orientalism." As discussed before, things like bindis, sarees, and henna body art have become very popular in Western fashion and art communities. In her paper, "'What can brown do for you?' Indo chic and the fashionability of South Asian inspired styles," Anita Mannur explains that at the same time "Indianness" is being "exoticized," South Asian people are still being discriminated against, fetishized, and underrepresented (*Mannur, 2011*). South Asian women find themselves caught trying to find a balance between falling into "mainstream exoticization" and finding their "ethnic authenticity" (*Maira, 2002*). This is where the importance of authentic representation comes into play. As Mannur points out, the new generation of South Asian artists have an opportunity to create an "ethical counter-narrative" (*Mannur, 2011*).

This counter-narrative has already started to form. Body art can be incredibly uplifting. We often separate ourselves from our bodies. That is the beauty of Indian body art and decoration. It is an outward expression of identity. In her article "*A Liberating Experience. On Becoming a Work of Art*," Maja Tabea Jerrentrup explains that during body transformation, we "remain in control," which "ensures coherence in the form of self-understanding" (*Jerrentrup, 2020*). The key point here is control over the body. Women in India and around the world do not always have control over their bodies. This is evident when looking at forced marriages that persist in regions of India today. Since henna body art is so integral to marriage ceremonies in India, it is hard to separate it from the history of sexism as well. However, it is important to remember that at its core, henna is a practice that is very focused on women coming together.

A "Ladies' Sangeet" refers to a wedding celebration in North India where "women of the bridal party come together to dance, sing, and have henna applied" (*Jain, 2020*). In this sense, henna is empowering and highlights women supporting each other. This is why, when thinking about the future of henna in popular culture, we must turn to Indian women to point us forward. Young artists are already starting to bring their own voices to this traditional art form. Prabhleen Kaur is a henna artist who understands the traditions of Mehndi inspiration found in modern design (*Sinha, 2022*). Her tattoo style is often minimalist and diverges from the traditional intricacy of henna designs. However, because Kaur understands the history of this art form, she is able to be playful with her creations. When audiences learn design histories and the context for cultural expression, the risk of misusing those art forms becomes less problematic.

The debate between appropriation and appreciation comes down to misrepresentation. Some would argue that although "Indo-chic" can be reductive, it is still moving the art form forward into the modern era. This thinking is flawed because henna has never been stagnant. The designs change based on region, artist, customer, or event. Each design means something to the person wearing it and the people around them. Henna artists have and will continue to develop their craft. The "Indo-chic" movement simplifies henna along with other Indian art and creates something hollow and without meaning. The limited view of Indian art that "Indo-chic" proffers only hinders an audience's exposure to the full breadth of Indian art — making it difficult to fully appreciate its value. Artists like Prabhleen Kaur offer hope that authentic Indian art will be amplified as people shift from mindless consumerism to thoughtful cultural engagement.

BIBLIOGRAPHY

1. JAIN, JESSICA. "Mehandi in the Marketplace." Museum Anthropology Review 14, no. 1-2 (2020): 18–107. https://doi.org/10.14434/mar.v14i1-2.5180.

2. JERRENTRUP, MAJA. "A Liberating Experience. On Becoming a Work of Art" Creativity. Theories — Research - Applications 7, no.2 (2020): 411-430. https://doi.org/10.2478/ctra-2020-0020.

3. MANNUR, ANITA, AND PIAK. SAHNI. 2011. "'What Can Brown Do for You?' Indo Chic and the Fashionability of South Asian Inspired Styles." South Asian Popular Culture 9 (2): 177–90. doi:10.1080/14746689.2011.569069.

4. MAIRA, SUNAINA. "Temporary Tattoos: Indo-Chic Fantasies and Late Capitalist Orientalism." Meridians 3, no. 1 (2002): 134–60. http://www.jstor.org/stable/40338549.

5. SINHA, ARUSHI. "Patterns of Change: Mehendi Artist Prabhleen Kaur Makes a Case for Minimal Designs." Vogue India. Vogue India, March 11, 2022.

1.

FIGURES

1. Unknown photographer, *A bride with traditional henna for her wedding day*, 2016. Source: Wikimedia, Creative Commons Zero.

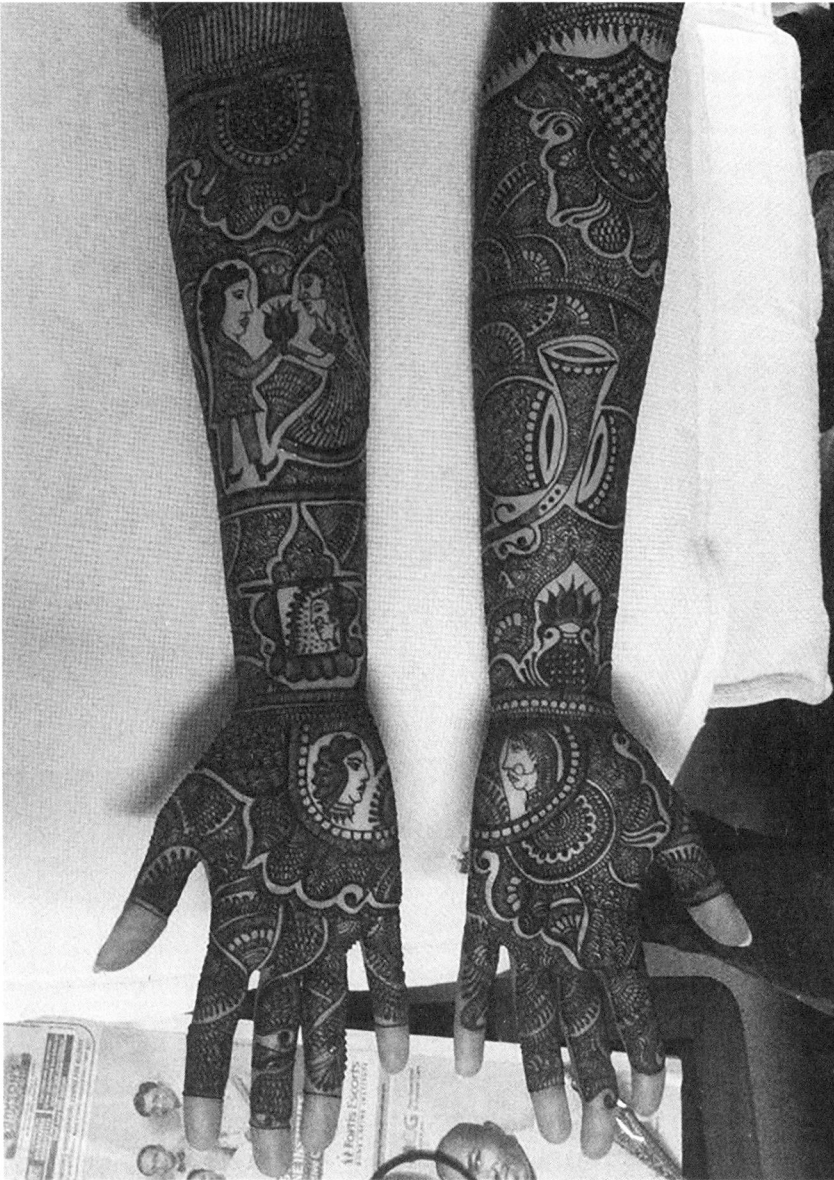

2.

2. Shypoetess (photographer), *A Hindu bride's arms decorated with Henna during the Mehendi Ceremony*, 2015. Source: Wikimedia, Creative Commons Attribution-Share Alike 4.0 International.

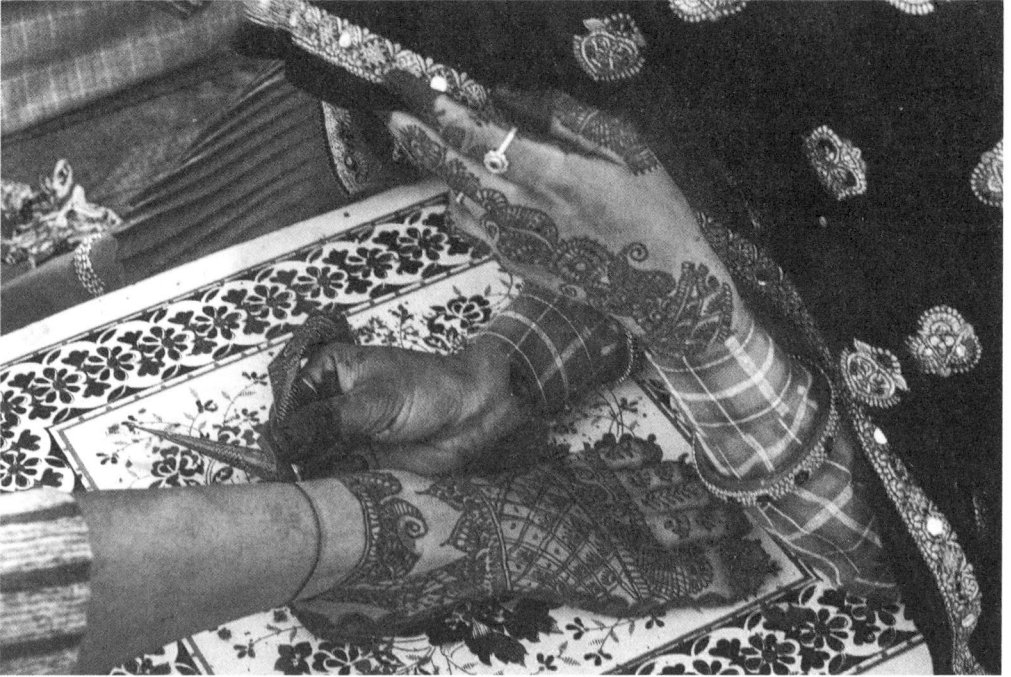

3.

RISA YAMAZAKI

Japonisme and Cultural Appropriation

The West's obsession with Japanese culture and art began when Commodore Perry entered Japan after the ports were forcibly opened for Western trade for the first time in over two hundred years in the late 19th century. The term Japonisme, coined by French art critic Philippe Burty in 1872, describes a wild fascination with Japanese style that coursed through Western consumer markets in the early 1900s (Hass, 2021). While the West attempted to show appreciation towards the impact of Japonisme, the aesthetic has descended into misuse, bordering on disrespect. Over time, the West's fetishization of Japanese aesthetics only deepened the discontent. Today, Japonisme as a style is so divorced from its philosophical origin that it's nothing more than a gross display of cultural appropriation across the consumer market.

Ever since trading opened between Japan and the West, Japanese culture and art have influenced Western aesthetics extensively. In 1837, Émile Hermès, the grandson of Thierry Hermès, incorporated Japanese designs into its brand. Hermès artisans created a leather handbag adorned with Japanese floral motifs carvings (FIGURE 1). Soon after, Hermès sold sandals that were "an innovation that was inspired by geta, the wooden clogs traditionally worn with kimonos" (Hass, 2021). Japonisme continued to influence beyond the art styles, namely the wabi-sabi philosophy, or "the acceptance of imperfection as a kind of perfection of its own" (Hass, 2021). Western expansion proliferated Japonisme across global settings.

In the 1850s, Impressionist painters in Europe observed the "bright colors, odd perspective, flat planes, and off-kilter compositions" seen in Japanese painting, which "ultimately liberated [the Impressionists] from the strictures of hyperrealism" (Hass, 2021). Notable Impressionist painters such as Claude Monet and Vincent van Gogh studied Japanese prints, yet few historians acknowledged the Japanese influence, as impressionists were lauded as two-dimensional geniuses. Van Gogh's move to southern France during his final years was, in fact, a quest to live in an environment more like the Japan he imagined since he had never actually visited the country (Siegal, 2018). Today, it's nearly impossible to parse out the Japanese influence on Impressionist painting which blurs the line between appreciation and appropriation of the Eastern aesthetic.

In 2015, the Museum of Fine Arts Boston (MFA) hosted an event inspired by Claude Monet's painting, *La Japonaise* (Camille Monet in Japanese Costume), that sparked controversy among the public (FIGURE 2). "Kimono Wednesday" invited visitors to try on a replica of the red kimono Camille Claudel wore in the painting. The inspiration for "Kimono Wednesday" came from an earlier exhibition in Tokyo, Kyoto, and the sister museum of the MFA in Nagoya. The exhibition in Japan was successful as the visitors tried on the replica of the red kimono. MFA Deputy Director Katie Getchall saw how successful it was in Japan and wanted to bring the experience to Boston (*Gay, 2015*).

But, in Boston, the event quickly drew outrage, and "Kimono Wednesday" was shut down following public disapproval. Getchell admitted to her and her staffers's surprise at the negative response, noting the event was positioned only as an educational enterprise (*Gay, 2015*). Detractors took issue with how the event was marketed, with an Orientalist mindset exacerbated by a complete relocation of Japanese art and culture. They claimed the event fetishized Orientalism and encouraged an imperialist perspective of the clothing that ultimately positioned Japanese culture as unfamiliar and exotic.

Adding to critique, "Kimono Wednesday" was a reenactment of the experience of a Parisian woman wearing a kimono that was clearly detached from the craftsmanship of kimono makers and the authentic culture behind it. In addition, Claudel is also wearing a blonde wig to highlight her European identity. The combination of a white woman wearing and gathering Japanese things while looking more "Western," felt like an affront, as if Monet himself was mocking Japanese culture. The MFA deprived audiences of the necessary positioning needed to fully honor the contextual origins of the work on view. Rather than celebrating the kimono tradition, it exoticized and commodified a treasured piece of Japanese history.

Commodifying symbols of Japanese culture persists throughout history. Art Nouveau painters Jules Chéret and Henri Toulouse-Lautrec used ukiyo-e inspiration to design a typeface (*Takagi, 2013*). The "bamboo font" is a decorative sans serif with calligraphic outlines, designed to feel more "Asian" with single triangular-shaped strokes that make up the character set (*Takagi, 2013*). In "Cycles Clément," Eastern and Western aesthetics collide as the "bamboo font" juxtaposes a woman in the center riding a bicycle (FIGURE 3). The "Amaryllis du Japon" poster shows a European woman wearing a kimono and holding a wagasa, a traditional Japanese umbrella (FIGURE 4). The Eastern and Western fusion lacked appropriate consideration for the Japanese traditions informing the aesthetics.

Japanese exotification is visible even today in contemporary design. Ray Masaki, a Japanese-American graphic designer and educator based in Tokyo, argues that designers must reconsider their design choices, claiming that borrowing and exchange are intertwined, blurring the line between appreciation and appropriation (*Masaki, 2022*). For example, Masaki cites non-native speakers who misuse kanji:

The first thing to note is the misuse of Japanese kanji. 酸音楽 (san ongaku) is a straight translation of 'acid music' and doesn't make sense for native speakers. 酸 (san) is the kanji for 'acid' or something that is sour in flavour, but not a character that represents the slang for the psychedelic drug, LSD. Curiously, doing a Google or DeepL translate of 'acid music' to Japanese outputs the katakana syllabary of アシッド (asiddo myu-jikku) as opposed to the kanji characters used in the design. My guess is that this designer broke up the translation of 'acid' and 'music' to output the three kanji characters of ミュージック to be more visually exotic (Masaki, 2023).

Like the adoption of Japonisme, consumers are not malicious, just naive. But the naivete can be just as dangerous when it impedes authentic cultural traditions, Masaki warns. Acid graphics that use Japanese text decoratively make no sense and only drive stereotypes deeper. Cliches and aesthetic stereotypes that purportedly represent another culture damage the legitimacy of an aesthetic.

Japanese art and culture have continued to impact modern design in expansive ways. Japonisme began with a fascination and appreciation of traditional art and culture. However, the Eurocentric intrigue of Orientalist traditions fetishizes Japanese culture and perpetuates racist cultural stereotypes. Extensive research on aesthetic origins can mitigate these outcomes and help audiences better appreciate styles embedded with cultural value.

BIBLIOGRAPHY

1. "The Art Institute of Chicago." Japanism and the Arts and Crafts Movement | The Art Institute of Chicago. Accessed February 22, 2023. https://archive.artic.edu/apostles-beauty/japanism/.

2. The Art Institute of Chicago. "When I Put My Hands on Your Body." Art Institute of Chicago. https://www.artic.edu/artworks/222004/when-i-put-my-hands-on-your-body.

3. GAY, MALCOLM. "MFA Backs down over Kimono Event in Response to Protests - the Boston Globe." BostonGlobe.com. The Boston Globe, July 7, 2015. https://www.bostonglobe.com/lifestyle/style/2015/07/07/mfa-backs-down-over-kimono-event-response-protests/lv9NHcnpW0lsRE77d9h-vkl/story.html.

4. HASS, NANCY. "How Japonisme Forever Changed the Course of Western Design." The New York Times. The New York Times, February 11, 2021. https://www.nytimes.com/2021/02/11/t-magazine/japonisme-paris-western-design.html.

5. KARATANI, KOJIN, AND SABU KOHSO. "Uses of Aesthetics: After Orientalism." Boundary 2 25, no. 2 (1998): 145–60. https://doi.org/10.2307/303618.

6. MASAKI, RAY. "Broken Japanese: Exploring Exoticisation and Stereotyping in Graphic Design." It's Nice That. Accessed April 3, 2023. https://www.itsnicethat.com/features/broken-japanese-opinion-part-two-creative-industry-170222.

7. PERSON, USERNAME, AND IGNORANCE1. "@ignorance1 On Instagram." Instagram, July 3, 2019. https://www.instagram.com/p/Bc-QRx5h71J/?hl=en.

8. SIEGAL, NINA. "Van Gogh Never Visited Japan, but He Saw It Everywhere." The New York Times. The New York Times, March 26, 2018. https://www.nytimes.com/2018/03/26/arts/design/vincent-van-gogh-japan.html#:~:text=Van%20Gogh%20Never%20Visited%20Japan,Everywhere%20%2D%20The%20New%20York%20Times.

9. TAKAGI, MARIKO. "'Bamboo Fonts' – Cultural Stereotypes Visualised by Display Fonts," 2013. https://www.academia.edu/12422507/_Bamboo_fonts_Cultural_stereotypes_visualised_bY_display_fonts.

1.

2.

1. James Tissot, *Young Women Looking at Japanese Objects, oil painting*, 1969. Source: Wikimedia, PD US/ EU copyright expired.

2. Claude Monet, *La Japonaise (Camille Monet in Japanese Costume)*, 1876. Source: Wikimedia, PD US/EU copyright expired.

3.

4.

3. Anonymous artist, E. Bougard (printer), *Cycles Clement Poster*, 1906. Source: Poster Corner, PD US/EU copyright expired.

4. Anonymous artist, L. Revon (printer), *Amaryllis Du Japon*, 1890-91. Source: Muzeo, PD US/EU copyright expired.

THE BLACK EXPERIENCE

Historically, African American narratives in graphic design were overshadowed, underrepresented, and, consequently, not widely known. This chapter seeks to amplify voices that persisted through centuries-old racism and discrimination. The work here was crafted by Black designers for Black audiences. For these designers, it wasn't just about aesthetics; it was about fostering belonging, unity, positivity, and identity for and within a historically marginalized community. By recognizing this work, we not only celebrate the contributions of Black designers in the Western graphic design narrative but also acknowledge the structural and institutional challenges these designers had to overcome to create such rich visual legacies.

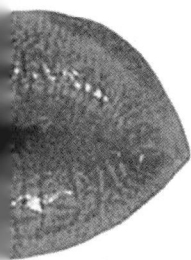

. . . .

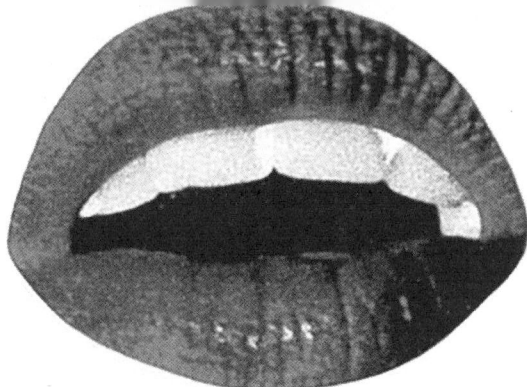

so easy to. . .

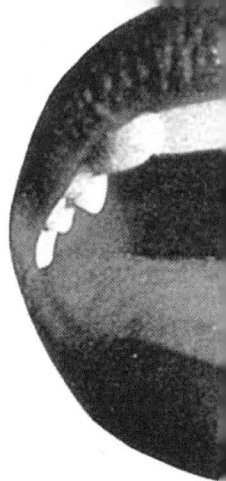

usy. . .

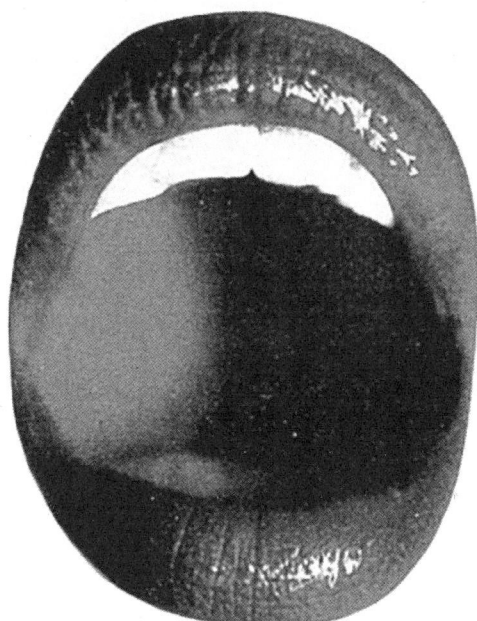

to idolize. . .

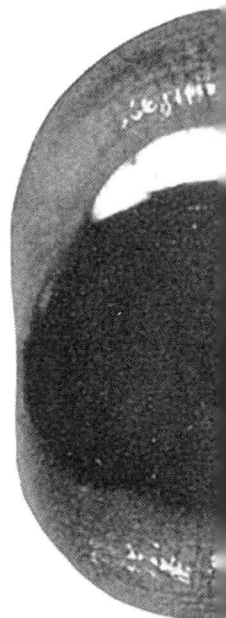

all oth

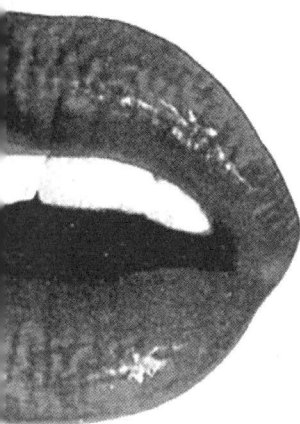

vorth. . .

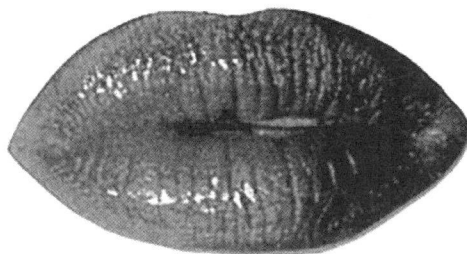

the yearning for. . .

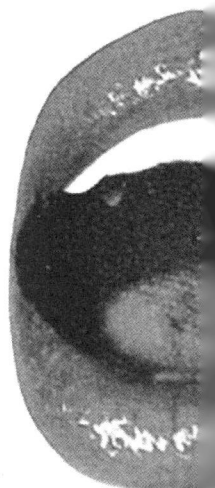

so si

Burt Goldblatt's Iconic Jazz Album Covers

In the 1950s, America experienced the full force of jazz music. This genre grew and evolved, embracing a variety of styles from diverse artists and musicians. The impact of the emergence of jazz can be traced to the present day. Alongside the growth of jazz music, a distinctive style emerged for jazz album covers. Notably, designer and photographer Burt Goldblatt pioneered the cool-jazz style, which became iconic in album covers during the 1950s. Through specific perspectives, collage and montage techniques, and abstracted caricatures, Goldblatt played a defining role in shaping the iconic jazz album cover style.

In the early 19th century, the genre of jazz emerged from a blend of traditional African music, blues, and ragtime. It began as a mode of expression and cultural identity for marginalized communities and gradually expanded to become a global phenomenon, giving rise to various subgenres. With jazz's rising popularity, the necessity for album covers became evident, serving as a way to package and promote the music, particularly with the prominence of LP records and vinyl as the primary distribution method for this new sound.

Eye-catching jazz album cover designs solved a critical marketing challenge. Traditional jazz music was absent of lyrics, which meant the album cover itself had to elicit the music and the album's mood. Album covers transformed from straightforward informational titles into a unique visual style with proven staying power, ultimately becoming synonymous with jazz and jazz culture.

While many designers contributed to this unique jazz aesthetic through album cover designs, Burt Goldblatt stands out as an artist whose prolific design career defined its visual style. After serving in World War II, Goldblatt ventured into the music industry, crafting numerous covers for various jazz musicians. Early on, Goldblatt's style suggested a visual simplicity that simply showcased illustrated musicians as the focal point of his compositions. Later, Goldblatt became more comfortable experimenting with dynamic typography and used typographic rhythm and expression to evoke the music within and, in doing so, forging an aesthetic that came to define his work and that of a timeless cover style (FIGURES 1-4).

Goldblatt continued to adapt stylistically by embracing new mediums and techniques. Goldblatt claimed he "[...] didn't want to get into a bag where everyone who saw a cover of mine would say, 'Oh, that's a Burt Goldblatt cover.' I didn't want that. I wanted a freshness" (Doherty, 2007). While Goldblatt initially depicted musicians with precise lines, he eventually found that using perspective helped capture the dynamism of jazz. FIGURE 5 features a close-up shot of pianist Ralph Sharon, while FIGURE 6 portrays the singer Johnny Hartman cast in a distinctive angle. In both instances, the synergy between imagery and typography directs attention toward the musician and evokes a soothing atmosphere sympathetic to the album's improvisational sounds. The musician appears rhythmic, balanced between typographic harmony and photographic intimacy, allowing the viewer to truly appreciate the artistry of both the design and the music.

Goldblatt established close friendships with all his musical collaborators, and frequent visits to the studio during recording sessions allowed him to immerse himself in their creative process. Not only that, but time spent in studios and night-clubs helped Goldblatt capture people dancing and singing, and these moments of authenticity made their way to his album cover designs (FIGURE 7). Pianist Bud Powell maintained a deep friendship with Goldblatt, eventually commemorating him with a song titled "Burt Covers Bud." Goldblatt's designs surpassed simplistic visual representations of songs by encapsulating his experience of the music, the creator, and the jazz world itself. His connection to the jazz culture helped elevate jazz album designs with renewed energy. Goldblatt's style would ultimately define and become a benchmark for jazz aesthetics at large, and the intimacy that defined his process would be one adopted by designers to come.

Goldblatt's jazz-style album covers represented a paradigm shift in jazz culture and aesthetics, mirroring graphic design's broader evolution. Avant-garde, Absurdism, and Cubism styles can be seen in an album cover for Carmen McRae (FIGURE 11). The choir of lips singing lyrics to the viewer imparts an absurdist quality to the piece. Similarly, in FIGURE 12, musician Mel Torme is depicted through a collage of cars and evokes abstract yet straightforward motifs. Goldblatt covers incorporate similar design elements that resonated with jazz audiences and aesthetics. He effectively conveyed requisite information while also underscoring the potency of visual design within the music industry.

The jazz album cover transformed from a mere marketing tool into an artistic expression that complemented and elevated the musical experience. Goldblatt played a pioneering role in shaping the realm of jazz album aesthetics, revolutionizing how jazz was introduced to audiences. His designs captured the intricacies and essence of jazz, inspiring countless artists and designers. The realm of jazz design remains an intriguing field that hasn't received extensive study, yet it holds valuable insights into the intersection of visual and musical arts. Burt Goldblatt offers a unique vantage point within Western design history and warrants further exploration.

BIBLIOGRAPHY

1. "And All That Jazz: Innovative Album Covers from the 1950s on — in Pictures." The Guardian, April 16, 2021. https://www.theguardian.com/music/gallery/2021/apr/16/jazz-albums-artists-covers-taschen-in-pictures.

2. "Bethlehem Records." Bethlehem Records - jazz album covers. Accessed June 24, 2023. https://birkajazz.se/archive/bethlehem.htm.

3. DOUGHERTY, CARISSA KOWALSKI. "The Coloring of Jazz: Race and Record Cover Design in American Jazz, 1950 to 1970." Design Issues 23, no. 1 (2007): 47–60. http://www.jstor.org/stable/25224088.

4. "The Golden Age of Jazz Covers - Angelynn Grant: Design." angelynn grant | design, July 2, 2018. https://angelynngrant.com/the-golden-age-of-jazz-covers/.

5. HELLER, STEVEN. "Burt Goldblatt, 82, Album Cover Designer, Dies." The New York Times, September 7, 2006. https://www.nytimes.com/2006/09/07/arts/music/07goldblatt.html.

1.

2.

3.

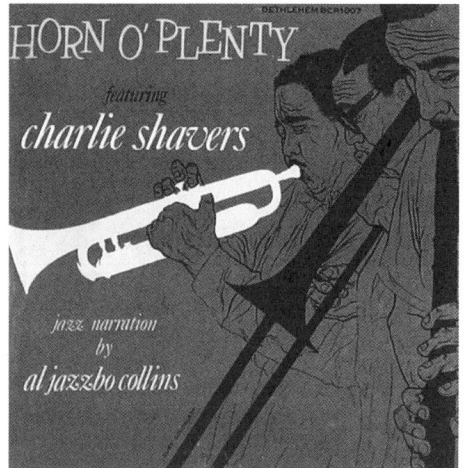

4.

FIGURES

1. Reid Miles, (graphic designer, photographer), (Donald Byrd, *A New Perspective*, 1964. Source: Discogs, fair use for educational use.

2. Jo Grey, (cover art), Cal Tjader, *Along Comes Cal*, 1967. Source: Discogs, fair use for educational use.

3. Unknown designer, *Billie Holiday Volume 3*, 1954. Credit: Dusty Groove, fair use for educational use.

4. Burt Goldblatt (cover art), Charlie Shavers, *Horn O'Plenty*, 1955. Source: Discogs, fair use for educational use.

5.

6.

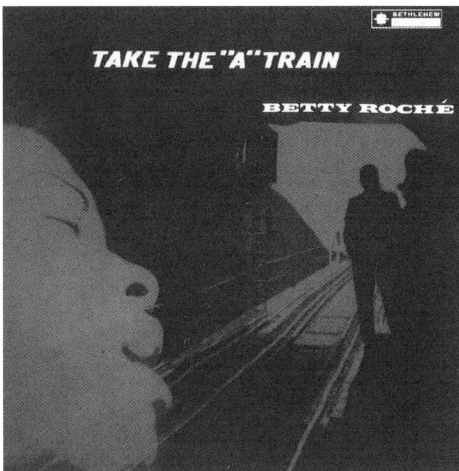

7.

8.

5. Burt Goldblatt, (cover art), Ralph Sharon, *Ralph Sharon Trio*, 1956. Credit: Dusty Groove, fair use for educational use.

6. Burt Goldblatt (designer, photographer), Johnny Harthman, *Songs From The Heart*, 1995. Source: Wikipedia, fair use for educational use.

7. Burt Goldblatt, (cover art), Betty Roché, *Take The "A" Train*, 1956. Fair use for educational use.

8. Robert Guidi (designer), Chris Connor, *Chris*, 1956. Source: eBay photo, fair use for educational use.

9.

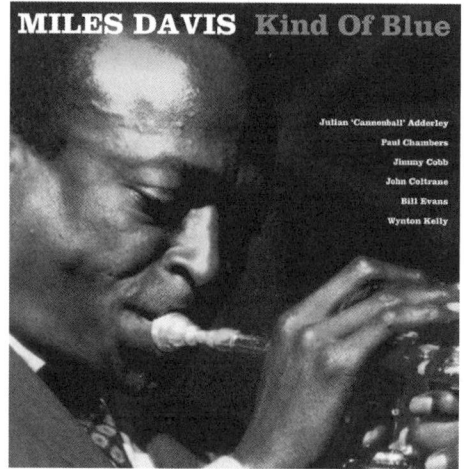

10.

11.

12.

9. David Stone Martin (graphic designer), Bud Powell, *Bud Powell Trio Vol. 2*, 1953. Source: Wikipedia, fair use for educational use.

10. Jay Maisel (photographer), Miles Davis, *Kind of Blue*, 1959. Source: Wikipedia, fair use for educational use.

11. Burt Goldblatt (designer), Carmen McRae, *Carmen McRae*, 1954. Source: Wikipedia, fair use for educational use.

12. Burt Goldblatt (Designer, Dave Pell (photographer), *Mel Tormé, Mel Tormé with The Marty Paich Dek-Tette*, 1956. Source: Discogs, fair use for educational use.

Designing Tomorrow: The Overlooked Impact of Afrofuturism

Yes, "There are black people in the future."

Wormsley's 2017 statement thrust into mainstream culture the concept of Afrofuturism, a vibrant cultural movement boldly reimagining tomorrow through a lens deeply rooted in Black experiences and aspirations.[1] Before Afrofuturism was even a word, musicians leaned into the idea that music could empower Black artists to redefine their narratives and envision themselves as the heroes and innovators of their own stories.

From Sun Ra in the 1960s, Parliament-Funkadelic in the 1970s, and Kendrick Lamar today, Afrofuturism is a potent instrument for expressing resistance, resilience, and empowerment within the Black community. It affirms the presence of and encourages agency in Black individuals to shape the future and firmly establishes Afrofuturism's place in the discourse of Western design history. This research demonstrates how Afrofuturism challenges traditional design narratives, redefines cultural identities, and asserts agency over creative expression through an examination of Afrofuturist pioneers.

The musician Sun Ra began his musical career in the 1950s as a little-known composer and embarked on a lifelong "project to re-envision the relationship between music, technology, society, and African American identity" *(Kreiss, 2012)*. Sun Ra blended avant-garde jazz with ancient Egyptian mythologies and futuristic imagery to challenge traditional narratives within jazz music — a fusion that resituated the Black identity in a universal, cosmic framework transcending earthly constraints. The transformative power of Sun Ra's Afrofuturist vision is visible in rare footage of Arkestra's televised performance on *Saturday Night Live* in 1978 (FIGURE 1). Even in black-and-white, the video radiates a "positively technicolor" vibe, vividly portraying the mesmerizing stage presence of Sun Ra and his ensemble. Through ecstatic dancing, blasting brass, and visually striking cosmic costumes, they create an otherworldly experience that transports viewers to a realm where music, art, and science fiction intersect. Sun Ra's *SNL* appearance introduced Afrofuturist themes in jazz to a mainstream audience, showcasing his innovative approach that incorporated elements of free jazz, modal jazz, and avant-garde experimentation. The footage captures Sun Ra's trailblazing influence and the transformative impact of Afrofuturism as a way

---

1 Coined by Mark Dery in his 1993 essay *Black to the Future*, the term 'Afrofuturist' is a "speculative fiction that intricately weaves African-American themes within the tapestry of twentieth-century technoculture" *(Dery, 1994)*.

to envision individual futures through art by claiming the cosmos as a site for Black creativity and emancipation.

Also, Sun Ra's striking album artwork served as an extension of his revolutionary Afrofuturist philosophy, redefining the visual culture surrounding jazz music. Sun Ra claimed complete creative control over the design process to challenge design industry practices that dictated artistic decisions from the top down. Sun Ra's sense of authorship showed how Afrofuturism empowered Black artists to assert agency over their narratives and cultural expression through an inventive fusion of ancient African symbolism with futuristic Afrofuturist aesthetics. The *Space Is the Place* album artwork transformed Western artistic conventions and notions of identity (FIGURE 2). William Sites notes Ra's use of the prominent *Eye of Horus* symbol "to connect ancient Egyptian culture to the African diaspora and black identity" *(Sites, 2020)* (FIGURE 3).[2] In the *Celestial Love* album artwork, the handmade, DIY nature of the covers reflected Arkestra's shared cosmic vision and collaborative process and infused the work with authenticity as physical manifestations of their collective identity (FIGURE 4). The covers helped listeners grasp the metaphysical, otherworldly qualities of Sun Ra's avant-garde compositions through distinctly analog futurism with handwritten text, collaged elements, cosmic shapes, and vivid colors. The innovative fusion of classical Egyptian iconography with science fiction aesthetics became a visual identity representing the experiences and aspirations of the African diaspora.

George Clinton and his collective Parliament-Funkadelic followed Sun Ra's lead[3]. Inspired by the Afrocentric elements present in Sun Ra's avant-garde jazz, Clinton famously joked that Ra was "definitely out to lunch — the same place I eat," acknowledging the profound influence of Sun Ra's experimentalism on his artistic vision. Clinton's music embraced science fiction imagery, technological metaphors, and interstellar mythology that reimagined Black identity through a cosmic lens. Albums such as *Mothership Connection* and *The Clones of Dr. Funkenstein* wove intricate tales of extraterrestrial funk entities and their cosmic voyages, melding infectious funk rhythms with Afrofuturist narratives (FIGURES 5, 6). This fusion challenged conventional portrayals of Black culture and provided a visionary outlet and imaginative escape for oppressed people. Furthermore, throughout Parliament-Funkadelic's height from 1975 to 1979, their live performances were not mere concerts but immersive experiences that transported audiences to realms of imagination and possibility.

Adorned in what Joshua Bird defined as "the most ornate, outrageous costumes and props imaginable," the band members became conduits of vibrant Afrofuturist mythology, embodying characters that defied traditional boundaries of space and time through their intricate funk grooves and psychedelic sounds *(Bird, 2013)*. Characterized as a "parade of tricksters" moving with the "anti-discipline of funk," they embellished themselves in primal, earthy outfits, alluding to ancestral, pre-colonial African aesthetics. The collective's diverse membership spanned races, genders, and sexualities and embodied a radical vision of inclusion and community that defied

---

2 The Eye of Horus is a concept and symbol in ancient Egyptian religion that represents well-being, healing, and protection.

3 The blend "Parliament-Funkadelic" was a fusion of Clinton's two bands in 1968, Parliament and Funkadelic, into a singular funk ensemble.

the conformity and exclusion often found in Western institutions (FIGURE 7). Parliament-Funkadelic carved out a space for self-expression, individuality, and the reclamation of their freedom through their subversive, gender-bending style. Their primal, earthy style served as a form of resistance against the cultural supremacy of the West, asserting the value and vibrancy of African American identity and creativity.

The female vocal trio Labelle explored the transformative potential of the performing Black body. Akin to Clinton's Parliament and Funkadelic, Labelle utilized the stage to redefine cultural narratives and challenge social norms. Their performances became a transient space for liberation and movement, transcending the boundaries of gender, race, and identity. Francesca T. Royster observed an "interest in the performing Black body as a space and conduit for transformation and movement" (*Royster, 2011*). Furthermore, the group's iconic *Space-Age Amazons* costumes, designed by Michael Vollbracht, were a striking departure from the traditional stage attire of female performers at the time. The costumes — featuring bold, geometric shapes, metallic fabrics, and exaggerated silhouettes that evoked a sense of the extraterrestrial and the divine — questioned the traditional expectations of female performers and offered a more empowered, feminist vision on the stage (FIGURE 8). Labelle's legacy can be seen in later R&B/soul groups such as En Vogue, Destiny's Child, The Pussycat Dolls, and Erykah Badu. As an Afrofuturist, Labelle challenged dominant narratives within the funk genre through bold, futuristic aesthetics and socially conscious messaging.

Artists in the 1990s and 2000s continued exploring the complexities of Black identity and history through Afrofuturist expression. Kendrick Lamar's *All the Stars* music video departs from hip-hop conventions. It blends themes of African mythology, the Middle Passage, and futuristic elements to create a visually stunning and socially conscious statement. The video opens with Lamar standing over a sea of people, evoking a majestic, Moses-like figure guiding the people who suffered the horrific transatlantic slave trade (FIGURE 9). While Lamar's lyrics directly confront issues of oppression, resistance, and the quest for truth, SZA's ethereal presence in the video, singing and dancing in a star-filled galaxy shaped like the African continent, adds to the Afrofuturist narrative (FIGURE 10, 11). Lamar's album artwork from *To Pimp a Butterfly* features himself seated on a throne with chains on his wrists — a juxtaposition of power and bondage that captures the essence of the Afrofuturist exploration of the African American experience (FIGURE 12). The muted grayscale of the image and the regal yet faded thrones suggest the idea of legacy and history that is often neglected or understated in mainstream narratives. Through his music, videos, and album artwork, Lamar infuses the voice of a community grappling with systemic injustice while asserting strength and resilience in a visionary future.

Integrating Afrofuturism into the canon of Western design history offers a more comprehensive understanding of visual culture traditions and enriches our perspectives on present and future design trajectories. My research on Afrofuturism changed my perspective about my Blackness — it is not a limitation but a source of abundant creativity, innovation, and visionary power. The work of Afrofuturist pioneers such as Sun Ra, George Clinton, Labelle, and Kendrick Lamar demonstrates how I, as a Black designer, can exalt my heritage and acknowledge the rhythms and traditions of my ancestors woven into the fabric of tomorrow.

BIBLIOGRAPHY

1. AGHORO, NATHALIE. "Agency in the Afrofuturist Ontologies of Erykah Badu and Janelle Monáe." Open Cultural Studies 2 (November 2018): 330–40. https://doi.org/10.1515/culture-2018-0030.

2. BANERJI, ATREYI. "The Cover Uncovered: The Story behind Miles Davis' Album Cover for 'Bitches Brew' by Malti Klarwein." Far Out Magazine, January 27, 2021. https://faroutmagazine.co.uk/miles-davis-album-bitches-brew-cover-story/.

3. BARNES, LOUIS. "Afrofuturism in Jazz Music." Medium, December 5, 2021. https://jazzvocate.medium.com/afrofuturism-in-jazz-music-72745abe32e9.

4. BIRD, JOSHUA. "Climbing Aboard the Mothership: An Afrofuturistic Reading of Parliament-Funkadelic." Occam's Razor 3, no. 1 (2013): 6. https://cedar.wwu.edu/cgi/viewcontent.cgi?referer=&httpsredir=1&article=1012&context=orwwu.

5. BOON, MARCUS. The Politics of Vibration: Music as a Cosmopolitical Practice. Durham, NC: Duke University Press, 2022. https://www.jstor.org/stable/j.ctv2vr9ct8.7?searchText=kendrick+lamar+afrofuturism&searchUri=%2Faction%2FdoBasicSearch%3FQuery%3Dkendrick%2Blamar%2Bafrofuturism%26so%3Drel&ab_segments=0%2Fbasic_search_gsv2%2Fcontrol&refreqid=fastly-default%3A0fd571947b-71f8a1545a48231346b525&seq=2.

6. BROOKE, DAVID. "Sci-Fi Afro-Futurism OGN 'Jimi Hendrix: Purple Haze' Coming November 2023." AIPT, May 17, 2023. https://aiptcomics.com/2023/05/17/titan-jimi-hendrix-purple-haze/.

7. CHEN, MIN. "Sun Ra's Legendary Album Art—Sometimes Handcrafted, Always Otherworldly—Has Been Compiled Into a Book for the First Time." Artnet News, January 17, 2023. https://news.artnet.com/art-world/sun-ra-art-on-saturn-handmade-album-covers-2243403.

8. DAVID, MARLO D. Mama's Gun: Black Maternal Figures and the Politics of Transgression. Columbus: Ohio State University Press, 2016. https://www.jstor.org/stable/j.ctvqsf2kp.8?searchText=Erykah+Badu&searchUri=%2Faction%2FdoBasicSearch%3FQuery%3DErykah%2BBadu%26so%3Drel&ab_segments=0%2Fbasic_search_gsv2%2Fcontrol&refreqid=fastly-default%3A37b73ec7c25b5f-579d32afc826d3f688&seq=1.

9. DERY, MARK, ed. Flame Wars: The Discourse of Cyberculture. "Black to the Future: Interviews with Samuel R. Delany, Greg Tate, and Tricia Rose." Durham, NC: Duke University Press, 1994.

10. HOSKING, TAYLOR. "'Black Panther' and the Magic of the 'All the Stars' Video." The Atlantic, March 2018. https://www.theatlantic.com/entertainment/archive/2018/03/all-the-stars-kendrick-lamar-sza-video-afrocentrism-afrofuturism/554306/.

11. KREISS, DANIEL. "Performing the Past to Claim the Future: Sun Ra and the Afro-Future Underground, 1954-1968." African American Review 45, no. 1 (2012): 197–203. https://muse.jhu.edu/article/502556/summary.

12. RAMBSY, HOWARD. "Beyond Keeping It Real: OutKast, the Funk Connection, and Afrofuturism." American Studies 52, no. 4 (2013): 205–16. https://www.jstor.org/stable/24589277.

13. ROYSTER, FRANCESCA T. "'Here's a Chance to Dance Our Way out of Our Constrictions': P-Funk's Black Masculinity and the Performance of Imaginative Freedom." Sexing the Colorlines: Black Sexualities, Popular Culture, and Cultural Production 7, no. 2 (2011): 88–115. University of Michigan Press. http://www.jstor.org/stable/10.3998/mpub.1586114.7.

14. SHARP, SARAH Rose. "Artist's Billboard Declaring 'There Are Black People in the Future' Taken Down by Landlord." Hyperallergic, April 9, 2018. https://hyperallergic.com/436763/alisha-wormsley-the-last-billboard-pittsburgh-there-are-black-people-in-the-future/.

15. SITES, WILLIAM. Sun Ra's Chicago Afrofuturism and the City. Historical Studies of Urban America. Chicago: The University of Chicago Press, 2020.

16. WASHINGTON, ANGELA. "Afrofuturism in the Stacks." Metmuseum.org, 2022. https://www.metmuseum.org/perspectives/articles/2022/6/library-afrofuturism.

1.

2.

3.

FIGURES

1. Saturday Night Live, *Sun Ra and his Arkestra*, 1978. Source: YouTube screenshot, fair use for educational use.

2. Chris Hall and Claude Dangerfield (designers), Sun Ra, *Space Is The Place*, album cover, 1973. Source: Wikipedia, fair use for educational use.

3. Egyptian, Eye of Horus, 3rd Century BC. Source: Wikipedia, Creative Commons Attribution-Share Alike Attribution-Share Alike 4.0 International, 3.0 Unported, 2.5 Generic, 2.0 Generic and 1.0 Generic.

4.

5.

6.

4. Sun Ra, *Celestial Love*, record sleeve, 1984. Credit: Sun Ra: Art on Saturn: The Album Cover Art of Sun Ra's Saturn Label, fair use for educational use.

5. Gribbitt (designer), Parliament, *Mothership Connection*, album cover, 1975. Source: Wikipedia, fair use for educational use.

6. Chris Whorf (designer), Parliament, *The Clones of Dr. Funkenstein*, album cover, 1976. Fair use for educational use.

7.

8.

9.

7. *Parliament-Funkadelic performing at Capitol City Carnival*, 2007. Source: Wikimedia, Creative Commons Attribution-Share Alike 2.0 Generic .

8. *Labelle in Afrofuturistic Costume*, 1975. Source: YouTube video screenshot, Top Pop, "Labelle - Lady Marmalade," fair use for educational use.

9. Kendrick Lamar, *All The Stars*, music video, 2018. Source: YouTube video screenshot, Kendrick Lamar, SZA, "Kendrick Lamar, SZA - All The Stars," fair use for educational use.

10.

11.

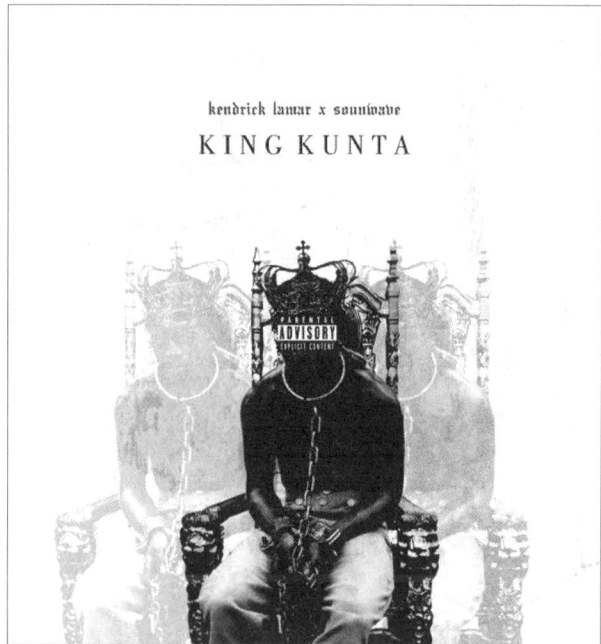

12.

10, 11. Kendrick Lamar, SZA, *All The Stars*, music video, 2018. Source: YouTube video screenshot, "Kendrick Lamar, SZA - All The Stars," fair use for educational use.

12. Kendrick Lamar, *King Kunta* song cover, 2015. Source: Filmaffinity, fair use for educational use.

RAYNE SCHULMAN

Aaron Douglas: African Influence on the Harlem Renaissance

1920s America is remembered as a time of prosperity and freedom, marking a significant shift in the United States' past and future. During the same time period, the Harlem Renaissance emerged as a groundbreaking force in Black culture. Stimulated by The Great Migration — where masses of African Americans moved to the North in search of economic opportunities and to evade racial violence in the South — the Harlem Renaissance represented a prominent and thriving epicenter of Black culture in America (Mitchell, 2010).

The city was "designed to secure the highest available social, economic, and artistic rewards for a generation that moved decisively beyond the horrors of old country districts" *(Baker, 1987)*. An environment where African Americans were uplifted and empowered provided a safe haven for Black writers, musicians, and artists to celebrate their heritage, which resulted in the influential artistic movement known as the Harlem Renaissance. Aaron Douglas, a painter from Topeka, Kansas, quickly became a pivotal artist and leader of the movement and has become known as "the father of Black American Art." He is credited as the first to incorporate iconography of African art into his pieces while integrating it with African American themes and being accepted into the culture *(Davis, 1984)*. Douglas' work has not only directly but powerfully influenced how Black art is portrayed and perceived in the United States — his role as a pioneer should not be overlooked in the Western design canon.

Before the Harlem Renaissance, African American portrayal in art was often reduced to demeaning and stereotypical depictions, such as minstrel shows. Alaine Locke, another prominent figure during the movement, scrutinized that "prejudice had made the Negro half-ashamed of himself, and racial subjects used to be avoided or treated gingerly in soft-pedaled Nordic transcriptions" *(Vechten, 1979)*.[1] The prevailing racism of the time treated African American subjects as ones not worthy of being discussed or severely downplayed from a Eurocentric perspective. Even educated Black Americans, who were taught a white perspective, were unable to look beyond the social precedent of the time, which "led to neglect his own experiential standpoint as a basis for knowledge" *(Thompson, 2000)*. The Black experience was not worth portraying. Douglas, however, wanted to change that. He believed that creating a shift in the perception of Black Americans could open up new opportunities and lead to a

---

1 The term "Negro" was historically used in the United States to refer to people of African descent, especially during the 19th and early 20th centuries. It is now considered outdated and offensive, replaced by terms such as "Black" or "African American."

wider range of social possibilities *(Thompson, 2000)*. Locke and Douglas led this shift, leaning into African art and black American folk culture — an arena untouched by white influence *(Thompson, 2000)*. However, the overall attitude of Douglas' artistic contemporaries was not as positive; they found it difficult to develop an aesthetic that could be both Black and American. Douglas argued that these were not two separate identities, for Black Americans are entitled to the same opportunities and rights as their White counterparts, and they also have important and unique perspectives to contribute to the culture *(Ragar 2008)*.

Stephanie Fox Knappe effectively summarizes Douglas' visual style: "This style comprised boldly flattened silhouettes that occupied complexly fractured spaces overlaid with transparent layers of geometric atmosphere. 'Blackness' — both in terms of his palette and as a conscious evocation of race — was at its core" *(Knappe, 2008)*. The geometric motifs in his work are often interpreted to be inspired by the Cubism art movement, which also found inspiration in African Art. In a series of murals, titled *Aspects of Negro Life: From Slavery to Reconstruction*, Douglas includes all those visual elements. In the last panel in the series **(FIGURE 1)**, Douglas uses concentric circles to draw the viewer's eyes to the highlight of the piece, a saxophone, a staple instrument in blues music (Takac, 2020). Cotton foliage grows on the bottom of his piece, and Art Deco-esque skyscrapers line the background. However, unlike Art Deco artists who used high rises as a symbol of progress, Douglas uses them as a metaphor to symbolize the contributions made by Black Americans to the future of the United States *(Thompson, 2000)*.

Douglas also drew heavy inspiration from Egyptian art, citing it as "ample support to the notion that non-Whites were just as capable as Whites when it came to producing great art" *(Ragar, 2008)*. In the example of a piece in the *Tomb of Nakht* **(FIGURE 2)**, the figures are standing in a composite pose, facing sideways while their shoulders are square to the font. Douglas utilized this technique in a wide array of his works, including the murals in *Aspects of Negro Life*. In "The Negro in African Setting" panel **(FIGURE 3)**, all figures are standing in composite in almost a non-natural way. The "wrong" perspective mimics the style of Egyptian art, but it also acts as a "refusal of the description of reality that those in power take to be obvious or natural or neutral" *(Thompson, 2000)*. Douglas is refusing the standards of a system that has undermined and eroded his community. *God's Trombone*, a series of paintings that Douglas created to accompany the writings of James Weldon Johnson, further highlights his visual style. In one piece **(FIGURE 4)**, a figure stands holding chains among repeated geometric forms that emphasize his strength. The chains entangling the figure are not shackled, signifying a transitional period for African Americans in the United States. The figure draws from African art, like relief sculptures **(FIGURE 5)**, to portray the Afro-centric features of the figure: slanted eyes with a wide nose and lips. The piece, *The Crucifixion* **(FIGURE 6)**, from the series tells a biblical story where Simon becomes the center point rather than Christ. Douglas distinctly uses Afro-centric features as well on Simon, reimagining this biblical story from a Black point of view. He challenges the preconceived racial standard that has been placed in the text and draws the focus to Black participation in biblical stories *(Carroll, 2002)*.

Some deem the Harlem Renaissance a failure — racial disparities persist and People of Color (POC) art still not entirely represented in mainstream media. Douglas acknowledged POC artists' hardships, such as a lack of financial support. There were essentially no Black art collectors who could fund Black artists *(Ragar, 2008)*. However, that is a narrow view of the situation, as Houston Baker writes, "The 'failure' of a movement that in the eyes of white America could never have been a success — precisely because it was Afro-American" *(Baker, 1987)*. The United States is still set in a very Eurocentric perspective, but we have the means to change that. The Harlem Renaissance was never meant to be just a short moment in history; it aimed to mimic the centuries-long influence of the European Renaissance *(Mitchell, 2010)*. Black artists need continued support, and Black art needs continued attention to remain a part of a long cultural continuum. Douglas began the conversation by stating that including art by Black artists in the modern art canon is the key to maintaining a vibrant "African diasporic locus" *(Powell, 2008)*.

BIBLIOGRAPHY

1. BAKER, HOUSTON A. 1987. "Modernism and the Harlem Renaissance." American Quarterly 39, no. 1: 84–97. https://doi.org/10.2307/2712631.

2. CARROLL, ANNE. 2002. "Art, Literature, and the Harlem Renaissance: The Messages of 'God's Trombones.'" College Literature 29, no. 3: 57–82. http://www.jstor.org/stable/25112658.

3. DAVIS, DONALD F. 1984. "Aaron Douglas of Fisk: Molder of Black Artists." The Journal of Negro History 69, no. 2: 95–99. https://doi.org/10.2307/2717601.

4. KNAPPE, STEPHANIE FOX. "Aaron Douglas: African American Modernist: The Exhibition, the Artist, and His Legacy." American Studies 49, no. 1/2 : 121–30. http://www.jstor.org/stable/40644203.

5. MITCHELL, ERNEST JULIUS. 2010. "'Black Renaissance': A Brief History of the Concept." Amerikastudien / American Studies 55, no. 4: 641–65. http://www.jstor.org/stable/41158720.

6. POWELL, RICHARD J. 2008. "Paint that Thing! Aaron Douglas's Call to Modernism." American Studies 49, no. 1/2: 107-119. https://www.jstor.org/stable/40644202.

7. RAGAR, CHERYL R. 2008. "The Douglas Legacy." American Studies 49, no. 1/2: 131–45. http://www.jstor.org/stable/40644204.

8. TAKAC, BALASZ. 2020. "Aspects of Negro Life, Aaron Douglas' Significant Mural Series." Widewalls. https://www.widewalls.ch/magazine/aaron-douglas-aspects-of-negro-life.

9. THOMPSON, AUDREY. "Great Plains Pragmatist: Aaron Douglas And The Art Of Social Protest." Great Plains Quarterly 20, no. 4 (2000): 311–22. http://www.jstor.org/stable/23532912.

10. VECHTEN, CARL V. 1979. "Aaron Douglas, Painter, at 79; Founded Fisk Art Department." New York Times, February 22, 1979, 9. https://www.nytimes.com/1979/02/22/archives/aaron-douglas-painter-at-79-founded-fiskart-department-perspective.html.

1.

2.

3.

2. *North Side of the West Wall of Nakht's Offering Chapel*,
1410-1370 B.C. Credit: The Metropolitan Museum of Art.

3. Aaron Douglas, *Aspects of Negro Life: The Negro in an
African Setting*, 1934. Credit: New York Public Library.

5.

4.

6.

4. Aaron Douglas, *God's Trombones*, 1927. Source: Wikiart, fair use for educational use.

5. *Equestrian Oba and Attendants*, 1550–1680. Credit: The Metropolitan Museum of Art.

6. Aaron Douglas, *The Crucifixion*, 1927. Source: Artchive, fair use for educational use.

COLOPHON

Design History Reader:
An Emerging Vision for Graphic Design History

Onomatopee #259
ISBN: 978-94-93382-08-4

Edited by: Kristen Coogan, 2025

With written contributions by:
Alexina Federhen
Amina Hachimura
Anna Doctor
Annabella Pugliese
Bella Bennett
Charles Li
Dar Saravia
Ellen Johnson
Flora Kerner
Grace Chong
Haya AlMajali
Julia Cheung
Kristina Shumilina
Leila Garner
Maidha Salman
Natalie Seitz
Niharika Yellamraju
Olujimi Taiwo
Rayne Schulman
Rhea Jauhar
Risa Yamazaki
Ruxian Wang
Shaimaa Sabbagh
Sheryl Peng
Sophie Zimbler
Tyler Best
Tzu-Hsuan Huang
Winnie Mei
Xiuqi Ran
Yue Luo

This project would not have been possible without
the tireless efforts of an incredible group of copy-
right permission seekers:
Alexina Federhen
Asya Tarabar
Katelyn Poe
Kristina Shumilina
Leila Garner
Niharika Yellamraju
Tyler Best

Published by:
Onomatopee Projects
Eindhoven, The Netherlands
Jesse Muller and Natasha Rijkhoff

Graphic design: Kristen Coogan Design
Kristen Coogan, Alexina Federhen

Proofreading: Irene de Craen

Typefaces: Grot10, Mencken, and Space Mono.

Paper: Holmen Book Cream, 80g;
Multi Art Silk UPM, 300g, FSC

Printed by: BALTO print, UAB

First Edition: 2025

Copyright: Copyright © 2025, Kristen Coogan /
Onomatopee. All rights reserved.

AN EM
VISION
GRAPH
DESIG
HISTO

How can we — as people, as designers, as educators — contribute to change? How can we foster more enhanced cultures of empathy and inclusion?

Design History Reader grapples with the paradox that while historians intentionally craft historical discourse based on collective knowledge, it often remains bound to a singular perspective. This book encourages a pluralistic approach to the teaching and narrating of the history of graphic design, presenting a history that actually reflects the diversity in the classroom and in the profession at large.

Throughout this book, the Western design history canon is challenged through written research, highlighting under-known designers and design movements who deserve representation. In collaboration with Kristen Coogan, the students of History of Graphic Design from Boston University embraced a plural design history pedagogy, multiplying perspectives and bringing their own authentic experiences and lived histories into conversation — resulting in a range of stories representing both dominant and minority cultures.

The concepts that tie these stories together become a contemporary vision of graphic design history and offer a new way to study, interact with, and perceive the narrative. *Design History Reader* is a dynamic starting point, open to interpretation and interrogation. It's not anywhere near being fully representative but, instead, a living archive that will continue to expand as our collective research advances.

Onomatopee# 259
ISBN: 978-94-93382-08-4